The Young Child and Mathematics

Juanita V. Copley

A 2000 NAEYC Comprehensive Membership Benefit

**National Association for the
Education of Young Children**
Washington, D.C.

**National Council of Teachers
of Mathematics**
Reston, Virginia

Photographs copyright © by

Nancy P. Alexander: 8, 76, 97, 163
BmPorter/Don Franklin: 9, 31, 33, 41, 133
Blakely Fetridge Bundy: 173
Juanita V. Copley: 50, 111, 122, 123, 137, 144, 149
Stephanie Feeney: 17
Ellen Galinsky: 70
Bill Geiger: 27
Jeanetta K. Hodges: 121
Jean Claude LeJeune: 2, 5, 57, 112
Ann Luce: 153
Robert Maust: 4
Jonathan Meyers: 129
Daniel Raskin: 129
Subjects & Predicates: 143
Francis Wardle: 93
Linda Werstiuk: 3

Children's art provided by Juanita V. Copley
Computer graphics by Malini Dominey
Illustrations by Natalie Klein

Permissions acknowledgments:

p. 73, "Treasure." Reprinted from L.B. Hopkins, *Good Rhymes, Good Times* (New York: Curtis Brown Ltd., 1995). Copyright © 1995 by Curtis Brown Ltd. All rights reserved.

p. 77, "two friends." Reprinted from N. Giovanni, *Spin a Soft Black Song: Poems for Children* (New York: Hill & Wang, 1985). Copyright © 1985 by Farrar, Straus and Giroux Inc. All rights reserved.

p. 123, cube diagrams. Reproduced from J.V. Copley, *PreK–K TEXTEAMS Institute* (Austin: University of Texas at Austin).

p. 158, graphs. Adapted from the National Council of Teachers of Mathematics, *Principles and Standards for School Mathematics* (Reston, VA: NCTM, 2000). Copyright © 2000. All rights reserved.

National Association for the Education of Young Children
1509 16th Street, NW
Washington, DC 20036-1426
202-232-8777 or 800-424-2460
www.naeyc.org

Through its publications program the National Association for the Education of Young Children (NAEYC) provides a forum for discussion of major issues and ideas in the early childhood field, with the hope of provoking thought and promoting professional growth. The views expressed or implied are not necessarily those of the Association. NAEYC thanks the author, who donated much time and effort to develop this book for the profession.

Library of Congress Card Number: 00-110024
ISBN 0-935989-97-8
NAEYC #119

Publications editor: Carol Copple
Editor: Catherine Cauman
Editorial assistance: Natalie Klein and Lacy Thompson
Cover and book design & production: Malini Dominey

Printed in the United States of America

Contents

About the Author

Juanita V. Copley is an associate professor in curriculum and instruction at the University of Houston in Texas, where she is coordinator of the early childhood program and director of a professional development project known as the Early Childhood Collaborative. For the past 11 years, Dr. Copley has been actively involved in teacher education at the university and has taught in early childhood programs in the public school system. For 10 years she served as a mathematics/science instructional specialist in the Alief Independent School District, with responsibilities for prekindergarten through fifth grade.

Dr. Copley is editor of the book *Mathematics in the Early Years* (1999), copublished by the National Council of Teachers of Mathematics and the National Association for the Education of Young Children.

Acknowledgments

Special thanks to children and teachers at Oates Elementary and Herod Elementary, Houston Independent School District, Houston, Texas; Lawhon Elementary, Pearland ISD, Pearland, Texas; and Hearne Elementary, Alief ISD, Alief, Texas.

And to early childhood teachers Mimi Lowdoski, teacher of 3-year-olds, and Susan McDaniels, prekindergarten teacher, River Oaks Baptist School; Kay Timme, early childhood director, Conroe ISD, Conroe, Texas; Michell Harper and Karen Walker, kindergarten teachers, Katy ISD, Katy, Texas; and Marianne Weber, mathematics consultant, St. Louis, Missouri.

Preface

The word *mathematics* makes many adults think of rote procedures for getting correct answers, a holdover from our own school days. But mathematics is essentially the search for sense and meaning, patterns and relationships, order and predictability. As Kathy Richardson and Leslie Salkeld (1995) write,

> Mathematical power develops in children who learn that mathematics makes sense and who learn to trust their own abilities to make sense of mathematics. The challenge for those of us interested in the education of young children is to help ensure that the movement to bring more and different mathematics to young children results in curriculum and assessment practices that are consistent with what we know about how young children learn. . . . In the past, *more* and *different* often meant adding pressure to the lives of children and assuming that more can be accomplished if we just start younger and expect more. The opportunity is here to develop mathematics programs that maximize children's learning rather than giving the appearance of high expectations while in reality engaging in inappropriate practices that interfere with children's developing understanding. (p. 23)

If the goal is to develop mathematical power in children, how should the enterprise of math education be changed? This was the question that mathematics educators and researchers considered for many months, culminating in 1989 in a publication by the National Council of Teachers of Mathematics (NCTM) titled *Curriculum and Evaluation Standards for School Mathematics*. A revised version followed in 1995. Now in 2000, NCTM has published *Principles and Standards for School Mathematics*. For the first time, the standards writers were charged with beginning at prekindergarten rather than kindergarten, as had been done in the past.

Response to the 2000 standards has been very favorable. The document presents standards for an entire age band ("In prekindergarten through grade 2 all children should . . ."), not specifying expectations further by grade or age, although supporting text does provide guidance to help teachers at different grade levels. NAEYC and NCTM want to ensure that states, districts, and practitioners do not misinterpret these broad-band standards and develop curriculum or standards that expect too much too soon—for example, pushing prekindergartners to master a concept that is reasonable for second-graders to acquire.

Accordingly, both organizations are eager to disseminate resources that clarify expectations as well as inspire early childhood educators to do *more* math and *different* math than they have done in the past. It is our hope that *The Young Child and Mathematics* will help to accomplish both of these goals. Nita Copley's engaging, practical approach communicates the main ideas of the NCTM standards within the context of effective, developmentally appropriate practice (NAEYC [1996] 1999). We believe that the book will help early childhood educators move well beyond present practice—to give children not only a first-rate start in mathematics but also a lifelong taste for its power and delights.

Carol Copple
Publications Editor
National Association for the
   Education of Young Children

James E. Schultz, Chair
Educational Materials Committee
National Council of Teachers
   of Mathematics

Chapter 1

The Child Learns,
the Child Teaches

An 8-year-old with spiky hair, an impish demeanor, and a seemingly permanent pout, Timmy entered my life late one October. He was referred to me because he demonstrated few skills in reading or mathematics, seemed unmotivated to attempt new tasks, and seldom if ever completed a readable assignment.

Jessica was quiet and compliant. She never caused problems, never showed any particular gift for mathematics, never volunteered in class. In fact, I had difficulty finding anything specific to say to her parents during parent-teacher conferences.

Armand was an enthusiastic ball of energy. With hands up in the air and a grin a mile wide, Armand entered the science lab with his kindergarten class and announced, "I'm here! I love science! I can't wait!" Within an hour I found Armand on the floor surrounded by dirt from the earthworm farm, every inch of bare skin and most of his clothing covered with dirt, holding an earthworm.

I have been a teacher for 26 years. I have taken courses, read books, earned degrees, conducted research, and published articles. I have learned mathematics, how to teach mathematics, how to assess mathematical understanding, how to understand child development, and so on. My teachers and mentors have been wonderful. They have taught me much, given me ideas, and broadened my beliefs about teaching. However, the lessons I learned from children—from Timmy, Jessica, Armand, and others—are the ones that have made the most difference in my teaching.

The Young Child and Mathematics focuses on children from ages 3 through 8 and their mathematical learning. The placement of *young child* before *mathematics* in the book's title is not accidental. It comes first because I believe that the child should be the focus. In this chapter I share some of the lessons that I have learned about children and their understanding of mathematics. Some of the ideas come from textbooks, some from watching other teachers teach, some from experts. However, most if not all of the ideas were greatly affected by children. In some cases their strategies changed the activities for my lessons, their interests changed the scope of the content, or their particular strengths or weaknesses changed the sequence of instruction. Whatever the case, I find that when the child is the focus of my teaching, I teach mathematics well.

Learning from Timmy

Let's talk about Timmy. After looking at his work and his records, I understood his teacher's frustration. Indeed, Timmy was a child with whom teachers found it difficult to work. He had demonstrated a very short attention span, and he showed little promise in mathematics or any other subject. I admitted him to a special program for "slow learners."

Because of an unexpected assignment, I didn't have time to work with Timmy that first day he appeared in my classroom. To keep him busy, I gave him a large box of electrical equipment from the sixth-grade electricity unit—switches, batteries, wire, and small light bulbs. I asked him to sort the box's contents and told him that I would return in a while.

Thirty minutes later, I walked back into the room. Timmy had created a working electrical system! Six bulbs were lit, three switches were incorporated, and within the connection he had produced a working model of both a parallel and a series circuit. I watched and listened as this difficult, unmotivated, and unskilled 8-year-old shared with me his creation, which was much more complicated than anything I could build. Timmy explained why certain bulbs were half the brightness of other bulbs, he told me how to predict whether a bulb would light or not light, he told me about resistance and the advantages and disadvantages of series and parallel circuits.

Timmy taught me an important a lesson: *Spend time observing, listening, and watching children.* Pay attention to what they like, listen to their reasoning, ask them to explain their creations, challenge them with tasks that seem impossible, and give them the opportunity to show you what they can do in the way they want.

A lesson from Jessica

Quiet Jessica was a child in my class during my second year of teaching. At the end of the year, I asked each child to give me a report card for being a teacher. I stressed the fact that they should tell me good things as well as things I could improve.

Jessica took my directions seriously. Her block-print note with her own spelling stated,

Ms Copley. You were real good with the dumd kids. They needed you and you halped them. You were real good with smart kids. You always keeped them buzy. but you should do better with the plane kids like me. I need to learn to!

Luv, Jessica

She was right; I had spent most of my time with the special children and I had ignored the "plain" kids. I learned an important lesson with that note: *Remember that every child is important!* It is my job to do my best teaching for those children who have special gifts, those who need concentrated help to overcome difficulties, and those quiet, plain children who have the right to learn.

The joy of Armand

Armand's fascination with earthworms began that first day in the science lab. He spent countless hours observing them, "reading" earthworm books in the library, and asking questions. During his study he became obsessed with finding the eyes of earthworms. Assuring me that "They gots to have eyes! They gots to see!" Armand kept asking for bigger magnifiers so that he could find their eyes.

Instead of discouraging Armand and correcting his error, I helped him set up experiments to test his hypothesis. During the last two months of the school year, Armand spent every free minute conducting experiments with colored mats, homemade earthworm houses, and colored lights. As he boarded the bus for his final trip home as a kindergartner, he yelled out the window, "I still think they gots eyes, Mrs. Copley!"

That statement taught me a great deal. Because I allowed him to investigate his hypothesis—in fact encouraged his exploration—Armand learned more about earthworms than anyone in the school. Because he had a need to know, Armand read fourth- and fifth-grade books about earthworms and could use the proper terminology to describe their parts. More important, because he was in charge of his own learning, Armand continued to be a powerful, excited learner.

When I heard Armand's final statement, I was reminded how important it is not to correct every error. Instead, *encourage investigation, and remember that children construct their own knowledge.* What an important lesson for someone teaching mathematics!

These three lessons should be in evidence throughout this book. First, spend time observing, listening, and watching children. Some of the many vignettes and dialogues I have recorded, videotaped, and remembered appear in every chapter. I believe that you can learn most from children and classroom examples; thus, such examples are abundant and (using pseudonyms) presented as realistically as possible.

Second, remember that every child is important. This volume presents a variety of examples and suggested activities that work for children with all types of needs in diverse settings. Because I have been privileged to teach in multicultural settings, in urban and rural communities, in private and public schools, and in 4-year-old, kindergarten, first-, and second-grade classrooms, the ideas here reflect those contexts.

Third, encourage investigation and remember that children construct their own knowledge. I value the joy of learning, exploration, and discovery. While mathematics is often considered a subject of right answers and prescriptive instruction, the ideas presented in this book foster investigation in the way children learn.

The intuitive mathematical knowledge of the young child

Young children are natural learners. They construct their own understanding about quantity, relationships, and symbols. They approach new tasks with curiosity and a sense of experimentation. Counting is a natural task, *more* is a word 2-year-olds know readily, and the concepts of addition and subtraction are actively used to describe and explain situations children encounter in their world. When a new idea or piece of information doesn't make sense to a child, Piaget theorized, the experience creates dissonance—that is, mental conflict that the child seeks to resolve. Thus the child develops and assimilates knowledge, making it his own.

The intuitive, informal mathematical knowledge of young children often surprises early childhood teachers. Yet, kindergarten curriculum tends to reflect the belief that 5-year-olds enter school as blank slates, with no concepts, no experience with quantities, patterns, shapes, or relationships!

Instead, research strongly indicates that young children have a strong, intuitive understanding of informal mathematics. To illustrate this point, listen to 3-year-old Jeffrey discuss his new set of blocks with his teacher.

Block Shapes

Ms. Wright: Tell me about your new blocks. What do you call them?

Jeffrey: Blocks with different shapes.

Ms. Wright: What can you tell me about these different shapes?

Jeffrey: This yellow one is a star. The blue one is a triangle.

Ms. Wright: Wow! Have you ever seen shapes like this before?

Jeffrey: *(sighing loudly)* Yeah, at my house, my Granna house, my Daddy house, outside.

Ms. Wright: You have all these shapes at everybody's house?

Jeffrey: No . . . *(picking up the orange circle)* This is like my Uncle Dee's basketball, but *(frowning)* it won't bounce up and *down.* This is a piece of pizza *(indicating a purple wedge-shape block),* this is a table *(a pink square),* this is my best book *(a rectangular block).*

Jeffrey proceeds to separate the blocks into two groups—five shapes on one side and one shape on the other side. The star-shape block is alone and the others—triangle, square, pizza slice, circle, and rectangle—are heaped together in a pile.

Ms. Wright: Why did you put the star on the other side?

Jeffrey: *(with a deep, long sigh that sounds as if he has lost his patience)* These belong in a house and this one *(the star)* doesn't. It belongs in the sky!

Did you notice Jeffrey's verbal labeling of the block shapes, his connection of the blocks to items he regularly sees, and his clarification of differences between the basketball and the round block? While his particular classification system (belongs in the house, doesn't belong in the house) is not found in state objectives, his system is perfectly correct and indicates a consistency not typical in such a young child.

Identification of two-dimensional shapes is an objective in kindergarten programs; Jeffrey has already shown that ability at age 3. The identification of shapes in the everyday world is also a standard objective in kindergarten curricula; again Jeffrey demonstrates that ability. I am not proposing that all 3-year-olds have Jeffrey's understanding and use of language; however, I do believe that many early childhood programs and teachers view young children as incapable, when in fact they already grasp many mathematical concepts at an intuitive level.

While reviewing research studies is not the purpose of this chapter, I have listed below some important points supported by research that illustrate the intuitive mathematical knowledge of the young child.

• Young children have a wealth of informal knowledge about mathematics as a result of everyday experiences and strategies they create to deal with events in their lives.

• The operations of addition, subtraction, multiplication, and division are often understood by young children. While they may not be able to complete a written equation like $5 - 2 = 3$, they can easily tell you how many buttons you would have on your shirt if you started with five and two fell off. Accordingly, they can figure out how many pieces of candy to purchase for a birthday party if everyone attending got three pieces.

• Children's understanding of rational numbers, while incomplete, is often more accomplished than expected. Their common sharing experiences, their use of the term *half,* and their fair distribution of quantities among friends are natural by-products of everyday experiences.

• The development of geometric concepts and spatial sense can often be observed when young children participate in free play. The young child directing a building block project uses words and motions to tell his friend how to make a castle. "Do it like me. You need a square block" (his description for a cube). "No, not that way. Turn it over!" When his friend says, "It doesn't matter, it's always the same," the child reaffirms his own understanding by saying, "Well that's 'cause now it's right!" Both boys are experimenting with beginning concepts of rotation and the language of geometry.

• A natural fascination with large numbers is evident with young children. While they frequently invent nonsensical numbers like "a million, dillion, killion," they often show a partial understanding of quantity and the need for counting.

Do we need to directly teach young children all they need to know about mathematics? Do we need to start from the beginning, drill in those basic facts, and fill all the holes in their understanding? Do we need to tightly define developmentally appropriate mathematics as *easy concepts all children can learn?*

The answer to all of these questions is a resounding *No!* Instead, we need to remember that young children possess a vast amount of intuitive, informal mathematical knowledge. Our job is to assess their prior knowledge, build upon their strengths, facilitate their learning, and enjoy the process.

The constructed mathematical concepts of the young child

Young children continually construct mathematical ideas based on their experiences with their environment, their interactions with adults and other children, and their daily observations. These constructed ideas are unique to each child and vary greatly among children the same age. Some of the ideas are perceptually immature, many of the problem-solving strategies are inefficient, and the verbal information necessary to discuss mathematics is often incorrectly labeled or modeled. The child who perceives *more* candy to be in the larger bag, the child who always adds together two sets of items using the counting-all strategy, and the child who counts, "6, 7, 8, 9, 10, oneteen, twoteen, threeteen," illustrate mathematical ideas that would be labeled incorrect for an adult but are often developmentally correct for a young child.

An early childhood teacher who frequently listens to ideas expressed by young children can provide materials and an environment conducive to the development of mathematical concepts. More important, by observing young children the teacher can ask questions that prompt them to make new discoveries and form their own questions. To illustrate this point, listen to some prekindergartners' responses to a problem presented by their classroom teacher.

Six Legs, Five Fingers

Miss Riley: I just bought this bee puppet *(shows a bee puppet attached to a black six-fingered glove)* and I have a problem. When I put my hand into the glove, I always have an empty leg on the puppet. I don't have enough fingers for all of the legs. I have only five fingers and there are six legs on this puppet. I don't know what to do! Maybe I'll just take it back to the store.

The children seem to be thinking about this problem. Some count their fingers, others talk to their partners, and still others shrug their shoulders.

Russell: Well, maybe you got your fingers in wrong.

Miss Riley: Maybe. Let's see. *(The teacher puts her hand in and out of the puppet a few times, each time showing the leg without the finger.)* No, it's still there.

Marta: Just cut it off.

Miss Riley: Well, that's an idea, but it's brand new. I don't want to cut up a brand new puppet!

Svetlana: I know. Let me show you. *(Svetlana tries to put one of the legs inside the glove. It leaves a hole, and Svetlana shrugs and sits down.)*

Miss Riley: Good try, Svetlana, but it still seems like it's not quite right.

Duane: Hey, maybe the guy who made it had six fingers!

This idea seems to satisfy many of the children, who nod. The children are excited about a possible solution.

Miss Riley: Maybe so. Let's see. How many fingers do you have on one hand?

Everyone spends time counting and recounting the fingers on their hands. Some repeat the counting three or four times.

Miss Riley: Does anyone have six fingers on a hand?

The children shake their heads no or respond verbally, saying they have five fingers. Others act like they do have six fingers, count aloud as they touch them, and then say that they have only five. After a few minutes they seem to be satisfied that no one in the class has six fingers.

Linda: *(excitedly raising her hand)* Umm . . . umm . . . maybe bees have six legs!

Duton: No. I have lots of bees at my house and they all have five legs! *(Linda looks disappointed; because Duton is a class leader, most students believe he is right.)*

Miss. Riley: Maybe Linda has a good idea. How could we find out?

The children suggest many ideas, including going to the library center. After a brief discussion, the children disperse to different activity centers, some looking for books with bee pictures and others becoming involved in other activities. Angelica is still sitting, counting her fingers over and over again.

Angelica: *(calling out after about five minutes)* Teacher, teacher, look! If I count my fingers real fast, I get six!

This brief classroom vignette illustrates beautifully the variability and wonderful creativeness of young children as they attempt to solve a real problem. Russell's notion—that if the fingers are taken out and put back into

the glove again, the extra leg would disappear—demonstrates a lack of number conservation, a characteristic common in many 4-year-olds. Russell seems to believe that if the appearance of the fingers in the puppet change, the number of legs will change as well. Marta's and Svetlana's subtraction methods were expedient yet did not take into account any reason for the extra leg. Duane's creative idea about six-fingered people may indicate his lack of experience with other people's number of fingers. The class's ready belief that Duton's five-legged house bees are like all bees reveals faulty reasoning based on insufficient evidence. Finally, Angelica's humorous response illustrates an inefficient and incorrect "fast-counting" strategy and also reveals her ability to persist in seeking solutions.

Again, many research studies report findings consistent with the idea that children construct their mathematical knowledge. In addition, studies have suggested that the teacher's significant roles of observing, facilitating, supporting, and questioning are essential to that construction.

• Mathematics is for everyone. If mathematics is taught properly at the early childhood and elementary levels, all children should develop proficiency in it. Instances that appear to be learning disabilities in mathematics are often caused by inappropriate teaching rather than intellectual inadequacy.

• Few, if any, differences in young children's ability to learn mathematics relate to gender or socioeconomic status. Rather, opportunity to learn is the primary factor in the development of that ability.

• Young children make sense of mathematical situations in different ways. Not all children in a group represent or solve problems in the same way. Not all children follow the same developmental sequence. However, there are some general guidelines that teachers can follow that will give children experiences with a variety of thinking strategies and modeling procedures.

Should we immediately correct young children's misconceptions about mathematics? Can we expect all children to solve problems in identical ways? Should we expect all the young children in a group to "get it" at the same time? Again, the answer is *No!* As teachers, we need to remember that young children construct mathematical understanding in different ways, at different times, and with different materials. Our job is to provide an environment in which all children can learn mathematics.

The power of positive attitude

In 1990 President Bush and the nation's governors established a list of national education goals to be reached in the year 2000. Goal one states, "By the year 2000, all children in America will start school ready to learn." While I understand that the panel was concerned about the physical, social, and emotional needs of the young child, my experience, supported by countless research studies, has demonstrated that the young child is more than ready to learn mathematics. In fact, she is already learning more complex mathematics than we might expect.

Young children are typically motivated to learn quantitative and spatial information. Their dispositions allow them to be positive and confident in their mathematical abilities. The highly prized characteristics of persistence, focused participation, hypothesis testing, risk taking, and self-regulation are often present and seldom acknowledged in the young child.

When discussing mathematics, the National Research Council (1989) described this disposition of the young child. After describing a young child's strong motivation to learn mathematics, the council stated that a gradual change occurs in early primary grades and described it as a shifting disposition "from enthusiasm to apprehension" and "from confidence to fear." Unfortunately, this gradual change is often completed by third grade.

After spending two years researching the motivation of 7- and 8-year-olds as they solve spatial tasks, I was amazed at the differences in motivation of children at that level. Let me illustrate the two contrasting situations by describing two children's actions during a spatial task.

According to a cognitive ability measure, Roberto and Mei-Chi possessed almost the same analytical and quantitative ability. English was the first language for both children, and they both participated in a program for gifted students. To assess their specific motivation to solve problems, each child was given the choice of an easy symmetry task or a hard one. Each child was asked to position a mirror vertically on a picture card (laid flat on the table) so that the image made by the picture and its reflection looked like the target picture. Unknown to the children, the easy tasks were quite easy and could be solved in less than 15 seconds by the average 7-year-old, and the hard tasks were impossible because of the target picture's nonsymmetrical characteristics.

Roberto and Mei-Chi were each given the choice of doing the easy activities or the hard activities during a 10-minute session. Listen to their contrasting responses to this problem-solving task.

A Matter of Motivation

Mrs. Evans: Mei-Chi, you may choose to do either the hard tasks or the easy ones. I don't care which ones you do, and you may stop at any time and change to another task. I will tell you if you have solved the problem or if you haven't solved the problem, but you do not need to solve the problem to move on to another task. It will be your choice. Understand?

Mei-Chi: I will take an easy one.

The task card is given to Mei-Chi, and she solves it in approximately 15 seconds. The teacher states that it is correct.

Mei-Chi: I will take another easy one.

Again, Mei-Chi quickly solves it, and the teacher states that it is correct.

The activity continues for 10 minutes. Mei-Chi solves more than 35 easy tasks, never asking for a hard one. Each time she solves one, she looks at the teacher and asks if it is correct.

Mrs. Evans: Mei-Chi, before you go . . . I noticed that you never tried a hard task. I was wondering why not. Could you tell me?

Mei-Chi: Yeah, I might get it wrong! You told me they are hard!

Mei-Chi leaves and Roberto enters. The same directions are given to Roberto.

Roberto: I will take a hard one.

Roberto eagerly takes the task card. He maneuvers the card, trying to complete the task in a variety of ways. Roberto works on the one hard task during the entire 10 minutes, ignoring the teacher and never completing the task correctly.

Mrs. Evans: Roberto, I am sorry, our time is up. You will need to leave the task here for now and go back to class.

Roberto: Aw, I was just about to get it. Can't I stay a little longer?

Mrs. Evans: No, I'm sorry. I promise to let you try again on another day.

As Roberto starts to leave, the teacher is busy preparing for another student. She glances up and sees Roberto place the task card in his back pocket.

Mrs. Evans: Roberto, I need that card. I'm sorry, you will need to leave it with me.

Roberto: If you would just let me take it home, I know I could get it!

What different responses! Mei-Chi completes many tasks successfully; Roberto never successfully completes one task. Mei-Chi requires a teacher's acknowledgment of success; Roberto seems to ignore the teacher. Mei-Chi attempts short, easy tasks; Roberto demonstrates great persistence on only one task. Mei-Chi takes no risks; Roberto even risks taking the task card against the teacher's wishes.

Both of these children are smart, capable mathematics learners. However, on this task they demonstrate quite different motivational characteristics. Mei-Chi worked for the teacher's approval, performing many tasks and never trying hard ones. Her motivation could be termed *performance oriented*. Roberto, on the other hand, worked to complete the task, persisting at a hard task in spite of his continual failure. His motivation could be termed *task-learning oriented*.

Research indicates that disposition is very important to the long-term learning of mathematics (Renga & Dalla 1993). Disposition concerns more than just attitude toward mathematics; persistence, risk taking, hypothesis making, and self-regulation are all important to a motivated disposition.

• All children seem strongly motivated to perform well in school mathematics. By around the third grade, however, important differences in both motivation and achievement begin to emerge.

• Performance-oriented children are motivated by others' approval and often "perform" to be successful. They frequently underestimate their successes and overestimate their failures. In addition, they demonstrate little persistence and, when confronted with a problem, can exhibit a state of "learned helplessness."

• Task-learning-oriented children are motivated by learning and view the task as something to be mastered or learned. They seldom express interest in what others think; in fact, they often ignore feedback about success or failure. They frequently take risks, demonstrate great persistence, and often continue a task in spite of many obstacles.

• Teachers can directly influence performance-oriented children. When teachers stress learning rather than performance, significant differences occur in children's motivation toward mathematics.

Should we ignore children's dispositions toward mathematics? Should we continually stress the importance of teacher-pleasing behavior when doing mathematics? Should we assume that young children fear mathematics and are as anxious as many adults when learning mathematics? Clearly, we should not.

Young children are motivated to do mathematics. Our job as teachers is to stress the importance of learning, model the joy of mastering tasks, and value errors as essential information to help us learn.

This book at a glance

This first chapter in *The Young Child and Mathematics* introduces young children and their characteristics as learners of mathematics. Throughout the book these ideas will be illustrated by descriptions of classroom situations, children's work products, and interactions between children.

The ideas expressed in this chapter are restated in their most simplified form below. Young children

- possess a large amount of intuitive mathematical knowledge
- continually construct mathematical ideas based on their experiences and observations
- are strongly motivated to do mathematics

Teachers of young children should

- encourage investigation of and experimentation with mathematical concepts
- spend time observing, listening, and watching children
- remember that every child is important

Chapter 2 integrates the curriculum, assessment, and instructional guidelines suggested by the National Association for the Education of Young Children (NAEYC) with the standards suggested by the National Council of Teachers of Mathematics (NCTM). Chapter 3 discusses the essential processes of mathematics. Chapters 4 through 8 detail the content of mathematics for the young child. Chapter 9 outlines the questions most frequently asked by teachers of young children as they relate to mathematics, along with some possible answers.

I am constantly intrigued by young children, their characteristics, and their ways of learning mathematics. As you read this book, I hope that my excitement is communicated and ignites your interest and efforts in educating the young child.

Chapter 2

Principles in Teaching Mathematics to Young Children

The fields of early childhood education and mathematics education have both addressed issues of curriculum, instruction, and assessment in published materials representing broad professional consensus in each field. Two major organizations that represent the early childhood community, the National Association for the Education of Young Children and the National Association of Early Childhood Specialists in State Departments of Education, adopted and published a position statement giving curriculum and assessment guidelines for programs serving children ages 3 through 8 in 1990 (NAEYC & NAECS/SDE 1990). Instructional decisions, developmentally appropriate practices, and a variety of teaching suggestions are proposed in this same document and other supporting volumes (Bredekamp & Rosegrant 1992, 1995; NAEYC 1996; Bredekamp & Copple 1997).

The National Council of Teachers of Mathematics (NCTM) published *Principles and Standards for School Mathematics* (2000), which is widely supported in the mathematics community by other national organizations such as the American Association for the Advancement of Science and the National Research Council. This document reaffirms NCTM's vision for school mathematics and for the first time includes the prekindergarten years as well as kindergarten through twelfth grade. Built on the foundations of the original NCTM *Standards* documents [1989, 1991, 1995] and designed to consolidate the classroom aspects of these documents, *Principles and Standards* contains five content standards and five process standards directed to teachers of children in prekindergarten through second grade, as seen in Appendix A.

The guidelines for curriculum, teaching instruction practices, and assessment defined by NAEYC and the curriculum, teaching and assessment principles developed by NCTM are strongly related yet distinct, with each perspective offering something unique. While the early childhood community is interested in the care and education of young children in all areas of learning and development, the mathematics community focuses on issues related to mathematics education of children across a broader age spectrum (prekindergarten through twelfth grade).

This book does not attempt to discuss fully each perspective. Both communities have already done that in a variety of useful resources. Instead, *The Young Child and Mathematics* blends the early childhood guidelines and the mathematics standards into a set of principles for curriculum, instruction, and assessment. These principles incorporate the special expertise and focus of each community.

As we consider mathematics and the young child through a variety of classroom vignettes and activity ideas, the principles guiding curriculum, instruction, and assessment often appear to be intertwined. This is as it should be: curriculum, instruction, and assessment are indeed closely connected. Illustration of these connections throughout the book, along with the guidelines and standards supported by the early childhood and mathematics communities, should contribute to teachers' better understanding of mathematics for the young child.

Curriculum principles

What mathematics should we teach to young children? Is content or process more important? What role does the child play in our selection of mathematics curriculum? What types of materials should we use? How does the environment in the early childhood classroom contribute to the mathematics curriculum?

Curriculum is the *what* of the education process, the planned experiences and the situations of instruction. The mathematics curriculum includes all aspects of mathematics content and processes, the learning environment and materials. Central to the curriculum is the child.

Curriculum Principles for Early Childhood Mathematics	
1. Content	The mathematical content should be rich, varied, and relevant to children.
2. Process	Essential mathematical processes are solving problems, reasoning, communicating, making connections, and representing.
3. Environment and materials	Effective curriculum includes a mathematically rich environment with a variety of materials to help children explore key concepts.
4. Child-centered choices	Curriculum decisions should take into account children's knowledge, abilities, and interests.

1 Mathematics for the young child is more than the old standbys—arithmetic, counting, and learning to identify a square, rectangle, circle, and triangle. The mathematical content for young children should be rich and varied and have a conceptually oriented, meaningful, and focused purpose. It includes (1) number and operations; (2) patterns, functions, and algebra; (3) geometry and spatial sense; (4) measurement; and (5) data analysis and probability. Content should be worthwhile, as accurate and clear as possible, and not over-simplified or presented with confusing or incorrect information.

> *Curriculum*
>
> 1 **Content**
> The mathematical content should be rich, varied, and relevant to children.

2 To *know* mathematics is to *do* mathematics. Mathematics curriculum must include opportunities for children to solve problems, reason and think, communicate in a variety of ways, represent concepts with symbols, and make connections between specific areas of mathematics, mathematics and other subjects, and mathematics and their world. These processes include investigating; applying; integrating; interacting with peers, materials, and the environment; and constructing knowledge.

> *Curriculum*
>
> 2 **Process**
> Essential mathematical processes are solving problems, reasoning, communicating, making connections, and representing.

3 The physical environment, including the math materials available to children, is basic to the mathematics curriculum. Math materials include concrete manipulatives (e.g., blocks, counters, base-10 blocks, pattern blocks, attribute blocks, two-color counters, plastic people, a variety of containers, measuring materials, tangrams), symbolic materials (dice, dominoes, number lines, graphs, specific computer programs, and other visual models), and more abstract representations (plastic numerals, 100 chart, price tags from store items, grocery store lists, building plans, calculators, computers, and telephone books).

> *Curriculum*
>
> 3 **Environment and materials**
> Effective curriculum includes a mathematically rich environment with a variety of materials to help children explore key concepts.

The environment should be mathematically rich with real situations, such as a grocery store in the dramatic center, daily calendar and attendance activities, and projects involving mathematics. The day's activities—art, science, language arts, blocks, music, water table or sandbox, physical activity—should be mathematically conducive and be adapted to a variety of settings (transitions, learning centers, small groups, circle time, outside and inside play, and at-home activities).

Curriculum

4 **Child-centered choices**
Curriculum decisions should take into account children's knowledge, abilities, and interests.

4 Teachers should base all decisions regarding the mathematics curriculum on their knowledge of children and their more specific knowledge of the children in the class. In constructing curriculum, teachers also need to consider research and professional opinion on how children learn mathematics. They should make curriculum decisions on children's prior math knowledge as well as individual dispositions and attitudes toward mathematics. Finally, young children's interests and their tendencies to explore and experiment should be taken into account at all stages of curriculum development and teaching.

To see these four curriculum principles in action, let's listen in on the discussion of a kindergarten team as they make their monthly plans.

Planning Curriculum in Mathematics

Sherri, Karen, Craig, Julio, and Helen are members of the same kindergarten teaching team. Karen serves as the mathematics expert for the team, and Sherri is the team leader. This curriculum planning meeting occurs in March.

Sherri: Well, let's get started. Any ideas for next week? We're getting near to the end of the year and there's a lot to do.

Karen: We have been neglecting measurement. I think the kids have the skills to understand nonstandard measurement and then progress to standard units as they need to. Does anyone have any ideas?

Julio: You know the model cars we've been building for our transportation unit? The kids want to race them. We could create an activity using the cars that would require the children to use measurement strategies.

Craig: We did something like that last year. I think we used licorice sticks to measure how far our cars went after going down a ramp, didn't we?

Julio: Yeah, don't remind me. We'll try a different method this year!

Helen: *(laughing)* Remember Carlos and how short his licorice stick was when we started to measure? No one could understand why his answers were so different from everyone else's.

Craig: That's right. Carlos *ate* his measurer! He didn't realize that having a shorter licorice stick would make a difference when he measured. I can still see his face! That gave me an idea. When it was my turn, I let my car go down the track, and then I measured it using a very small piece of licorice. When we tested the kids' cars, we used a large piece. For a long time the kids couldn't figure out why my car went 10 licorice sticks and theirs only went 5 when they could see that theirs had traveled farther. It was great!

Helen: What did the kids learn, besides having fun?

Karen: They were certainly doing a lot of reasoning. And an important concept in measuring is understanding the need for a constant or standard unit of measurement. So that activity works for mathematics!

Helen: As the resident science guru, I can see some science concepts we could integrate. Children could hypothesize about what would make their cars go farther, and then to test their hypotheses, we would have to measure! Let me work on that for next week. First we'll need to teach measurement skills and then provide some good practice.

Craig: I know some books that will help us set the context— like *How Long Is a Foot?* or Shel Silverstein's *A Giraffe and a Half* or *Let's Measure It!* or even *Who Sank the Boat?* We used that one before, remember? We put boat-making materials in the water tub. Maybe we could tie that activity into measuring—you know, find out what weight it takes to sink the boats.

Sherri: O.K., those are some good ideas for using math in the learning centers. And don't forget about the calendar. I'm sure there are some possibilities for measurement there.

Measurement is an often neglected mathematics topic for young children. Because these teachers know the importance of a broad mathematics curriculum, they know that measurement belongs in their curriculum.

The teachers also want to promote children's use of the processes of mathematics. Trying to explain the puzzling results in the car competition challenged the children to use their reasoning abilities. Connecting mathematics to other subjects and experiences is another key process skill. Science concepts involved in the car race have connections to mathematics and measurement skills, which can be incorporated and highlighted. These teachers plan to introduce books with measurement elements and give the children many communication opportunities.

At this stage in children's learning about measurement, it is appropriate to use materials they are familiar with or to encourage them to determine what they could use for the purpose. The teachers plan to coordinate the many different places in the environment where measurement can be explored, and they mention learning center activities, the library corner, calendar time, and circle time activities as possibilities for exploring and teaching measurement concepts.

Finally, throughout this planning session the teachers consider the children's own choices. With their interest in racing, race cars, and contests, children see the purpose in measuring and thus in trying to understand measurement ideas. Children also have choices about what to make and where to work during much of the day.

All of the curriculum principles are evident in this short vignette. The content is broad and meaningful, reasoning and connections are stressed as important processes, concepts to be learned are placed within a variety of settings, and children's interests and use of exploration and experimentation are considered.

Instruction principles

How does a teacher support children's learning in mathematics? What does a teacher do to help young children develop their mathematical reasoning? What kinds of classroom interactions and other instructional strategies promote math learning? How can relationships between family and school encourage mathematics learning? What can a teacher do to encourage family-school relationships?

Instruction typically describes the *how* of the education process. It involves (1) planning learning experiences, (2) interacting with children and mathematics, (3) orchestrating numerous classroom activities, and (4) facilitating family-school relationships.

Although often debated, the directive role versus the nondirective role of the teacher is not an either/or issue. Instead, the teacher continually selects from a continuum of behaviors ranging from directive to nondirective on the basis of the goals for the learning experience.

Instruction Principles for Early Childhood Mathematics	
1. Planning experiences	To effectively plan experiences, teachers must make a variety of decisions based on their knowledge and focusing on the needs of individual children.
2. Interacting with children	Interacting with children and promoting interactions between children are key roles of the early childhood teacher.
3. Orchestrating classroom activities	The teacher must orchestrate various contexts and ways in which children engage in mathematical experiences, such as whole group, small group, project teams, and other strategies.
4. Facilitating family-school relations	To facilitate effective family-school relations, the teacher must encourage reciprocal communication between teachers and families in mathematics as in other areas.

The instruction principles are presented here as they specifically apply to mathematics instruction and the role of the early childhood teacher. As with the curriculum principles, guidelines and standards from NAEYC and NCTM support the instruction principles.

1 When planning learning experiences in mathematics, teachers must make decisions based on many considerations. They plan based on their knowledge of young children's development and learning, as well as their knowledge of mathematics and how children acquire math understanding and skills. Also essential in teachers' planning is their knowledge of children's interests and of the social and cultural context of the classroom. Teachers need to plan mathematics experiences at different levels to meet the needs of individual children.

Children's learning is cyclical in character, and it reflects the process of constructing knowledge (Bredekamp & Rosegrant 1992). Four components—awareness, exploration, inquiry, and utilization—make up the process of learning that occurs over time (see "Cycle of Learning and Teaching" box on page 172 in Chapter 9). Teachers should bear in mind that children need numerous opportunities to explore materials and processes before proceeding to more goal-directed learning.

For example, to teach the mathematical concept of combinations, a teacher decides to set up a 31-flavors ice cream store in the creative dramatics center.

Awareness: Children are introduced to the ice cream store, are given a chance to see what is there, and hear a story about going to an ice cream store.

Exploration: Children have the opportunity to play with the new materials, making different double- and triple-decker ice cream cones using color blocks or Styrofoam balls to represent the ice cream flavors.

Inquiry: Children are given a particular challenge, such as determining how many different double-decker combinations they could make from their three favorite flavors.

Utilization: Children are able to represent and explain a solution to a similar problem involving a variety of ice cream toppings.

2 The early childhood teacher must decide when to let children struggle with a problem; when to give a direct or indirect clue or demonstrate a process; and when to pose a new, more challenging question. The teacher also needs to decide when to give a child feedback about a response and when to comment about a child's result or product.

Just as important, the teacher makes a set of *how* decisions concerning interacting with children to promote math thinking and learning. For example, the teacher decides how to provide support when children are frustrated; how to pose

Instruction

1 Planning experiences

To effectively plan experiences, teachers must make a variety of decisions based on their knowledge and focusing on the needs of individual children.

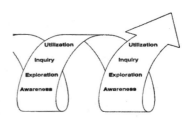

The Learning Cycle

Instruction

2 Interacting with children

Interacting with children and promoting interactions between children are key roles of the early childhood teacher.

problems in ways that engage children; and how to respond to answers or offer cues to encourage further thinking. The learning cycle is also relevant here; teachers use different strategies at different stages in children's learning.

This principle emphasizes that classroom discourse is an essential component in the learning of mathematics, and the teacher's decisions about interactions are critical.

Instruction

3 Orchestrating classroom activities

The teacher must orchestrate various contexts and ways in which children engage in mathematical experiences, such as whole group, small group, project teams, and other strategies.

---

3   The effective early childhood teacher works to enable each child in the group to attain a number of learning goals in mathematics and other areas. To do this the teacher orchestrates the many activities, groups, experiences, schedules, small- and whole-group times, projects, and centers during the day and over time. Through the physical environment, schedule, learning contexts, and materials, the teacher can encourage self-regulation and facilitate the learning of mathematics.

Instruction

4 Facilitating family-school relations

To facilitate effective family-school relations, the teacher must encourage reciprocal communication between teachers and families in mathematics as in other areas.

---

4   Because of their own prior experiences with mathematics, which may be mostly negative, parents often communicate to their children that math cannot be learned easily. Unfortunately, these attitudes can influence a child at a very early age and can affect the child's mathematical learning.

For children to get off to a good start with attitudes and experiences that support math learning, families must be aware of the importance of mathematics, the ways that they use mathematics daily, and how they can share their child's success in mathematics. The role of the teacher is to communicate methods to teach mathematics, listen to families identify children's natural mathematical knowledge, introduce games and activities appropriate for use at home, and share with parents an informative picture of the child's mathematical understandings.

Planning and Orchestrating Classroom Learning

In a large elementary school in a culturally diverse urban setting, Ms. Henekee teaches 25 second-graders who show varying levels of ability. Often children work on a variety of activities, independently and in learning centers, while the teacher works with one small group and then another. So the children can do this, Ms. Henekee every morning prints clear, concise instructions on the chalkboard.

This morning she writes an estimation question: How many times could you snap your fingers in a minute (if your fingers didn't get tired)? The children are getting index cards from the middle of the table, talking to each other, and recording numbers. As children practice snapping their fingers, the teacher walks around answering questions, showing children how to snap their fingers when they ask for help, and encouraging them to record their estimates.

Ms. Henekee: *(stopping at Jeffrey's table)* Jeffrey, what's your estimate?

Seth: *(shrugs)* I don't know what it is.

Ms. Henekee: I don't either, but I wonder . . . maybe 1,000! Do you think 1,000 is too much? Or what about 5—too little?

Seth: *(small smile)* No . . . you're silly. It can't be that big or that little. Umm, maybe 20? *(doubtful, waiting for a response)*

Ms. Henekee: *(smiles)* Who knows? Could be. *(pats him on the shoulder and whispers)* I'm glad you're trying!

When everyone has recorded an estimate, the children form a number line, arranging themselves in order from the smallest estimate to the largest and holding up their estimates.

Children: *(talking to each other)* I have 34. Is my number bigger? . . . No, you are smaller than me . . . I have 28 . . . Hey, you are out of order! You belong over there! . . . Wow, I've got 100. I'm probably way over there . . . *(in a few minutes the line gets quiet)*

Ms. Henekee: We are ready to look at our data. Alicia, I think it is your turn to be data director. I will hold your place in the number line.

Alicia: O.K., everybody say your number. Listen for the number that's said the most because I will ask you when you're done. *(pointing at the beginning of the line)* Start here!

The children say their numbers one at a time. Several children are out of order and change places as the errors are discovered.

Alicia: O.K., What number did we hear the most?

Sam: Twenty-five—there were three of those.

Alicia: That means 25's the mode. Fernando, please be the recorder *(Fernando goes to the board and records the mode under the question)*. Now, what about the range?

Paula: It starts with a 3 and goes to 200!

Some of the children start to giggle about the large guess. The teacher gives a "teacher look" to those who appear to be making fun.

Alicia: I think we are done. Paula, would you please write it? Ms. Henekee, is that everything?

Ms. Henekee: Thank you, Alicia, but I think there is one more thing we need to know. What about the middle number, the median?

The class finds the median by returning to their seats two at a time—one from each end of the line. When only Chet is left standing, he gives his number. Ms. Henekee reminds the children that the number in the middle of data arranged in a number line is called the *median*. Paula records Chet's number on the board.

> **Ms. Henekee:** Remember that we will work on getting a closer estimate at the end of class today. Alicia, you were an excellent data director. Thank you. Everyone, think about what kind of sample we will need for our better estimate. It should be interesting to see how close we get.

While the teacher meets with two groups of children for about 20 minutes each, the others continue to work independently or together in various centers or at their seats; some work on a video project.

Next, Ms. Henekee returns to the finger-snapping activity, asking the children to give suggestions for making a better estimate. The best suggestion (as determined by a class discussion) is to count finger snaps for half a minute and then double that number. Ms. Henekee times the 30 seconds, and the children begin their calculations.

Conversation is lively as the children try to determine the most accurate estimate, sharing methods and discussing calculations. Some children get calculators; others count on their fingers. Several get place-value blocks, while still others calculate on paper.

When the lunch bell rings, Ms. Henekee reminds her class that they can do more estimating at home. She asks them to time someone at home snapping his fingers for 30 seconds and record the number of times he snaps. The next day they will check the sums and make a new number line.

Ms. Henekee has thoughtfully planned the schedule, activities at the learning centers, small-group meetings, and various levels of the learning cycle used throughout the activity to contribute to a mathematics experience that meets children's individual needs. The teacher's interactions with children are highly dependent on the children's responses. While children are talking, helping each other, and comparing numbers, Ms. Henekee appears to be very nondirective. Then she steps out of the teacher role, facilitates Alicia's leading of the activity, and, taking Alicia's place in the number line, participates in the activity as the children are doing.

The teacher continually encourages self-regulation and communication among the children. Her role is that of facilitator when Alicia acts as the data director. Ms. Henekee briefly lends her a hand when the children forget to calculate the median. The organization and structure provided by Ms. Henekee, though not obvious to the children, underlie all aspects of the math activities. The schedule too encourages self-regulation and management, as is demonstrated by the children's behaviors. Finally, the homework assignment is a fun extension of a classroom activity that facilitates family-school relations.

This classroom vignette illustrates a well-organized, planned classroom experience in which children are principally at the exploration and inquiry phases of the learning cycle. The teacher's role varies throughout the lesson. She actively orchestrates the many classroom activities so that children can learn, and she assigns homework that links school and family. The teacher must be ready to react and adjust plans if she sees that more time or assistance is needed for any activities or if she sees a good opportunity to go further than anticipated with a particular concept. The plans are a general framework, not a rigid timetable.

Assessment principles

How does a teacher assess what young children know about mathematics? How can a child's reasoning or problem-solving skills be assessed? And how can busy teachers do the myriad tasks necessary in working with young children—organize an inviting learning environment, plan and carry out the curriculum, interact with children to enhance their learning—and still find time to assess the mathematical understanding of each child in their care?

There are no easy answers. But with practice and persistence, continuing to learn about children's mathematical thinking, teachers are able to make the processes of thoughtful observing and questioning part of their natural routine. To develop these important skills, teachers should plan daily observations that involve watching, listening, talking with children, and carefully listening to their responses.

To make the best instructional decisions for children, teachers need to assess each child's pattern of development, knowledge, attitudes, and interests. Both the early childhood community and the mathematics community emphasize that assessment should be the basis for educational decisions that affect children (NAEYC & NAECS/SDE 1990; Bredekamp & Copple 1997; NCTM 2000).

When people hear the word *assessment*, they often think of testing, but assessment has a much broader meaning. It is the process of observing; gathering evidence about a child's knowledge, behaviors, and dispositions; documenting the work that children do and how they do it; and making inferences from that evidence for a variety of purposes.

Assessment Principles for Early Childhood Mathematics	
1. Benefiting children	The primary purposes of mathematical assessment are to benefit children and identify their strengths and specific needs.
2. Observing and listening	Observing and listening are essential skills for the early childhood teacher.
3. Using multiple sources of evidence	To best assess mathematical understanding, teachers should use multiple sources of evidence collected on a systematic basis.
4. Assessing learning and development	Teachers have a responsibility to assess their own teaching effectiveness as well as children's learning and development in mathematics.

Assessment should always be designed, carried out, and used in ways that benefit children. With young children, effective assessment includes observing them, as well as documenting and collecting their work. Equally important is the teacher's reflection on and conceptualization of what she has seen and heard. Such thoughtful reflection occurs only when the teacher has an understanding of the mathematics involved and of young children's thinking and learning. As this author previously wrote, "A teacher who continually learns *from* children and *about* children can become the most effective assessor of the young child's mathematical understanding" (Copley 1999, 188).

> *Assessment*
>
> ## 1 Benefiting children
>
> The primary purposes of mathematical assessment are to benefit children and identify their strengths and specific needs.

1 For mathematical assessment to accomplish its central purpose of benefiting children, it should take place before, during, and after instruction. Teachers assess before instruction to plan learning experiences. During the learning experience the teacher observes and asks questions, listening to children's responses and watching what they do. After the experience the teacher uses assessment to determine what the children have learned.

If aspects of a child's work or responses indicate a misconception or lack of understanding, the teacher uses this information to make needed adjustments in the curriculum or her teaching practices to enhance the child's learning and understanding. If assessments show a mathematics program to be ineffective with a number of the children, with respect to either their learning or their developing positive dispositions toward math, the teacher may want to consider a new curriculum or new instructional methods. Most important, assessment of mathematical understanding should identify strengths and specific needs of young children.

Assessing children's understanding of mathematics in real, natural settings helps teachers adapt their teaching styles and curricular materials to children's diverse learning styles. Moreover, when assessment becomes a routine part of the ongoing classroom activity, learning is not interrupted.

> *Assessment*
>
> ## 2 Observing and listening
>
> Observing and listening are essential skills for the early childhood teacher.

2 Young children often are not proficient in expressing themselves in writing or conversation. This is especially true when children's home language is not English. Teachers must observe children's actions, behaviors, and interactions and listen carefully to them as they talk. Systematic, planned observations, sometimes with the aid of audio or video recordings, help teachers to make valid, objective observations (Bergen 1997).

Teachers also need to work to develop effective questioning skills and pay careful attention to children's responses. By using these skills in both informal observations and interactions and in conducting systematic, planned assessments, the teacher gets a good picture of each child's understanding and can use the information in planning instruction.

3 Assessment includes the process of gathering evidence about the mathematics that children know, their ability to use it, and their attitudes toward math. Multiple sources of evidence—samples of children's mathematical work, audiotaped descriptions of their problem-solving discussions, anecdotal records describing children's work at centers and on mathematical tasks—should be collected and used on a systematic basis.

4 Teachers must assess their own growth as well as children's progress in learning mathematics. To evaluate their teaching behaviors and effectiveness, teachers observe, listen, collect, and document children's learning and use this evidence to consider what is working and what is not.

To assess children's growth in mathematical understanding, teachers observe and document what children can do independently and with assistance. Assessments must occur systematically over a period of time to fully analyze and assess growth. And because different children show what they know and can do in different ways, assessment should include multiple approaches in order to give a well-rounded picture and allow each child to show his or her strengths (NCTM 2000).

The activity described next provides examples of the four assessment principles in a kindergarten classroom.

Observing and Assessing

It is circle time, and the children are participating in a weekly activity involving a particular type of reasoning. The gathering provides many assessment opportunities for Mr. Garza, the teacher.

The activity requires children to place their vote in either the YES bag or the NO bag to answer the question of the day. The question of the day, "Do you have a dog?" is represented in rebus form.

Mr. Garza Can anyone tell me how many children are in our class?

Ian: Twenty-two. There always is unless somebody's gone!

Mr. Garza: Is everyone here? Has everyone voted?

Antonio: Maria's gone and so is Lisa. So we just got . . . uh . . . *(looks at the numbers on the calendar, finds 22, and goes back two numbers)* 20, I think.

Mr. Garza: Let's listen to Antonio tell us how he got his answer.

Antonio describes and demonstrates his procedure using the calendar board, which shows the month's dates in calendar form and as a number line.

Mr. Garza: Does everyone agree with Antonio? Amy?

Amy: Yeah! I just counted us and I got 20.

Everyone quickly counts the class members present and a consensus is reached. The numeral 20 on the calendar board is circled.

Mr. Garza: Let's see. *(pointing to the question of the day)* What is our question today? *(The YES bag has a picture of a dog, and the NO bag has the same picture with a large **X** over the dog.)*

Children: "Do you have a dog?" YES or NO.

Mr. Garza: All right, let's empty the NO bag. *(As the teacher empties the NO cubes, he assigns counters.)* Hunter, Joanne, and Jorge, you are the counters today. Remember that the three of you must get the same answer before you report back to us.

Hunter, Joanne, and George: *(returning to report their findings after a quick count)* We got five in the NO bag, so five people don't have a dog!

Mr. Garza: O.K., now comes the hard question. I wonder how many cubes are in the YES bag. Remember, 20 people voted and there are five NO votes. . . . I wonder how many cubes are in the YES bag. . . . Let's think about it for a while. Remember, good thinkers don't yell out answers; they put them in their heads and think about them.

The teacher observes the ensuing flurry of activity. Some children seem to be counting the class again and trying to eliminate five children. Others use their fingers and ask friends to help. Still others focus on the calendar board, counting backwards. A few children watch everyone else and seem totally confused. Patrick sits quietly, looking confident. Mr. Garza makes notes in a notebook.

Mr. Garza: Well, I think everyone is ready. Please share your answer with a partner. *(The children are used to this request and quickly share their results.)* Now, who would like to share their answer with the class?

Answers are shared, discussed, and demonstrated for the class. As children tell their answers, Mr. Garza takes more notes. Here are some of the responses.

Eleana: It's a lot. More than 10 because I counted the five cubes in the NO bag on one hand, and I needed Terry's fingers and mine to count the blue ones.

Federico: It's 22 because I know it.

Patrick: It's 15! I know because we have done this one lots of times before. A 5 and a 10 always make 15!

Silvie: I think it's 16 because I counted on that. *(points to the calendar)*

Tatanene: It's five! *(When asked if there were five cubes in both the YES and the NO bags, he responds)* Yeah, I guess so. That way it would be fair!

Dominique: Can I count the cubes?

Using anecdotal records, Mr. Garza jots down phrases describing some of the children's responses. Patrick understands the part-part-whole relationship of 5, 10, and 15. Eleana has good number sense about the value of the cubes in the YES bag. Federico demonstrates no understanding of the problem and answers using the one piece of information he remembers. Silvie has almost mastered the counting backward strategy. Tatanene has this concept confused with an equalization problem done the previous week. Dominique can solve the problem only by counting the cubes in the NO bag.

From his notes, Mr. Garza can plan further experiences that will address individual children's needs as well as continue the weekly YES/NO activity during circle time.

Mr. Garza listens to responses to this problem-solving activity so he can plan activities to benefit children's learning. To best accomplish this, teachers must spend a great deal of time observing and listening to children, a process detailed in the second assessment principle, Observing and Listening (p. 24). Note the many opportunities for the teacher to listen and observe children's thinking throughout the lesson. Finally, because this is a weekly activity, the teacher can assess children's mathematical understanding regularly as it develops (see p. 25, the fourth assessment principle, Assessing Learning and Development.) Based on his notes, the teacher can compare the growth of individual children as well as analyze the effectiveness of his teaching.

In this learning activity the four principles of assessment are evident, as well as many of the instruction and curriculum principles. Good assessment benefits children and involves observing and listening, collecting and documenting evidence, and assessing growth. Effective assessment enhances instruction, which in turn is grounded in a well designed-curriculum. All three sets of principles are essential and intertwined in good educational experiences.

As we look at specific mathematical ideas in the chapters that follow, many examples of the assessment, instruction, and curriculum principles will be apparent.

Chapter 3

Mathematics Processes in the Early Childhood Curriculum

E arly childhood educators say that children learn by doing. The statement is true, but it represents only part of the picture. In reality a child learns by doing, talking, reflecting, discussing, observing, investigating, listening, and reasoning.

The processes involved in learning mathematics are especially important to teachers of young children. Both the National Association for the Education of Young Children and the National Council of Teachers of Mathematics emphasize the learning processes—thinking, integrating, interacting, applying, and investigating—and children's active involvement in learning.

This chapter discusses the five mathematics processes described in *Principles and Standards for School Mathematics*: problem solving, reasoning, communicating, connecting, and representing.

Problem solving

Mr. Ketner's second-grade class enjoys frequent games of Hidden Tiles. Mr. Ketner hides different color square tiles and gives the children clues describing the tiles and their whereabouts. During the games he introduces math vocabulary. Here is an example of a Hidden Tiles game conducted early in the year that illustrates the process of problem solving.

Hidden Tiles

Mr. Ketner: I have some color tiles hidden under the file folder. Your job is to be detectives and figure out which tiles are under the folder by using the word clues I give you. There are lots of tiles for you to use to show your guesses. Now, I've just told you that I have *some* tiles. Using that clue, show me what I might have underneath the folder.

Children make various arrangements of color tiles on the table. Some children watch their friends and copy arrangements; others are clearly creating unique tile arrangements.

Clarice: Is this right?

Jonah: Is mine like yours?

Diego: Why don't you just show us?

Mr. Ketner: I want you to use your words and your brains to figure out the answer. Let's see, *(pointing to one child's design)* could this be right? Are there *some* tiles in this picture? Yes, in fact, all of these could be right, so I'll give you the next clue. I have *more than* three tiles and *fewer than* five tiles. *Now* show me what the hidden tiles might look like.

Children again become busy working on their answers. Some realize readily that there are four tiles in the solution. Others use only one part of the clue, making a solution that has more than three but not fewer than five, or fewer than five but not more than three. In each case the teacher asks the children to share their solutions with a partner and decide if the solutions could be correct. The teacher circulates, reviewing children's guesses by describing their tile configurations using the words in the clue.

Mr. Ketner: *(pointing to a child's guess)* You have more than three tiles and fewer than five tiles. That could be right! *(pointing to another child's guess)* You have more than three tiles. Let's see, do you have fewer than five tiles?

Becky: No . . . *(changes her tile answer to show four tiles)* Yes, now I do!

Mr. Ketner: Oh, what a good problem solver you are. You changed your answer when you remembered the other clue. A good problem solver changes her answer when she gets more information. Ready for another clue? Here it is: the four square tiles are put together in one large square. Try it!

Mr. Ketner continues to provide clues, reviewing children's guesses and reminding them to make sure their tiles fit all the clues. Finally, only two solutions are possible. With partners, children share the possibilities with the class and give justifications for their solutions.

As children share their guesses, the teacher records notes about their guesses and behaviors on a checklist. He will use this information to plan follow-up experiences and questions for the group and for individual children.

This particular game of Hidden Tiles took longer than 30 minutes. The children were highly involved, asking questions that demonstrated their reasoning, discussing the meaning of clues, and listening attentively to ideas and questions posed. The teacher gave clues that required negation ("I do *not* have any blue tiles") as well as clues that used mathematical terms ("My tiles form a big square." "The yellow tiles are diagonal to each other." "The red tile is on the top row.") After solving a few Hidden Tiles problems posed by the teacher, the children create their own problems and share them with their classmates.

Problem solving in the early childhood setting

All young children solve problems; yet even among preschoolers, differences in children's dispositions toward problem solving may be seen. One 3-year-old persists for 10 minutes in building a graduated tower, while another quickly gives up in frustration. One 5-year-old keeps trying the same unsuccessful strategy again and again, while her friend seeks another way to solve the problem.

Disposition is more than just a positive attitude toward math. An effective problem solver perseveres, focuses his attention, tests hypotheses, takes reasonable risks, remains flexible, tries alternatives, and exhibits self-regulation. Young children have far to go before their dispositions reach the level of mature problem solvers, but they are already learning (or failing to learn) key lessons. Just as so-called math minds are not distributed at birth, so children are not born with dispositions suited to problem solving. Instead, their accumulated learning experiences combine with their inherited characteristics to contribute significantly to their dispositions.

Letting children solve problems themselves. Informal opportunities for problem solving occur all the time in an early childhood classroom. When distributing materials to their classmates, children may need to determine if there are enough items to go around and if not, figure out how their class-

mates can share fairly. Teachers often resolve classroom problems themselves just to keep things running smoothly so children have time to do the "real lesson." But when teachers solve all the routine problems, children are robbed of the learning experiences that occur in authentic situations. In fact, problem solving very often *is* the real lesson.

Mrs. Nix is a prekindergarten teacher who was at the point of interrupting a child's problem-solving efforts when she caught herself. Four-year-old Steven decided to build an upside-down volcano using the new beveled blocks in the block building center. As he worked at this difficult task, which required him to balance and position blocks in an alternating pattern, Steven spent more than 30 minutes in deep concentration. Several times he watched his structure fall and then tried again.

Just as Mrs. Nix prepared to intervene, Steven discovered the position pattern required for the blocks to stand in an inverted volcano. Steven threw up his hands and shouted, "I got it! I got it!" The look of excitement on Steven's face testified to his strong motivation in problem solving, and all the children could see his enthusiasm. During circle time Mrs. Nix asked Steven to share his discovery, emphasizing the hard work Steven put into solving the problem and the great satisfaction he felt when he succeeded.

Later Steven sat in the block center explaining the solution to his peers and helping them with their projects.

Steps in problem solving. The approach most commonly taught in problem solving involves four steps:

1. understanding the problem

2. planning how to solve it

3. carrying out the plan

4. reviewing the solution (Polya 1957).

For young children this process is seldom linear or automatic. In fact, even adults go back and forth among steps or omit a step.

Taking time to explore the materials and possibilities in a problem situation, a natural process for children, is the first step. Having uninterrupted time to explore is critical in the problem-solving process, especially for young children. They gain understanding of the problem and have a much better chance of generating possible solutions when they have had the opportunity to play with materials and experiment.

Second, the problem solver needs to plan. Planning involves thinking ahead and considering alternatives—both challenging processes for young children. Teachers can model the planning process and encourage children to plan by asking questions to scaffold children's learning and using other strategies to get children to think ahead. In Hidden Tiles, for instance, children have time to consider the solutions they will put forth, and the teacher can ask them about their reasons, get them to check clues, and so on—all before they find out whether their ideas are right. The teacher also acknowledges children's thinking, planning, and reflecting on solutions. Thinking ahead and considering alternatives are processes children have to learn through experiences. As children see planning processes modeled, explore a variety of alternatives, and experience the positive results when planning occurs, their planning skills gradually develop.

The next problem-solving step is to carry out the plan—to try it out and see if it works. If the plan does not work, the problem solver modifies it and tries again.

Young children, however, often get an idea and immediately put it into action, so there may be little or no separation between the second and third steps. Children tend to quickly try a solution, then another, and then another. Yet reflection is key to effective planning. To promote the development of reflection and planning, teachers must get children to pause—not in every instance, of course, but at times—and take time to think about what will happen before they try out their plan.

Finally, looking back is a critical but frequently neglected step in the problem-solving process. Mr. Ketner kept drawing the children's attention to the earlier clues and reminding them to check to see if their solutions still fit *all* the clues. This step often occurs quickly if at all. Young children need reminders to "see if your answer works" or "check back with your clues" or "look back to see if your answer makes sense."

Promoting children's problem solving

A key teaching role is to provide a setting rich in possibilities for solving problems. Early childhood teachers should design and stock the learning environment so that it offers interesting problems and an array of materials for children to use in solving them, such as counters, geometric shapes, blocks, and puzzles.

Another task for teachers is to help children identify and work on those problems. Children encounter problems every day in their lives at home (Do I have enough money to buy the book? How many different outfits can I make with my favorite shirt? How many days until we see grandma?) and at school (Do we have enough calculators for everyone? How could we plan our day so that everyone who wants to, gets to work at the sand table? How many cars do we need for our field trip?). Often, teachers or parents solve problems that could be solved by the children themselves if given the time and opportunity. Instead of offering solutions, the teacher can help children clearly state a problem, provide time to listen and talk about problems, and connect to mathematics learning some of the problems occurring in children's lives.

Children gain a great deal when teachers model problem-solving strategies and dispositions. They learn a powerful lesson when the teacher conveys the joys of solving problems *and* acknowledges the frustrations, giving them encouragement and strategies to handle the taxing moments in problem solving.

By posing questions and making comments along the way, teachers help children learn to stand back and consider possibilities and evaluate various ideas before deciding what to try. Children become more reflective when they are encouraged to share their thinking with others, verbally or through other methods of representing and communicating. As a further bonus, teachers find out what children are thinking. Knowing a child's interests and how she constructs and understands problems enables the teacher to present a problem that extends the child's mathematical thinking and problem-solving skills—to tailor instruction to the child's needs.

Young children frequently solve problems using the guess-and-check strategy: make a guess, check it out, and try something else if that idea fails. Although this method may lead to eventual success, children need to learn to consider why the first solution did not work in order to become better problem solvers.

An unspoken stratagem, however, exists among young children that allows them to short-circuit such thinking: they take a guess and then check the teacher's reaction. Teachers are often so quick to reinforce children's right answers and dismiss their wrong ones that they do not give young children the time or encouragement to rethink a problem. Focusing on the teacher's reaction cuts off problem solving and reflection, not only for the child giving the answer but also for all those who hear the teacher's response or see the *yes* or *no* on her face. For this reason teachers do well to cultivate an interested but noncommittal expression that conveys, "Hmmm, that's an interesting idea . . . ," and leaves plenty of space for children's thinking to continue.

Reasoning

Reasoning opportunities are abundant in the life of the young child. In early childhood classrooms, children play games, classify and label sets of objects, solve problems, and observe and listen to others as they think. Guess My Cage is a game to promote reasoning and is played often in this class during circle time.

Ms. Lim's class of 4-year-olds returns from a "creature hunt" in which they searched the playground for red-paper and blue-paper creatures. They will use the creatures to play Guess My Cage.

Guess My Cage

In Ms. Lim's classroom, are six "cages" each labeled to indicate a single characteristic—Red, Blue, Big, Little, Horns, and Hair. The children survey the cages and place each creature in an appropriately labeled one. Ms. Lim then launches the second part of the activity.

Ms. Lim: Wow, we have done a great job! All the creatures have a cage. Let's see if every creature is where it belongs. Myra, why did you put this creature in this cage?

Myra: *(after a pause)* Because it's blue, and the sign says blue.

Ms. Lim: Good. What about this one, Jackie?

Eli: 'Cause it's big, like this one. *(points to another creature in the same cage)*

Ms. Lim: Do you agree with Eli, Jackie?

Jackie: *(nodding)* Uh-huh, and it's red.

Ms. Lim: So, could I put it in this cage too? *(indicates the cage labeled Red)* Where else could it go? What else do you notice about this creature?

The discussion continues, with children discussing the distinguishing characteristics of creatures and justifying their placement in the labeled cages. Ms. Lim introduces a new twist.

Ms. Lim: Would you like to play a game? It's called Guess My Cage. *(Mr. Allen joins the group.)* Let's see if we can fool Mr. Allen. Mr. Allen, we are going to try to fool you. Look at our cages. In just a minute we are going to send you out of the room. Then we will choose one cage, take away the label, and see if you can figure out which cage it is from the children's clues. We are not going to tell you. You'll have to figure it out by yourself!

Mr. Allen leaves the room, and Eli accompanies him to make sure he doesn't peek. Ms. Lim asks the children to choose a cage. They quickly decide on the Red cage, and Ms. Lim takes out the creatures and removes the label. The children then put away the other cages, redistributing the creatures among themselves.

Ms. Lim: Now we are almost ready. Let me show you again the card for the cage you chose. Put it in your heads and remember. *(She shows the card labeled Red and motions for the children to put it in their heads and lock their lips. She asks Dick to sit on the card so Mr. Allen can't see it.)* Evangelina, please tell Eli to bring Mr. Allen back into the room. Remember, don't tell Mr. Allen!

Eli brings Mr. Allen back. There is a great deal of giggling and excitement.

Mr. Allen: I wonder which cage that is. Will you tell me?

Children: No! . . . No way!

Ms. Lim: No, Mr. Allen, we won't tell you what the cage is, but we will give you some clues. Jo-Lin, will you be first? Pick one of your creatures, and tell Mr. Allen if it belongs in the cage.

Jo-Lin picks up a red, big, horned, hairy creature and places it in the cage.

Mr. Allen: So, your creature belongs in the cage? *(Jo-Lin nods.)* Pete, how about one of your creatures? *(Pete nods and places his red, little, horned, hairy creature in the cage.)* How about one of your creatures, Evangelina?

Evangelina picks up a blue, big, horned, hairless creature and looks at Ms. Lim. Ms. Lim shakes her head no, and Evangelina shakes her head no and sets the creature outside the cage.

Mr. Allen: I have just learned something new.

Mr. Allen continues questioning children, and the children place creatures in the cage until there are 15 in it. More than 10 creatures, all blue, remain outside the cage.

Mr. Allen: *(appears to be thinking)* Oh, I think I know the cage! At first I thought it was *Big,* but then this creature was little. And then I thought it was *Hair,* but this creature has no hair. And then I thought it was *Red,* and I checked, and every creature in the cage was red, and all the creatures outside are blue! *(indicates all the blue creatures)* So I think your cage is *Red!*

Children: *(groaning)* He's so lucky . . . Did you tell? . . . Man, he guessed it!

Ms. Lim: Let's see if you are right, Mr. Allen. Dick, would you give me the card? Let's see. *(shows the* red *card to everyone)*

Eli: He got it right!

Ericka: He's so lucky!

Jo-Lin: Let's play again!

Jo-Lin's enthusiasm is shared by her classmates. They will play this game over and over. Each time they try to fool an adult, and each time the children express surprise that the adult "got it right!" But over time the game changes dramatically as children learn to listen to the reasoning of the adult and eventually discover that they too can find the solutions. After many experiences, children and teachers change roles and the children try to "guess my cage." Later, children play the game as partners during choice time as they challenge each other with new attributes or objects.

Reasoning in the early childhood setting

The children's reactions in playing Guess My Cage are typical of 4-year-olds. For instance, they believe that someone who solves a problem correctly is lucky—that thinking has nothing to do with it! Preschool children do not yet understand that people use reasoning to solve a problem; they have even less understanding of how reasoning works.

Another example of 4-year-olds thinking is that the children consider clues to be useful only if they concern the creatures *in the cage.* When Mr. Allen indicates creatures not in the cage, the children want to dismiss those creatures as irrelevant. They do not comprehend that finding out about a creature *not* in the cage can be even more revealing than learning about creatures in it. Children typically need extensive experience with such problems before they see that eliminating possibilities is important in solving the problem.

Reasoning experiences with the concept of *not* can be emphasized during routine activities. For example, children learn important reasoning words when teachers give directions such as, "Those people *not* wearing red may get their jackets to go outside" or "Those boys and girls who did *not* have a turn yesterday . . . "

Preschool and kindergarten children tend to focus on only one property or attribute at a time. Picking up a blue fish, a child will say, "This is blue," and put the fish in the *blue* pile. Or she may say, "A fish!" and put it in the *fish* pile. By second grade, however, children recognize that objects have multiple properties, and they use classification schemes that take into account more than one property. Now the child might sort a collection of animals into sets of blue fish, green fish, blue crabs, and green crabs.

Young children reason, but their reasoning tends to be intuitive; they are not aware of how they arrive at an answer. They tend to respond to *why* questions with short, unrevealing answers. Shoulder shrugs and phrases such

The Young Child and Mathematics

as "I just know it" or "Just because" are typical. One first-grader used a calculator to correctly answer a number pattern problem. When asked how he figured it out, he responded in a characteristic way: "I thunk and I thunk and I mashed and I mashed and out came the answer!" Although we chuckle over such explanations, we also need to keep in mind the value of persistently encouraging young children's justifications and reasoning.

Promoting children's reasoning

Even in the early years, children need to have experiences that help them begin to develop clarity and precision in their thinking. To give children familiarity with the language of logic and reasoning, teachers should get into the habit of using words and phrases such as *or, not, if . . . then, because, some, all, never,* and *probably*. For example, a teacher could say, "You may choose apple juice *or* grape juice to drink with your crackers," or "*All* of you have families, and *some* of you have sisters in your family."

Teachers should also encourage children to make conjectures, and to investigate and justify them as well. For instance, when children make their own conjectures about natural phenomena, teachers should encourage them to investigate their notions, no matter how unlikely the premise. Armand in Chapter 1 was certain that earthworms have eyes. Encouraged to investigate his idea, he created charts and graphs to justify his beliefs. Although he was wrong, Armand used reasoning and other mathematical skills to support his conjectures—powerful mathematics!

A second-grader who told his teacher that an even number added to an odd number is always an odd number explained his reasoning by first showing examples using numbers: 1 + 2 = 3 (odd), 5 + 10 = 15 (odd), 7 + 2 = 9 (odd). Then he built an even number with paired cubes (two 3s) and he built an odd number with paired cubes and one odd cube (two 5s and one 1). When he put them together (two 3s, two 5s, and one 1), he still had one lone odd cube (the 1) and thus an odd-number sum.

The teacher's role in fostering children's reasoning processes is critical. Teachers should ask questions that require investigation and reasoning, such as

- Are you sure?
- How do you know?
- Why do you think . . . ?
- What else can you find that works like this?
- What would happen if . . . ?
- I wonder how this could be changed?
- What would the pattern be?
- What if . . . ?
- I wonder why . . . ?
- Perhaps it's because . . .

In addition, teachers should continually use reasoning language in every-day occurrences. Thinking out loud and expressing their own thoughts about problems can facilitate children's thinking. Finally, and most important, if teachers are to emphasize the reasoning process, they must listen to children's own reasoning. Only when a teacher knows and understands a child's justifications can he best encourage more sophisticated and reason-able conjectures.

Communicating

To communicate about mathematics ideas, children must articulate, clarify, organize, and consolidate their thinking. As they struggle to capture their ideas and processes in words or other modes of communication, children become more conscious of what they know and how they solve problems. At the same time the teacher finds out more about what children think and know. Peers also listen, observe, and learn, becoming aware of other children's perspectives and strategies and asking questions that push their classmates to be clearer and less egocentric in communicating.

First-grader Ong creates a picture of fish and dogs during a classroom drawing activity. His teacher, Mrs. Wyman, uses questions to get Ong to de-scribe how he calculates the total number of eyes belonging to the fish and dogs in his picture.

Animal Eyes

Mrs. Wyman: Ong, would you tell me about your picture?

Ong: My dogs and fish have lots of eyes. There are 16!

Mrs. Wyman: But I don't see 16 eyes. How do you know how many there are?

Ong: (places two fingers on one fish) There are two eyes, but one is hid-ing. I will show you!

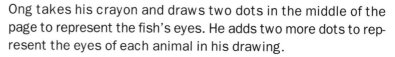

Ong takes his crayon and draws two dots in the middle of the page to represent the fish's eyes. He adds two more dots to rep-resent the eyes of each animal in his drawing.

Mrs. Wyman: Are you sure there are enough?

Ong: (holding two fingers over each animal's face and then pointing to the corresponding dots in the cen-ter) They all have two. This fish has two eyes, and this fish also has two eyes, and this dog has two. See, I was right! Sometimes you have to count stuff you only see in your brain.

When Mrs. Wyman asks Ong about his drawing, Ong responds by explain-ing the drawing, elaborating on his explanation by adding the dots, and then acting out the completed solution using his fingers. In this way he articulates information about his drawing that would not otherwise be clear.

Communication in the early childhood setting

In mathematics-rich classrooms, children use a variety of means—verbal and nonverbal—to communicate their mathematical ideas to others. They manipulate objects, draw pictures, use fingers, and devise other ingenious ways to show what they mean. They also learn to explain their answers in writing, use diagrams and charts, and express ideas with mathematics symbols.

When children are deeply invested in an undertaking, they are often particularly keen to share their ideas and creations with others, even when doing so takes some hard work. In the block-building center, 4-year-old Teddy created an ornate pattern using curved blocks of various colors. He spent more than 15 minutes describing his pattern to Andy and directing Andy to make his pattern "go the other way." Teddy named his pattern The Wave and described each step using specific color, position, and size words.

In the end Teddy and Andy created a 10-foot-long symmetrical pattern of wooden blocks. With a strong motivation to cooperate in making The Wave, the two boys eagerly strove to communicate with each other. Thus the experience enhanced their math communication skills far more than an artificial communication task would.

Interactions involving math occur from child to teacher, from teacher to child, and between children (NCTM 2000). To learn to express themselves clearly, listen attentively, ask for clarification, and use other communication skills, young children need to observe these skills in action and have many opportunities to practice them. Children are not adept at listening to others share ideas; nor are they skilled at stating their ideas with clarity and precision. However, with practice, they can learn to listen to each other and describe their reasoning. As children strive to express their ideas, they organize and consolidate their mathematics thinking and concepts.

While young children have not yet acquired advanced writing skills, they can draw pictures, write simple words, or frame sentences that communicate their own mathematics ideas. Samples of children's written work indicate their intuitive and often inaccurate understandings and their emerging skills in written communication. What they write or draw is generally more comprehensible when they add a verbal explanation. Such explanations also help teachers to assess what the child understands, both about math and about mathematics communication, and to make instructional decisions accordingly.

Promoting children's communication

To help children develop in mathematics communication, teachers find it helpful to verbalize and restate concepts and processes. They ask questions and describe what they see the child doing, and they listen carefully to children's communicative efforts.

While it is important for teachers to use clear, age-appropriate mathematical language and to ask questions that help children clarify or extend their ideas, the most important teaching skill in promoting communication is listening attentively to what children say. Observing in early childhood classrooms, one frequently hears well-meaning teachers ignore important clues and information that children are giving them. In comments and questions, children reveal what they are focusing on, what they understand and misunderstand, and the aspects with which they are struggling. By listening well, teachers gain an important window into the child's mind.

To foster math communication, teachers also should give children many opportunities to talk with and listen to their peers. Working in small groups or pairs on a reasoning game or task is particularly helpful. When children find it difficult to follow a classmate's reasoning, their questions and misinterpretations provoke the speaker to restate her idea or try other ways to communicate it. At times teachers may provide encouragement and support during this process, saying, for example, "Can you find another way to help James understand how you figured that out?"

Connecting

In outlining the connections standard for children in prekindergarten through second grade, *Principles and Standards for School Mathematics* (NCTM 2000) states,

> The most important connection for early childhood mathematics development is between the intuitive, informal mathematics that students have learned through their own experiences and the mathematics they are learning in school. All other connections—between one mathematical concept and another, between different mathematical topics, between mathematics and other fields of knowledge, and between mathematics and everyday life—are supported by the link between students' informal experiences and more-formal mathematics. Students' abilities to experience mathematics as a meaningful endeavor that makes sense rest on these connections. (p. 132)

Elaborating on the value of seeing connections for children, the *Principles* document goes on to say,

> Understanding connections eliminates the barriers that separate the mathematics learned in school from the mathematics learned elsewhere. It helps [children] realize the beauty of mathematics and its function as a means of more clearly observing, representing, and interpreting the world around them. (p. 132)

Exploring Pennies

Miss Hewitt is listening and observing during center time in her kindergarten classroom. Three children are in the science exploration center using magnifiers to explore pennies from a jar she put there. After having some fun using the magnifiers on each other and giggling at their magnified eyes and fingers, they began looking at the pennies. Miss Hewitt overhears them talking.

Arun: I have numbers on my penny! I got a 1 . . . a 9 . . . an 8 . . . and a 6.

Julie: Where? *(after a brief consultation with Arun)* Oh, so do I! I got a 1 . . . a 9 . . . a 7 . . . and a 5!

Roger: Me too. I got a 1 . . . a 9 . . . Man, this is weird!

After a few minutes, Miss Hewitt comes over and asks the children about their discoveries.

Julie: Well, every penny we look at has a 1 and a 9 on it. Roger says it's weird!

Miss Hewitt: I wonder if this is just true about *our* pennies. Do you have pennies at home? What if I let you take a magnifier home, could you check them out?

The investigation continues for several days. Children bring in pennies and record on a graph the numbers they find on these pennies. To their amazement they find a 1 and a 9 on every penny! Rather than give the children the explanation, Miss Hewitt encourages them to graph the results and engages them in discussing possible reasons for this weird phenomenon.

The children offer a variety of reasons, and Min mentions the calendar date. (If no one had thought of the calendar, Miss Hewitt would have brought it, along with other items, for the children to search for clues to account for the many 19s.)

More discussion ensues as children make conjectures about this intriguing connection. Finally, comparing the years pennies were "born" with their own birthdates, the children make a wonderful timeline.

Miss Hewitt did not anticipate the children becoming interested in the numbers on the pennies; she put them out simply as objects to magnify. When the children notice the pervasive 19s, however, the teacher capitalizes on their interest and helps them see mathematical connections.

Connections between mathematics content areas and other content areas often occur quite unexpectedly. Mrs. John's kindergarten class had just finished reading *Where the Wild Things Are.* Each child was creating a costume for her own wild thing. Having made patterns during recent math experiences, many of the children put color patterns in their costumes. When Mrs. John remarked about the patterns she saw, all the children immediately added other patterns to their costumes. A wide variety of patterns resulted, some made with geometric shapes, others with design patterns, and still others with color patterns. Later, children made patterns on lined music paper with color dots and performed their music dressed in their costumes as Wild Thing Rock Stars! Lasting several weeks, this project had many connections between art, music, reading, and the mathematics content of pattern, geometry, and number.

Connections in the early childhood setting

Mathematical experiences and opportunities can occur in any content area. Mrs. Bresselman's class of 3- and 4-year-olds was reading a familiar read-aloud book, *Chrysanthemum*. Dana, who had just learned to write her name, said, "Wow! Her name is stupid. It's too hard to write!" Pointing to the Name Wall (on which each child's name appears along with his or her photo), Mrs. Bresselman asked the children if they could find any names that were long, like Chrysanthemum.

The children became very excited about long names and short names and those in between. During the following week, children began to count the letters in their name and constructed a class graph showing short names, in-between names, and long names. Although Mrs. Bresselman had not planned to teach mathematics during a reading activity, children's interest led naturally to the connection.

To the observant early childhood educator, many mathematics connections present themselves every day. Besides keeping an eye out for connections between mathematics and everyday contexts, teachers can link different mathematical ideas—for example, a geometric concept with a concept in number or pattern. Finally, mathematics connects to other content areas. Children tapping out patterns in the music center, identifying patterns in the ceiling tiles, or creating patterns on the tie-dye project in the art center are making connections.

Although children sometimes find such connections themselves, they would miss many useful and interesting connections if teachers did not spotlight them.

Promoting children's awareness of connections

Teachers play an important role in helping young children connect mathematics to other parts of the curriculum and to their wider world. They commonly highlight connections between math and children's experiences using calendars and clocks, cooking, counting books, and some aspects of science. But there are countless potential connections that are not so commonplace.

The teacher who incorporates number in a movement game by asking children to "stop and make five elbows" is making an explicit connection between movement and math. The teacher who enlists children's help in counting class materials by fives is illustrating the important uses of mathematics. When a teacher asks children to sketch their building creations before they are taken down, he fosters geometric awareness and visual representation. Many art projects and activities with sand and water help to develop measurement concepts and skills as well as spatial sense.

An infinite number of connections can be made quite naturally between mathematics and literature, language, science, art, construction, physical movement, and music. For the early childhood educator, it is important that these connections be natural and not forced. Contrived experiences or stories are not necessary and can inhibit a meaningful understanding of mathematics.

When children represent ideas mathematically or connect representations to mathematics, their understanding of math is enhanced. Representation is also crucial for recording information, communicating solutions, and explaining reasoning.

Young children convey their mathematical ideas and methods in a great variety of ways. They make use of concrete objects of all sorts, including their own fingers. Children draw, produce diagrams, and make tallies, symbols, and markings of various kinds. They also use language, of course, sometimes on its own and often in conjunction with other representations as well. As the representation standard for prekindergarten through second grade (NCTM 2000) states,

> Through interactions with these representations, other students, and the teacher, students develop their own mathematical representations of mathematical idea. . . . Representations make mathematical ideas more concrete and available for reflection. Students can represent ideas with objects that can be moved and rearranged. Such concrete representations lay the foundation for later use of symbols. (p. 136)

Representation is very closely linked to communication, each contributing to and supporting the other.

Hungry Ants

Mrs. Petri has taught kindergarten for 10 years. She frequently uses literature to discuss mathematical concepts and she constantly "talks mathematics" with her students. After reading *One Hundred Hungry Ants*, the children line up for lunch, forming two equal lines at the door. Their discussion as they line up prompts the use of mathematical representation.

Mrs. Petri: Let's see, we have two lines that are exactly the same in number. How many are in each line?

Everyone is busy pointing and counting.

Eunice: I think there are 10 in mine.

LeRoi: Yeah, 10 in my row too.

Mrs. Petri: So, do we have even rows, rows like the marching ants? How can you tell?

Michelle : Well, it's like our bar problems when we do our graphs. Everyone has a partner to shake hands with. There's no extra!

Mrs. Petri: Let's check.

Children begin shaking hands with their corresponding partners in the other line.

Mrs. Petri: Ten in each row. Hmmm. *(sighs)* How can we remember how we are lined up? Who is our recorder today? Bob? Would you write on the board about our lines so we can remember?

Bob readily consents and goes to the chalkboard to record. He looks uncertain, counting but not knowing exactly what to write.

Mrs. Petri: Would you like someone to help you? How about Michelle?

Bob and Michelle work at the board. Bob begins to draw stick people in two rows while Michelle makes tally marks for each line. Michelle finishes first, shows Bob, and returns to her place in line.

Mrs. Petri: Bob and Michelle, that looks great. Now, I wonder if we could line up any other way and still have even lines? Let's see . . . we have 10 in this line *(holding up 10 fingers so everyone can see)* and we have 10 in this line. *(holding up two hands again so everyone can see)* I wonder what we could do.

Keith: *(standing in the middle of one of the lines)* We could split the lines here maybe *(pointing to the middle of the line in which he is standing)* and then have *fair* lines, you know, like the ants!

Geraldo: I know! One line will have five, the next line will have five, and then five, and then five! That would work!

Mrs. Petri: Wow, let's check it out. Five here . . . five here . . . five here . . . five here . . . Shake hands. It does! It works! Five in every row! How did you know that, Geraldo? What did you do?

Geraldo: Well, see, you had 10 in each line, like this *(holds up two hands)* and 10 in the other line, like this, *(holds up two hands again)* so you put one hand for one line, one hand for another line, one hand for this line, and one hand for this line *(places one hand at a time in front of each line)* and it works!

Bob records the four lines of five children using tally marks like Michelle's. When the class returns after lunch, the teacher suggests they use their math journals to see if they can find any other ways to line up like the ants.

Representation in the early childhood setting

Representations for number, operations, patterns, and geometric and statistical concepts are all essential to the young child's mathematical understanding. Representations often help to make mathematical relationships more obvious. These include common mathematical representations introduced by teachers as well as child-created representations.

In the Hungry Ants discussion, representations helped children solve a problem originally presented in a story. Bob's picture representation of stick people, Michelle's use of tally marks, and Geraldo's use of fingers helped children visualize and remember solutions, represent number quantities, solve problems, and explain their reasoning.

Teachers and parents often introduce children to common forms of numerical representation—tally marks, finger models, domino pips, pictures of objects, and dots used with ten frames. Even very young children use fingers to show their age—not always understanding what the fingers stand for but gradually getting the idea. The use of fingers is a common representation in part because the concept of 10 modeled by five fingers on each hand is easily learned and often serves as a useful benchmark.

For example, during circle time in a prekindergarten classroom, 4-year-old Lucas told his teacher that only six people could play a particular partner game because "you only got three boards!" When the teacher asked Lucas to explain his reasoning, he held up two fingers three times, saying, "One game, two games, three games. See, six people!" Lucas used his fingers to appropriately and purposefully represent the solution to a problem.

Promoting children's mathematical representation

To encourage flexibility in mathematical representation, early childhood teachers should introduce children to a wide range of representations—pictorial (drawings, maps), graphical (bar graphs made from stacked objects, timelines, pictographs), and symbolic (tables, prose descriptions) (Greenes 1999).

Providing meaningful contexts that encourage children to represent and communicate their understanding is part of the teacher's role. Children should also learn that representation helps them remember what they did and explain their reasoning. In addition, teachers should often ask children to verbally or concretely represent a concept by showing the number in another way or by using their words and objects to communicate their ideas.

When children see teachers referring to representations they have created ("Let's check back to your diagram and see how many were in each group"), the usefulness of representing is reinforced for them. Teachers should also make it a point to connect children's emerging mathematical representations with commonly accepted representations in mathematics.

The processes of mathematics are critical to the young child and his understanding of mathematics. As outlined in *Principles and Standards for School Mathematics* (NCTM 2000), the processes include problem solving, reasoning, communicating, connecting, and representing. It is impossible to describe in this chapter alone each process in the detail necessary; however, without specific content, the processes are not relevant. Thus, in the chapters that follow, these processes will be referenced frequently and stressed as they relate to specific mathematical content.

Chapter 4

Number and Operations in the Early Childhood Curriculum

National Council of Teachers of Mathematics publication *Principles and Standards for School Mathematics* (NCTM 2000) lists content standards in five areas for prekindergarten through twelfth-grade mathematics:

- number and operations
- algebra
- geometry
- measurement
- data analysis and probability

Consistent with these standards, the first curriculum principle introduced in Chapter 2 (see p. 15, Content) supports a mathematics curriculum for young children that is broadened to include more than arithmetic and shape identification.

The mathematics presented in this chapter and the subsequent chapters on content standards is varied and rich—and all of it can be very meaningful to young learners. Here the content standard of number and operations is the focus. However, because mathematics content standards are all interconnected, the other standards are interwoven as well.

In the math curriculum, the teacher's role is to provide a bridge between the child's informal knowledge of mathematics and the more formal "school" mathematics. As described in Chapter 1, young children enter school with many intuitive mathematical understandings. This is especially true of number and operations content. The teacher's job is to gain insight into the child's interpretation of number and to assess what each child knows and doesn't know. The subsequent teaching can then move the child from present concepts and constructions to more formal school mathematics.

When considering the content standard on number and operations, we first look at a classroom vignette. Then examples that occur spontaneously in play, during routine events, or while children are at centers are shared. Examples of planned learning experiences follow, accompanied by several unplanned, informal illustrations of classroom situations occurring in early childhood settings. These examples show the curriculum, instruction, and assessment principles (detailed in Chapter 2) in action in the teaching of number and operations.

To write an exhaustive list of mathematics activities for young children would be impossible. This is especially true for number and operations; this standard is the one most often addressed in books, texts, or curriculum documents for young children. The examples presented here are for teachers' use only if appropriate or for adaptation to particular situations.

Early childhood teachers are the primary decisionmakers in their classrooms. Effective teachers evaluate their decisions continually as they interact with children. To convey necessary information, early childhood teachers carefully choose appropriate activities and then, mindful of children's interests and needs, adapt the activities accordingly. The result: children doing mathematics and learning about number and operations!

The development of number concepts does not occur in one lesson, one unit, or even one year. It is a continuous process that provides the foundation for much of what is taught in mathematics. The following vignette occurs in a kindergarten program. Most of the children are 5 years old and their proficiency in English is limited. Ms. Scott is the teacher.

The Octopus Story

Children sit on the floor in a semicircle facing the story chair. Ms. Scott sits in the story chair holding a covered basket. The children have just finished a project about "minibeasts"—all types of insects and spiders. Using magnifiers, they counted legs, created their own minibeasts, and collected lots of data about where minibeasts live. In addition, they used insect and spider puppets in the creative dramatic center. All of the puppets are realistically made with the appropriate number of legs.

> **Ms. Scott:** Today I want to introduce to you a new puppet. But before I do, you must solve a riddle. Listen carefully . . . First clue: The puppet I have in my basket has eight legs.

Ms. Scott pauses. Children are counting on their fingers, pointing to the spiders still on the project table, or excitedly raising their hands or shouting out, "*Spiders!*"

> **Ms. Scott:** Ooooh, listen to my second clue: My new puppet is *not* a spider.

Again the teacher pauses. Some children look disappointed; however, it is clear that others do not understand the use of *not* and still believe the puppet to be a spider. Still others seem confused and begin talking and looking around the room for more clues.

Ms. Scott: Talk to your neighbors and see if they can help you.

Children: *(to each other and the teacher)* It's a spider . . . It can't be a bee, a bee has six legs . . . No, it's not a spider, that was the other clue . . . Hey, I heard about a weird dog that had eight legs . . . Oh, you're silly . . . That can't be . . . What about those things that live at Galveston . . . We saw one once, their legs sting and hurt . . . Octopus . . . *Pulpo* . . .

Ms. Scott: O.K., I am hearing lots of ideas. Listen now as I give you one more clue: I have a special book, and the illustrator, Eric Carle, put this creature on the front cover of the book. See if you know what it is.

Ms. Scott shows the front cover of Eric Carle's *Animals, Animals*.

Children: Octopus! *Pulpo!*

The teacher brings out the blue octopus puppet and shows the eight legs.

Ms. Scott: Now I have another tough question for you. Let's see, there are eight legs on this puppet . . . eight places for my fingers. If I put the fingers of one hand in the legs, I wonder if there will be any legs that don't have a finger.

Ms. Scott begins to slowly put her fingers into the puppet. Some children count on their fingers, others watch the teacher, and others excitedly shout out an answer.

Rena: You have extra legs, I think.

Tomas: No, it will be just right.

Mario: I know, you will have three legs empty! Just like the spider puppets. 'Cause they have eight legs too. The answer's not going to change!

Ms. Scott: Let's see if you are right. *(shows the puppet with her fingers in the legs, emphasizing the three empty legs)* Wow! Such good thinking! Now tell me what you know about an octopus.

A lively discussion ensues, with interesting stories and myths and partially correct facts—the black ink the octopus uses for protection is mentioned. The teacher decides to focus on a mathematical concept for the rest of the lesson, and she makes a note that octopi would provide an interesting focus for a project on the ocean.

Ms. Scott: I wish I had a puppet like this for each of you. This one will go back to our creative dramatics center later. But for now, I have a different kind of octopus puppet for you. The only thing is, you will have to make the legs.

She brings out a small paper plate with two large "googly eyes" glued on the bottom. Holding the plate between the palms of both hands, she wiggles her fingers. After questioning Ms. Scott about the number of legs, the children seem satisfied that her new puppet has eight of them.

The teacher distributes plates to each member of the class. Children experiment with ways to hold their octopi and create exactly eight legs.

Ms. Scott: We are going to do a play. Everyone will get a chance to be an octopus. Half of the class will be the octopus actors, and half of the class will be the audience. Then we will switch places. O.K., first group, over here, you are actors. Audience, over here.

Spontaneous dramas are a common occurrence in Ms. Scott's classroom. Children often work in two groups. While *dividing in half* is not a concept that they have been explicitly taught, children are very aware that it is a fair way to act out stories. They know that everyone will get a chance to be actors and audience members.

Ms. Scott: First, let's read the play lines:

(reading from a poem she has written)

> 1 octopus, 2 octopi, 3 octopi, 4 octopi, *5,*
> 6 octopi, 7 octopi, 8 octopi, 9 octopi, *10 . . .*
> 10 octopi swimming in the sea,
> Everyone's swimming, happy as can be.
> Oh, no! Black ink's a'coming . . .
> Some run hiding . . . everyone's a'running.
> How many octopi do you see?

Now, before we practice our lines, our actors must practice being octopi. Let's see, do you have eight legs? *(observes children holding plates and creating eight-legged octopi)* All right, let's see you swim happily. *(children wear large smiles as their octopi swim happily)* Can you show your octopi running? How about hiding and being very still?

O.K., we're ready! Audience, let me introduce our characters. Octopus number one, Yodit! *(audience claps as Yodit steps forward, wiggles her octopus's legs, and smiles).* Octopus number two . . .

After the teacher introduces all the octopi, octopus actors go through the actions as the audience reads the verses. There are 10 octopi standing at the front of the room. When the words "Oh, no!" are read, a teacher aide brings over a large piece of black butcher paper—the black ink—and covers four actors and their octopi. Children in the audience can still see the eight feet of the four hidden children showing under the black paper.

Ms. Scott: So, how many octopi do you see?

Chere: Six.

Ms. Scott: Are you sure? Show me with your fingers.

Most children easily show six fingers, five on one hand and one on the other; others look at their neighbors and model responses after theirs.

Ms. Scott: Can you show me another way to make six?

The children are familiar with this question. Some immediately show three fingers on one hand and three on the other. Others try different configurations. Still others, satisfied with their first way, only observe their friends' fingers.

Ms. Scott: Now, here's the tough question. How many octopi are hiding in the black ink? They are being very still so you can't see them. I wonder how many are hiding. Listen as I think out loud. Let's see, we started out with 10 octopi, and now we see six.

There is a flurry of activity as children count using their fingers, look at the black ink covering and count legs underneath, or talk to their friends about possible answers. Ms. Scott ignores children who respond verbally and seems to be thinking about the problem herself. After a long pause, she asks the children for their ideas and explanations of their thinking.

Jimmy: I think there's six hiding because I see six.

Chris: Me too!

Rachelle: No, there's four because a 4 and a 6 make 10 octopi, (showing fingers) see?

Phillippe: I counted the feet. There's eight!

Huong: No, people gots two feet. See? (Huong models by placing two fingers in front of each person hiding under the black paper. Then he turns to Phillippe and smiles expectantly, as if he is sure Phillippe will understand. Phillippe shrugs.)

Juanita: No, there's three because Hernando, Eduardo, and Phong are back there. I remember!

Ms. Scott: Oh, I like your thinking. I can tell you are all working very hard. Now I want everyone to show me with your fingers what you think, and then we will see. Show me!

When everyone has shown their finger answers, the teacher aide removes the black paper and the children count the four octopi that were hidden. The actors and audience then change places, and the play is performed again, but with a different number of octopi hidden by the ink.

Ms. Scott: I liked seeing how hard you worked to think about this problem. Now I would like you to make up your own stories. (shows a half strip of large manila paper) Make your ocean on this piece of paper. Then make as many octopi as you want in your ocean. Fold one end of your paper over . . . it's the black ink! When you finish, tell your story to a friend. See if your friend can tell how many octopi are hidden!

Children excitedly begin creating their octopus stories. Their pictures will later become permanent fixtures in the classroom. Months afterward children will still be trying to guess how many octopi are hidden in Mario's or Susie's picture.

Children at play—With number and operations

Opportunities to emphasize number and operations concepts abound in early childhood settings. For example, Mrs. Nielson observed four prekindergartners in the housekeeping center. "Brother" Allen was setting the table for his pretend mommy, brother, daddy, and company. Joshua, as the daddy, was reading the newspaper upside down, and "Mommy" Amanda was cooking the meal. Jennifer watched but was not involved in the dramatic play. There was one place setting each for the mommy, daddy, brother, and company; however, the company place setting included all of the extra dishes stacked in a pile.

Mrs. Nielson asked, "Could I please be the company? And what about Jennifer?" After Allen and Amanda agreed, Mrs. Nielson said to Jennifer, "Oooh, this meal looks great. I hope they have enough dishes and spoons and cups for both of us."

Immediately Allen and Amanda began to match dishes with spoons and cups and to make two places for the company. They quickly noticed that there were more than enough plates for the company but not enough cups. They sent Daddy Joshua to the store to buy more—"just one more cup." When Joshua returned with one paper cup from the classroom sink, the imaginary meal was served and enjoyed by all.

Beginning literacy activities often provide opportunities for number and operations exploration. Kindergartners learning to use a computer software program in Ms. Tank's class selected pictures and wrote words to tell about their pictures. When children discovered the *copy* command, they began to make many pictures of the same thing. Ms. Tank decided to ask children to write a number story to tell how many they created. Children loved the activity, and their pictures soon became number stories complete with number equations. Interpretations:

```
5 lit ing a en 4 ubg = 9
```
5 lightnings and 4 umbrellas equal 9 pictures

```
2 fr ad 3 elefhs = 5
```
2 flowers and 3 elephants equal 5 pictures

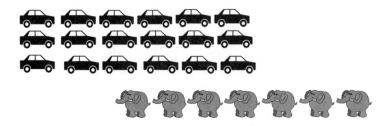

18 curs + 7 elphets = 25

18 cars plus 7 elephants equal 25 pictures

Shared reading experiences generate number stories as well. As part of an ecology project, Mr. Lathan read J. Pellowski's *The Messy Monster* to his class of kindergartners. Children retold the story and counted all of the items the monster threw away. Then Mr. Lathan asked them to write their own word problems about the animals of the forest. The children's stories included their own invented spellings, a question involving numbers, and numbers.

Sam Skunk was eating popcorn in the trees. He ate up five boxes. He didn't know where to put it, so he threw it on the ground. How many now?

Bob Bunny planted 18 carrots. He planted 7 more. How many now?

Number and operation concepts can be emphasized when children are working in various areas of the classroom. Abigail and Samantha were arguing in the block area about who had more blocks. The aide, Ms. Lazarow, asked each girl how many she had. Abigail said she had only 14: "See . . . 1, 2, 3, 4, 5, 6, 7, 8, 9, 10, 12, 16, 18, 14." Samantha said, "That's not right. Let me show you . . . 1, 2, 3, 4, 5, 6, 7, 8, 9, 10, 12, 13, 14, 15, 20, 22, 20, 26, 28, 40, 41, 42, 43, 20, 21, 22. Abigail has 22 blocks!"

Rather than count them correctly, Ms. Lazarow suggested a method for comparing quantities: "Let's match Abigail's blocks with Samantha's blocks to see who has more." Having some familiarity with this strategy, the girls made two long rows, matching one of Abigail's blocks to each of Samantha's. When Samantha ended up with two extra blocks, she gave one to Abigail and they continued their play.

Development of Mathematical Knowledge

In Piaget's (1965) classic conservation task, a child is first shown two lines of items exactly the same in number and length. When the child is asked if the lines have the same number, the child readily answers yes. Then the items are spread out in one of the lines. Again, the child is asked if the lines have the same number. Young children typically respond that the longer line has more items; that is, they do not *conserve* number.

Ginsburg (1977) describes this behavior as Phase 1, Direct Perception, in a three-stage model. Stated differently, the child's judgment is based primarily on the appearance—the length of the lines—rather than on the number of items in the lines.

Line 1 □ □ □ □ □ □

Line 2 □ □ □ □ □ □

In Phase 2, children begin to develop their understanding of number and quantity by counting items in different arrangements. Ginsburg (1977) labels this second developmental phase Informal Knowledge. In this phase children's concrete knowledge is based on everyday experiences to determine their answers to the Piagetian task. The young child looks at the differently spaced lines and either counts to check the answer or immediately answers the question correctly without counting, knowing that merely stretching out the line leaves the quantity unchanged.

As children learn in more formal settings, they progress to Phase 3, Formal Knowledge. At this stage children learn the meaning of symbols (=, <, >) and numerals (6, 4, 20) and their use in representing relationships between quantities.

Research over the last two decades suggests that with changes in the wording of questions posed to children, they show earlier understanding of number than was demonstrated in Piaget's research. Researchers have shown that young children possess considerable informal knowledge (Phase 2) even before entering school.

A great many young children learn to count to 10 or higher before reaching kindergarten (Van de Walle & Watkins 1993). When introducing their children to the kindergarten teacher, parents may proudly assert, "This is Suzanne. She can read her name and she knows most of her letters and she can count to 100!" Counting is indeed an important component of number and operations. However, it is only one small part of mathematical understanding.

Number sense is defined as "good intuition about numbers and their relationships. It develops gradually as a result of exploring numbers, visualizing them in a variety of contexts, and relating them in ways that are not limited by traditional algorithms" (Howden 1989, 11). Understanding of number and operations and sense about number do not just naturally occur. Number sense cannot be taught in one month-long series of lessons, nor does having number sense mean a child always responds correctly and with certainty. It is complex and develops gradually over time. It can and should be promoted through teaching.

Let's start our exploration of young children and number sense with *counting*, a key number skill that we begin to see in early childhood and that generally receives considerable adult attention.

Counting

Many teachers and parents have had the experience of listening to a young child count to 100 with no actual items to count. Taking a deep breath, the child begins counting with 1, continues with an unintelligible stream of numbers, and ends with 100! When asked to tell the number that comes after 20 or the number that comes before 5, the young child may begin the long counting sequence again, demonstrating little or no understanding of the question or a possible answer.

Counting is a skill requiring several abilities. Reciting the sequence of number names—one, two, three, and so on—is a memory task, like reciting

---

Finger Counting and Patterns

Researchers have determined that finger counting plays an important role in the development of mathematical understanding of young children. Using fingers to count, compare, and perform simple operations can provide children with a basis for understanding relationships between numbers up to 10.

A natural way of working with numbers, finger patterns give children the opportunity to represent a particular quantity with their fingers using different models. For example, children asked to show *five* with their fingers can show all the fingers on one hand, two fingers on one hand and three fingers on the other hand, or four fingers on one hand and one finger on the other (Baroody 1987; McClain & Cobb 1999).

---

the alphabet. Many children can do this before they are 3. Children who have not learned this verbal sequence are clearly not able to count, at least in the usual sense of the word. Yet learning the sequence of words does not ensure that children can actually count with accuracy and understanding.

To progress in counting, children must recognize the patterns involved in counting numbers greater than 9—for example, after a number ending in 9, a new decade (10, 20, 30) begins; or after a new decade number (20), subsequent numbers require the addition of the numbers 1 through 9 (21, 22, 23). Researchers have discovered that many children beginning kindergarten can count to 12 or higher (Payne & Huinker 1993; Van de Walle & Watkins 1993; Baroody & Wilkins 1999).

The teen numbers are often the most difficult for children, at least in English. If the teen numbers followed a logical pattern, as in some languages, the number 11 would be called *one ten, one* or perhaps *oneteen*, while the number for 15 would be labeled *one ten, five* or perhaps *fiveteen*. However, the English words for the numbers 11 through 15 must simply be memorized, and teachers can use a variety of materials and strategies to make the meaning clear.

The names for the decade numbers (10, 20, 30, 40) also deviate from the pattern of number names and need to be learned as distinct items within the counting sequence. Anyone who has listened to children count remembers the long pause before they change decades, whether correctly or incorrectly (25, 26, 27, 28, 29 . . . 50!).

Early Development of Counting Skills

Many researchers have investigated young children's object counting and oral counting (without objects). Here are some of their discoveries.

• The development of oral counting skills may begin as early as 2 years of age (Fuson 1988).

• Children first begin to memorize the sequence of number words, often missing portions of the sequence (Baroody & Wilkins 1999).

• Preschoolers may be able to say the counting sequence accurately and be able to tag objects as they count them. However, they often have difficulty keeping track of what they have or have not counted (Gelman & Gallistel 1978).

• Kindergartners typically know the 1–9 sequence and a bit beyond but often have difficulty identifying the counting patterns for decades (10, 20, 30) and transitions (for examples, that 39 signals 40 next) (Baroody & Wilkins 1999).

• Kindergartners typically can count out collections of at least five items accurately. With instruction they can learn to count out six or more objects, touching each object with their finger as they count it and retagging the last item counted as they tell the number of objects in the set (the *cardinal-count* concept) (Baroody 1987; Baroody & Wilkins 1999).

After children have become comfortable with the verbal sequence for counting by ones, they go on to learn counting in groups, that is, by twos, by fives, or by tens. Children's familiarity with the counting sequences increases when they join in songs, fingerplays, and rhymes that include counting ("One, two, buckle my shoe").

One-to-one correspondence. Beyond knowing the number words in sequence, counting requires linking a single number name with one object—and only one—at a time; that is, one-to-one correspondence. Many young children simply recite the counting sequence as they touch items, with no awareness that each item corresponds with one word in the counting sequence. Often during center time or outdoor play periods, children look and sound as though they are counting—counting out grocery items at the cash register, distributing toys to others in their play group, or telling a friend how many pretzels each child has for snack.

When we listen closely, however, we may find that children do not grasp the concept of counting, at least not entirely. They sometimes touch more than one item when they say one number, or conversely they say several numbers and touch only one item. In fact, children's verbal counting often seems to have no relation to the objects they are trying to count. A child counting six items may run through the verbal sequence very quickly and declare she has 20. Or a child who produces the number words very slowly may only reach three instead of six! One-to-one correspondence for the counting sequence is a skill that must be modeled and often directly taught.

Khan was a first-grader in my class who had great difficulty with the idea of matching one number to one item in counting. After many attempts, I invited him to stand on my feet and we walked around the room counting every footstep. After he felt, heard, and saw the counting skill, he better understood the process and was able to count accurately with other objects. Although my feet were sore, Khan had grasped the meaning of one-to-one correspondence in a way that connected for him.

Keeping track while counting. To count correctly, the child also has to keep track of those items she has already counted, making sure not to count any twice. Young children often count an object several times and get an inaccurate result, despite having consistently used the correct verbal sequence and one-to-one correspondence. Moreover, at some point in their mathematical understanding, some children may not see a problem if they count five marbles one time and six marbles the next time. Other children are puzzled when they get five marbles one time and six another but do not know how to keep this from happening.

Teachers can give children strategies to help them keep track of items they have already counted. For instance, children can count objects into sections of an ice cube tray, making sure only one object is in a section. Or teachers can introduce a keeping-track strategy by placing a line down the center of a paper or workspace and instructing children to slide each object over the line as they count it. In a first-grader's words, "Put the balls you have counted into piles—one pile for counted ones and one pile for the others—then you won't forget."

In learning to keep track, understanding one-to-one correspondence, and mastering counting, children benefit from exposure to a range of strategies and examples and lots of practice. Recall the varied counting experiences in the octopus vignette. Children joined in reciting a songlike poem that emphasized the verbal counting sequence 1 to 10. They had occasion to count by twos when only the feet of the other children were showing. At several points children used their fingers to count out amounts. And the teacher asked "how many" questions various times, eliciting a variety of answers.

Another example in which a counting issue came up was the block argument between Abigail and Samantha. Neither child had mastered the decade pattern in counting; therefore, they could not do an accurate comparison using only counting strategies. The problem was resolved when the teacher proposed a comparison method using concrete objects—the blocks themselves.

Quantity

Enumerating the objects in a set is central to the understanding of number and operations. When children realize that they can tell how many objects are in a set of items by saying the last number in a counting sequence ("1, 2, 3, 4, 5, 6—there are six cups"), they have begun to understand number quantity. To develop the concept of number, children should have experiences with representing quantity in a variety of ways. Ten frames, domino and dice pips, tally marks, and finger patterns are all representations that help young children to understand quantity.

Part-part-whole relationships. Basic in developing number sense are experiences that help children recognize part-part-whole relationships. For instance, a whole of 7 can be represented as a 4 and a 3, a 5 and a 2, or a 6 and a 1. Any whole number can be represented in parts. A precursor to number operations, the part-part-whole representation helps children develop an understanding of the relationship between addition and subtraction.

Three-year-old Rodney showed me how old he was using two fingers on the left hand and one finger on the right. He then changed hands, showing two fingers on the right hand and one finger on the left. His words indicated that he was beginning to understand part-part-whole relationships: "See, Miss Nita, I can make three like this. But I can't make all the fingers on one hand, like Mommy!"

Five-year-old Rebecca looked at bug counters on the table and said very confidently without counting, "There are five bugs there. I know because, see, you have two there and three there. A 2 and a 3 always make 5, you know." Rebecca had not learned this as an addition fact; indeed, she was unaware that addition was involved. Rather, she was stating a part-part-whole relationship that was part of her mathematical construction of five.

When two bug counters were hidden, however, Rebecca's incomplete understanding was evident. Asked how many bugs were hidden when only three of the five counters were visible, Rebecca said, "Well, three or maybe two." Her belief that a 2 and a 3 always make 5 was not quite strong or versatile enough to help her with the basic subtraction relationship of $5 - 2 = 3$.

Three- and 4-year-olds are often able to describe the parts of small numbers (2 to 5). Understanding of the relationships for larger numbers (6 to 10) typically does not develop until a year or two later. When the teacher makes a point of providing many experiences with part-part-whole relationships, including hiding tasks (for example, the Bears in a Cave game described below), children's understanding is enhanced and solidified. Regardless of age, a wealth of experiences should precede children's introduction to the more formal meaning of addition and subtraction.

In exploring octopi and number, Ms. Scott asked children to represent numbers using finger models. She also asked children to think of other ways to show the numbers using their fingers. Confronted with the challenges of the hidden octopi, the children gained experience with part-part-whole relationships. If children understand 10 as a quantity made up of a 4 and a 6, they are beginning to see the relationship between a whole (10) and its parts (4 and 6). The independent work that children completed as they drew their own problems and story models of octopi swimming in the ocean gave them further opportunity to work with part-part-whole in various contexts.

"Let's Play Bears in a Cave"

Materials and games designed for children to use on their own make it possible for them to explore number relationships, as well as concepts and skills in any other mathematical domain, without a teacher being involved. An example is Bears in a Cave (Nelson 1999), a partner game through which children explore part-part-whole relationships and are able to extend and consolidate their understanding as they play.

Using an overturned plastic sorting tray or box to represent a cave and seven or eight plastic counting bears, two children act out a scenario in which a group of bears having a picnic decide to play hide-and-seek. While one child covers her eyes, the other child takes some of the bears and hides them in the cave, leaving the remaining bears in plain sight. The child who has been covering her eyes now tries to guess how many bears are hiding in the cave—a highly motivating and challenging task for preschoolers, who tend to focus on the visible bears rather than the hidden ones.

Using representations. Multiple representations are essential for understanding number and developing number sense. Representations for 11 include the following.

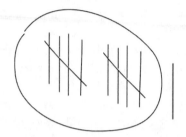

Tally method

"Eleven is two 5s and 1 extra."

Finger method

"Eleven is two hands and a finger."

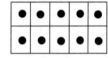

Ten-frame method

"Eleven is one ten frame and one more."

Domino method

"Eleven is 4 on each side and 3 in the middle."

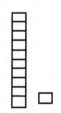

Base-10 blocks method

"Eleven is one 10 and one 1."

Real-life example

"There are 11 players on a football team."

Children represent number quantities in a variety of ways. The sample below shows three different representations by 5-year-olds.

This real-life picture was drawn by Chad in response to the teacher saying, "There were nine baseball players on the team. Four got sick and had to go home. How many were left to play the game?"

Stephanie used a modified tally method to express the number of pennies she had.

Juan used a ten-frame representation to show the number 8. He said he crossed out one box because "I got too many in the top line. There's supposed to be only five."

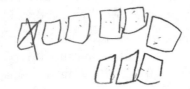

Change operations

The easiest number operation problems are active in nature and often can be solved by very young children. Two common change operations are *add to* and *take away*.

Teachers can best ask a question or pose a problem by relating it to children's real-life experiences. When 3-year-old Ryan was given three pieces of candy and asked how many he would have if his brother gave him one more, he readily answered, "Four!" Adding more was something he valued—it meant more candy for him—and he could tell how many he would have if he got one more.

Likewise, when 6-year-old Jordana was discussing the trade of some of her 105 special rocks, she knew exactly how many rocks she would have left if she gave Christina 15. Again, this active operation was one whose answer was important to Jordana, and she calculated it easily.

Research (Baroody & Standifer 1993; Carpenter et al. 1999) suggests that children in all cultures follow a three-step developmental progression in solving such operation problems:

1. They count all objects. For example, when adding 3 apples to 4 apples, they first count the four apples one by one and then the three apples one by one.

2. They count on. In other words, they already know they have four apples, so they say, "Four, five, six, seven."

3. They perform the necessary arithmetic in their heads through mental representation. Perhaps they manipulate objects in their heads or perhaps they have actually memorized the operation.

In the octopus story, the operation used was a part-part-whole relationship, a more static one than the active change stories. The children were later given other octopus stories that used change operations.

Learning Addition and Subtraction through Games

Young children informally learn addition and subtraction by playing simple games that they enjoy. Shane (1999) describes three activities that provide opportunities for young children to talk about adding and subtracting in a familiar context.

Bowling: Children roll balls toward plastic toy pins. They receive one counter for each pin they knock down. After three turns they count their counters and the scores are recorded. In a more challenging version, the pins can be labeled 1, 2, and 3. The rules are the same as above, except that children earn the number of counters indicated on each pin they knock down.

Store: Children are given dollar bills in play money. Items for sale are clearly labeled with dollar amounts ($1, $2, $3, $4). The cash register contains $1, $5, and $10 bills. Playing store is a natural addition and subtraction activity as children buy items, sell items, and count out change.

Beanbag Toss: Three hoops laid on the floor are labeled 1, 2, and 3. Children toss a beanbag into one of the hoops. If it lands inside the hoop, they get that number of counters. If it lands touching but outside the hoop, their score is one less than the hoop's value. After five turns, scores can be totaled (p. 134).

Comparison

Comparison terms like *more than, bigger than, greater than, less than, smaller than, fewer than,* or *the same as* are invaluable to children when relating two or more number values. Children tend to have difficulty with the language of comparison. For example, when waiting at a bus stop with a teacher aide one day, a 4-year-old asked the aide if she was bigger than his real teacher. Surprised that the child thought her heavier than the teacher, the aide responded, "I am taller. Is that what you mean?" The child said, "No, I mean more numbers." Realizing that the child meant *older,* she laughingly responded, "Oh yes!" and the 4-year-old was satisfied with the answer.

Comparing numbers is more than knowing the right words; the child must understand number quantities. A child may describe 100 as more than 10, much bigger than 10, or more than twice as big as 10. In each case the child uses comparative language to discuss the numbers. In the last two examples, however, the child uses greater comparative knowledge to describe somewhat more specifically the relationship between the two numbers. When children state that "ten 10s make one 100" or "100 is 90 more than 10," they are describing a numerical relationship and using the operations of addition and multiplication. A conceptual understanding of number is necessary both to compare quantities in general and to assess specific number relationships.

Using ice cube trays or some other system in which children can sort and place objects of one type in one row and objects of a different type in the other row can help young children compare two number quantities.

Number lines are a good visual strategy for showing children increasing numbers, and thus allowing them to compare. The teacher can begin a number line to show the number of teeth lost by children in the class or the number of school days that have passed. Using tally marks on a roll of paper (for example, adding-machine tape) gives children a visual model of number quantities growing progressively larger. The tape must be unwound from the roll, getting longer as the number line progresses. Tally marks can be used to represent each number. Then when children compare numbers on the number line, they can see that the numbers at the beginning represent fewer items (teeth, days, and so on) than the numbers farther down the number line. The *before* or *after* position of a number in relation to another number also can be used to determine which number is larger or smaller.

Later, when children are ready to work with tens and ones, the adding-machine tape can be cut into strips of ten numbers to make a hundreds chart. Using the hundreds chart, children can visualize the numbers in rows at the bottom being larger than the numbers in the top rows. Both visual models can be helpful in the comparing process.

Beginning number line

Two strips put together to begin 100s chart

The comparing operation occurs frequently in daily situations and everyday language. For example, teachers ask when passing out individual cartons of milk, "Do we have enough for everyone? How many more milks do we need so that everyone can have one?"

In the octopus activity Ms. Scott asked a comparison question that engaged the children's interest. She wondered aloud if the fingers on her hand would fill in all the legs of the puppet—a very precise comparison question. Some of the children were able to grasp the concept, while others needed to watch Ms. Scott demonstrate the action so that they could see before and after Ms. Scott tried on the puppet. Also in Abigail and Samantha's disagreement over the number of blocks each had, when the girls matched the two sets block-for-block, they were able to easily see that one set had two blocks extra. Again, direct visual information was necessary.

The comparing and equalizing question is a difficult one because it cannot be visualized as easily as *take away* and *add to* change operations. However, teachers' comments and questions in a variety of contexts help children think about questions of the "how many more" variety.

Recognizing and writing numerals

To progress in mathematics, children need to be able to use the standard written numerals of their society. In the United States and many other nations, this means becoming familiar with the Arabic numerals—1, 2, 3, and the rest.

There is a parallel in literacy. During the early childhood years, children are learning to recognize letters of the alphabet and over the same period are constructing their understanding of key skills and concepts that are basic to literacy—the alphabetic principle, phonological knowledge, structures and patterns in language, and so on. Similarly, during the same months and years when they are building an understanding of number, young children should be learning to identify and use numerals.

Moreover, just as effective early childhood teachers create literacy-enriched classroom environments to promote children's recognition of letters and words, they need to make sure children encounter written numerals and word names in a range of meaningful contexts. In the octopus lesson, Ms. Scott points to each word and numeral as she reads the poem. Although many children cannot read the words or the numbers, she wants to help them learn to recognize the numerals as representing quantity. The numbers are presented in context as the children act out the poem.

Just as in literacy, children first recognize the symbol for a number, connect it to the meaning, and then learn to write it. Describing the numeral 8 as a snowman without a hat, the numeral 1 as a stick, and the numeral 6 as a ball and stick together, the teacher provides word pictures that help children recognize and later write numerals. Numerals can be classified into groups, such as those that have curves and those that don't or those that have straight lines and those that don't.

The teacher can provide numerous opportunities, formal and informal, for children to become familiar with numerals. Children can go on scavenger hunts looking for particular numerals, identify the numerals in their phone numbers, cut out numerals from magazines, or find page numbers in their books. The numerals they find can be listed on butcher paper under the title, "Look Where We Found a 3!" or "Can You Help Us Find 9?"

Researchers (Payne & Huinker 1993) propose that the number symbol be accompanied by some representation for quantity whenever possible (see the number line on p. 63). The particular representation is not important; the fact that there is a representation is the critical part.

Writing numerals is a fine motor skill requiring muscle control and copying skills. Again, just as in early writing activities, children need to practice writing numerals in many different media. Children can create numerals with rolled clay, pipe cleaners, or Popsicle sticks. They can trace numerals in shaving cream, sand, salt, hair gel in a plastic bag, sandpaper, or cornstarch and water. Children can practice their writing skills with different writing implements (felt-tip pens, paints, chalk, crayons, pencils) on a variety of writing surfaces (sidewalk, color paper, posters, easels, journal pages).

When children are learning to recognize and write numerals, it is important that teachers constantly describe the meaning of the numerals. Equally important, teachers should listen to children as they use their words to describe their meaning of the symbols they write.

Veronica, a 5-year-old kindergartner in a bilingual class, recorded the results of a buried treasure activity. When asked about the numbers on one side of the paper and the numbers written upside down on the other side, she responded, "Oh, these numbers are for my teacher. She only speaks English. See, they say, one, two, three, four, and five. These other ones are for my mother. She only speaks Spanish. They say [pointing to each one], *uno, dos, tres, quatro, cinco.*" Although the symbols were written exactly the same, in Veronica's mind one set was Spanish and the other was English. The symbols represented two distinctly different counting sequences, yet the same quantities.

Place value

Understanding our decimal system requires the child to recognize that the place of a digit matters—12 is not the same as 21; 56 is not the same as 65. At the heart of the decimal system is the exchange principle: ten ones for a 10, ten tens for 100, and so on.

In the early years children are in the process of learning the number names for two-digit and even three-digit numbers. But the number names are only the tip of the iceberg. To fully understand 25, children must grasp that it means 2 tens and 5 ones.

Children need easily identifiable benchmarks for 10 and 100 if they are to grasp and confidently use our decimal system. Real-quantity representations that fit in their world can help children develop these benchmarks. For example, there are 10 fingers on two hands, there are 100 pennies in a dollar, there are about 20 children in our class, and so on.

Young children often respond to estimation questions (How many jelly beans do you think are in this jar? How many people are in the cafeteria?) with silly numbers (zillion-killion-dillion is one of my favorites!) or large overestimates or underestimates. Relating estimates to benchmarks or visual models helps children give more realistic estimates and provides many opportunities to develop the meaning of larger numbers as well.

First-grader Tish illustrated the importance of benchmarks in her journal entry when she described her solution to the problem of the day: "How many hours are there in four days?" Although Tish had never learned the formal algorithm for adding 24 four times, she had often used the ten blocks and one blocks to represent numbers greater than 10. Her journal response illustrates her solution using the ten and one blocks. It says, "Tell how you would find the number of hours in four days. 20 + 20 + 20 + 20 + 4 + 4 + 4 + 4. I did it by using 20s and 4s which = 96."

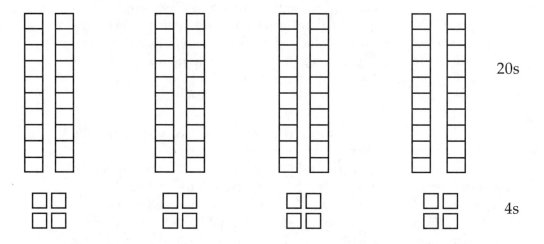

Six-year-old Tish's solution to the problem, "How many hours are there in four days?"

Providing a mathematics-rich environment

Just as print should be prominent in children's environments, so should numbers. It is particularly important to display mathematical terms and symbols in meaningful situations.

Many signs, labels, and papers contain numbers and mathematical symbols. Children often recognize numbers because they have seen them in restaurant menus or advertisements. Children growing up in the 1950s recognized the numbers 5 and 10 easily because the old five-and-ten stores were common. Today dollar stores are more prominent and children have as a benchmark items that can be purchased for one dollar. Prices of Beanie Babies, brand-name tennis shoes, or other popular items are familiar numbers and also become a reference point for children. Knowing a favorite item costs five dollars, the child has a rough idea what five dollars is worth—far less than the cost of a bicycle or computer but more than a candy bar.

Teachers should place labels and advertisements with prominent numerals in the creative dramatics center and change them often. In addition to familiarizing children with numbers and their everyday uses, such real-life items can also be used in presenting children with simple mathematics problems.

Calendar

Most teachers engage children in a daily activity with the calendar, perhaps centering on the day of the week, the date, and the weather, but they may fail to take full advantage of many of the calendar's mathematical possibilities. Calendars can convey information important to the children about schedules, such as the weekly visit to the neighborhood public library. Children can calculate the number of days until an eagerly anticipated event—a field trip to a firehouse or a visit from a storyteller—or the days elapsed since the beginning of the school year.

The hundredth day of school is a time for celebration in many classrooms, and children participate in a variety of activities emphasizing sets of 100. Children can keep track of the number of days that have passed with numerals placed on a blank calendar shell, or teachers can use adding-machine tape to make a number line, adding a numeral each day (see p. 63). Children's finger representations can indicate sets of 5 or sets of 10 when counting by fives or tens on the number line.

Teachers can also introduce tallies as a way of recording days elapsed or days when something happens, such as all the days in the month when it rains. Of course, tallies or other representations can record other events, such as someone losing a tooth, that can be kept as a total for each child and for all the children together.

$$1 \quad 2 \quad 3 \quad 4 \quad 5 \quad 6 \quad 7 \quad 8 \quad 9 \quad 10$$

Manipulatives

Using concrete materials known as *manipulatives* can help children develop a sense of number and operations. One basic kind of manipulative for math experiences is a counter. Counters should be uniform in size so that children can focus on number without the distraction of size variations. For example, dominos that use a large dot to represent a value of one but six smaller dots to represent the value of six erroneously convey to children that one is bigger than six.

School supply stores and catalogs offer a wide variety of counters, including Unifix cubes, connecting cubes, base-10 blocks, and plastic counters in a variety of animal shapes. Teachers can also find an array of counters at discount stores—little pom-poms (the fluffy balls that dangle from sew-on fringe edging), "squashed" marbles or smooth glass beads, Popsicle sticks—or use materials such as beans, small stones, or straws from children's daily environments.

Another useful kind of material for exploring number is strings of colored plastic beads. A particular color can be cut up into sections of a particular number. For example, a string of blue beads can all be cut so that all the beads are separate. Six green beads can be cut into sections of two, orange into sections of three, yellow into fours, and red beads into fives. With these beads children can make sets of six, seven, eight, nine, or 10; or, using the beads as another way to emphasize the part-part-whole model, children can describe their sets of six as two greens and four yellows or one blue and five reds.

The Young Child and Mathematics

The following sample of activities emphasizes number concepts. While they are organized roughly in order of difficulty, many can be simplified or expanded to be much more challenging.

Make Four Elbows!

Children form a circle and begin slowly walking in one direction. At a signal from the leader, they stop and listen to instructions. When the leader states, "Make four elbows," the children touch one or both of their elbows to other children's elbows to make a total of four connected elbows. After everyone shares their methods for accomplishing this task, new directions, such as "Make 12 fingers," are given. Some favorites: Make three ankles, Make nine shoulders, Make seven feet.

Children delight in working together to make the required number of body parts. Their solutions are often creative and unusual. Two 4-year-olds, Rudi and Elise, made five shoulders by standing back-to-back, shoulders touching, with one other friend touching one shoulder to their shoulders. When asked how they made five, they responded, "We each got two. That makes four, and one more is five!"

Asked to make 12 fingers, three kindergartners touched four fingers each, stating that they wanted to "be fair." For seven feet, four 4-year-olds put their feet together, one child holding one foot off the ground. They explained that they had eight feet and they had to get rid of one, "so John held one up."

Tees and Tees and More

Children create sculptures using pieces of Styrofoam, plastic stirring straws, pipe cleaners, and golf tees. Although the golf tees can be pushed quite easily into the Styrofoam, children often like to use plastic hammers and other workshop tools to make their sculptures. This is a good activity for the classroom's constructing center.

When they are finished, children describe their works of art using numbers and position words. For example, Charles and Kendall each used four tees in their constructions. In Charles's sculpture all of the tees were at the top of the Styrofoam piece, while in Kendall's, two tees were at the top and two at the bottom. The language the boys used to describe their constructions was delightful and included position words as well as number words.

More/Less Concentration

Sixteen number cards with representations of numbers (using ten frames, numerals, tally marks, or pips like those found on a domino) are placed face down in a 4-by-4 grid. A More/Less spinner (half of the spinner is labeled More, the other half, Less) is spun to determine if the More game or the Less game will be played.

The first child turns over two cards. In the More game, if the numerical value of the second card is greater than that of the first card, that pair of cards now belongs to the child and she takes them from the grid. If the value of the second card is less than that of the first card, the cards are turned face down again and the next player takes his turn. Remembering the value of the cards previously turned over helps. The game is over when all 16 cards have been collected by the players, but there is no need to compare which child has the most cards or to declare a winner.

The Less game is played in the same way, but for a player to claim a pair of cards, the value of the second card turned over must be *less than* that of the first.

Children 5 years and older generally find *more* an easy concept; *less* is harder for them to grasp, and they may need some assistance from the teacher when playing the Less game. Children love to play the More and Less games in small groups and with partners during center time. Some children need to count the representations on the cards and look at a number line to help them determine which one is greater. Others compare both numbers using a visual one-to-one correspondence. Some players clearly do not know which number is larger or smaller, so their partners can help them find the solution.

How Many Legs?

Children make playbills or advertisements for a puppet show to be presented in the creative dramatics center, featuring insects, animals, and other creatures. Each puppet character needs to be accurately drawn in the advertisements and playbills!

Children's pictures often illustrate their understanding of number. In many of the pictures, the creatures initially may not have enough legs or antennas or spots. A few key questions—"Did you draw enough legs?" or "Does your ladybug have the same number of spots as our puppet?"—help the children to correct their pictures so that the numbers of legs, spots, or antennas in their drawings match the puppets'.

Block Towers

A die with two ones, two twos, and two threes is added to the block center. The teacher may want to explain that this die is special, and that a regular die has numbers from one to six. The children throw the die and build towers with the indicated number of blocks. The towers are then compared by height. Number cards representing one, two, and three in a variety of different ways can also be used instead of a die.

Children's thinking is very evident in this activity, which is excellent for prekindergartners. Often, children change the activity by throwing the die a number of times and building many towers before comparing. They also figure out that the way the blocks are stacked affects how tall the towers are. Two blocks stacked "the tall way" are taller than three blocks stacked "the wide way."

Priscilla's Bows

Priscilla is a puppy puppet with beautiful bows on her ears—red bows on the right ear and lavender ones on the left ear. (*Red* helps the children remember *right*, and *lavender* helps them remember *left*.) She wants to be "equally" beautiful, so she wears the same number of bows on each ear. When Priscilla falls asleep, her friends take some of her bows to tease her. To get them back, Priscilla has to decide how many bows of each color are missing. After solving this puzzle several times, children tell their own stories, using story mats with a picture of a puppy and red and lavender cubes.

The children often tell the same exact story as the one modeled with the puppet. They pretend to be Priscilla and employ interesting strategies for finding out how many bows are missing. Shawna, a 4-year-old, said, "You just look real hard and when you close your eyes, you keep trying to remember how many were there until you open your eyes again." Amelia, another 4-year-old, said, "You just count how many are on one ear and then you know that's how many you need when you wake up. If you 'member, it works!"

Making 8

Children use a variety of materials—such as cubes, pennies, or fingers—to construct the number 8 (or any other number) as many ways as possible. They then record this process by drawing pictures (which may also include written numerals) illustrating their methods for constructing 8. For example, a child who uses red and blue connecting cubes might draw a train of three red cubes and five blue cubes. A child who uses pennies might draw two heads and six tails. Another drawing might show four fingers on one hand and four fingers on another hand. Many children know only a few ways to express 8. By modeling or asking questions, the teacher can encourage children to see and make 8 in other ways.

Ten-Frame Cookie Sheet

The teacher constructs a ten frame by dividing a metal cookie sheet with colored tape. He then represents a number on the ten frame using magnets and asks the children to look quickly and tell the number by showing the same number of fingers. The procedure can be repeated over and over representing different numbers as the teacher removes or adds magnets. The sound of the magnets being added to or removed from the metal cookie sheet helps children keep count.

Children learn to tell the number of magnets by simply looking. When asked how he knew so quickly there were five magnets on the cookie sheet without counting, Troy answered, "I just know. It filled up all the top line and that's always five!" When Crissy was asked how she knew there were seven magnets on the cookie sheet, she said, "Because there's two more than five—a row and two more!"

Number Necklaces

Children make number representations on paper plates or index cards using a ten-frame format, domino pips, tally marks, and/or numerals. The plates or cards are made into necklaces using yarn, and each child wears one.

Many games can be played outside with the necklaces. Holding hands, children can run or skip in a circle until a whistle is blown. The teacher then

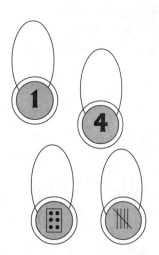

calls out the name of a game. Find a Match requires children to find someone with the same number represented on his or her necklace. In Make a Train, the children make the number sequence 1 to 10 by joining hands to make a train.

Kindergartners love to play games with number necklaces. When children need physical activity, the teacher can take them outside to play Make a Sum. The children run or skip clockwise in a large circle until the teacher blows the whistle twice. Children then stop and listen as the teacher announces, "Make 10."

Timmy, whose necklace shows the number 6 in tally marks, and Bill, who has 7 shown on a ten frame, are best friends and check each other's number first. Timmy says, "Uh-oh! We make too much. I need something littler." He then runs and finds Corinne, who has a 4 on her number necklace. After a careful check, Timmy and Corinne decide they make 10 and stand together.

When everyone has shared their solutions, the children go back to their circle and skip again until the whistle blows and the teacher calls a new number.

What's in Your Pocket?

Using books (for example, *Katy No-Pocket* by Emmy Payne), puppets, or poems ("Treasure" from *Good Rhymes, Good Times,* by Lee Bennett Hopkins), children create stories about what is in their pockets, and then make pockets out of paper.

Treasure

A rusty door key,
A part of a tool,
A dead bee I was saving to take in to school;
A crust of pizza,
Sand from the shore,
A piece of lead pipe,
An old apple core;

My library card,
A small model rocket—
I guess it is time
to clean out my pocket.

—*Lee Bennett Hopkins*

Front

To make a pocket, children fold a piece of paper in half, then cut a horizontal slit across the middle of the front flap so that the top and bottom of the pocket can be opened separately. Placing items on the paper pockets, the children tell stories about what is in their pockets. They are then asked how many items are in the top part of the pocket, how many in the bottom part of the pocket, and how many in the whole pocket.

Inside, top

Each child then records the items by drawing them inside the pocket and writing the numbers on the back of the front flaps. The total number of items in the pocket is written on the back page. The front of the pocket is decorated according to the child's whimsy.

Inside, whole pocket

Children's pockets can be very creative and make a good addition to the library center. Children love to play Hide the Pocket with a partner, in which both children try to guess the number of items in one part of a pocket or the total number.

Back

Twinkle Music

"Sheet music" (music staffs with numerals instead of music notes) is added to the music center and corresponding numerals are written on a xylophone, with 1 written on C, 2 on D, 3 on E, and so on. Children play the xylophone following the numerals written in the music: 1, 1, 5, 5, 6, 6, 5; 4, 4, 3, 3, 2, 2, 1 represents the beginning of "Twinkle, Twinkle, Little Star," a song familiar to most young children.

Children constantly return to the music center to play Twinkle music. Once they understand the procedure, they quickly memorize "Twinkle, Twinkle, Little Star," and the tune is frequently heard in the center. Children can create their own music by writing numbers on the music paper and asking their friends to perform concerts.

Music can also be made with large plastic bottles. Six 2-liter plastic soda bottles are taped together in a row and labeled 1 through 6. A small amount of water is poured into the first bottle, and each subsequent bottle is filled with more water than the previous one. The children make music by blowing across the tops of the bottles. The notes are not exactly those of a regular musical scale, but they make wonderful music nonetheless. Adding water to plastic bottles to make musical instruments is also a great way to connect mathematics with music and science.

Counting Books

The most identifiable mathematics books in the library are counting books. The variations are fascinating and applicable to almost every subject or theme. Children can read them, add more pages, or create their own type of counting book. Asking "What page comes next?" provides a lesson in prediction.

One Tortoise, Ten Wallabies: A Wildlife Counting Book, by Jakki Wood, illustrates counting baby and adult animals. It pictures only the numbers 1 through 12, 15, 20, 25, 50, and 101, giving children a reason to add pages. *Mouse Count,* by Ellen Stoll Walsh, and *Bat Jamboree,* by Kathi Appelt, provide good beginnings for children's number stories. After reading and acting out the stories, children select new characters and a new setting for their stories. They create, write, and read their own stories to the class, asking questions in the form of "How many . . . ?"

Children love books that can be acted out, but they are sometimes so familiar with a story that they become "functionally fixed" on an event or a number. For example, whenever a non-English-speaking 4-year-old was asked to show three fingers, she always said, "Cha-Cha-Cha!" because the three bats in *Bat Jamboree* always say "Cha-Cha-Cha!" She needed to be introduced to a broader range of stories and a broader experience of the number three.

If resources are available, these amazing stories by children can be captured on videotape. At the end of each story, the child can pose a question. A large question mark indicates that viewers should give the answer. The question mark can be made with special effects, but filming a question mark drawn on a piece of poster board works just as well. Videotapes can be exchanged between classes. Children not only enjoy the dramatized stories, they work hard to solve their classmates' puzzles.

I Spy

I Spy Two Eyes: Numbers in Art, by Lucy Micklethwait, shows 20 famous works of art. Each picture contains a particular number of some objects. For example, *The New Year,* by Picasso, contains 17 birds.

Children can create their own art gallery, modeled after Micklethwait's examples. Each child selects a specific item and a number from 1 to 25, then paints or draws the item that number of times. The children's pictures are framed and displayed to create an art gallery; the exhibition is titled "I Spy." Children from other classes enjoy the art and have fun hunting for and counting the special items in each picture.

How Many Windows?

After counting the number of windows, doors, or lights in the school as a class project, children are asked to count the windows, doors, or lights in their homes. Using tally marks is an important part of the assignment. Helping children record and accurately report the count involves family members in school work. The results can later be used for classroom discussions.

This activity can accompany a social studies unit on community helpers and responsibility. Using the results, the class discusses the jobs of glaziers, carpenters, and electricians. The teacher poses questions about work and time, and asks children to make predictions: What would happen if someone broke all the windows in the school? If the glazier took five minutes to fix every window, how many minutes would it take to fix all the windows? How many hours? If we made our school [or your home] twice as big, how many doors, windows, and lights would be needed?

After engaging in this activity, one class saw a large skyscraper from the bus window while on a field trip. When the children saw a window washer near the top, they spent 10 minutes trying to discover how many windows were in the skyscraper and how much a window washer would charge for cleaning the windows. Because there wasn't time to count all the windows while on the bus, when the children returned to the classroom they discussed possible solutions to the problem by arraying colored tiles on their desks in rows, like the windows of the building. The children compared different ways to array the tiles and, as a group, decided which setup most closely resembled the skyscraper. They then counted the number of tiles to determine how many windows there were.

Where's the Bear?

Upside-down plastic cups are labeled with a number from 1 to 20 and displayed in order on a chalk tray. A child hides a small plastic bear under one of the cups. The other children take turns asking questions—referring to the cups by their numbers—to determine under which cup the plastic bear is hidden.

Sample questions: Is the bear under cup [4]? Is the bear in a cup before cup [16]? Is the bear in a cup after cup [6]? Is the bear in a cup between cups [7] and [10]? The child who hid the bear can respond giving as many clues (visual and verbal) as he wants until the children find the bear.

Children love this game, and the position words they learn (*between, before, after, in front of, behind*) are helpful, as are the problem-solving strategies they discover. When one child finds out that the bear is hidden in a cup after cup 6, another child may guess cup 7, another guess cup 8, and so on. After one such case in which the children finally discovered the bear hidden in one of the last cups, Amy said, "Hey! We shouldn't guess the numbers right in a row. Next time let's skip around and we can find out faster!"

Where Are the Minibeasts?

In this activity, a search for minibeasts, mathematics skills can be easily linked to science investigations. *Minibeasts* are any creatures smaller than

the length of a child's pinkie finger. Children predict different places in which they will find minibeasts, such as in the air, on a tree, on the sidewalk, in the grass, or in the bushes. Predictions are recorded indoors, and then the expedition begins. Children work with partners, select a likely minibeast environment, and tally the number of creatures found. Upon returning to the classroom, the results are graphed and discussed.

Tallying and recording the numbers counted are important skills for young children. Teachers also gain insight from watching children count and tally moving minibeasts. Children are often stumped upon encountering a large group of squirming creatures. As one child remarked when investigating an ant colony, "How can we count this many? We don't have any more numbers!" A problem like this naturally leads to a discussion of really big numbers and sampling strategies.

How Many Pips Are Hidden?

Children learn that a die has six sides (or faces) and that the dots on the die are called *pips.* Each side has a different number of pips, ranging from one to six. By investigating, they learn that adding the numbers on opposite sides equals 7. For example, 5 is opposite 2, and 6 is opposite 1. To play the game, children sit in a circle and one of them throws a large foam die into the middle. Children try to determine the number of pips hidden on the bottom of the die. They typically solve this dilemma by counting the pips on each side and locating the side that is missing in the sequence 1 through 6. However, if they know that opposite sides add up to 7, then the task is much easier. If the top of the die shows one pip, then six pips are hidden; if three pips are on top, then four are on the bottom, and so on.

A similar but more challenging activity involves making dice towers. For example, if three dice are made into a tower, the bottom die will have seven pips hidden, the second die will also have seven pips hidden, and the top die will have seven minus the number of pips on the very top hidden.

And One Good Friendship

This activity helps the teacher recognize and assess social development as well as children's understanding of number. Using as a model the poem "two friends," by Nikki Giovanni, children can draw pictures of their own friends. The pictures are then described using number words similar to those in the poem.

two friends

lydia and shirley have
two pierced ears and
two bare ones
five pigtails
two pairs of sneakers
two berets
two smiles
one necklace
one bracelet
lots of stripes and
one good friendship

—Nikki Giovanni

Pom-Pom Jacks

Colorful pom-poms are placed on the floor inside a yarn circle about 20 inches in diameter. Use enough pom-poms to almost fill the circle. A number is selected and labeled The Number. Children estimate how many pom-poms adding up to The Number can be collected during the time it takes the teacher to bounce a ball The Number of times. The pom-pom sets collected are placed outside the circle.

After conducting the activity, children compare their results with their estimations. The chosen number is changed often and new experiments are tried. Note that this activity requires estimating a measurement (for example, children estimate that the time it takes to bounce a ball three times is less than the time it takes to bounce a ball seven times) as well as estimating the number of sets of a specific number of items that can be made within.

Observing children's comments during this activity provides insight into their learning processes. For example,

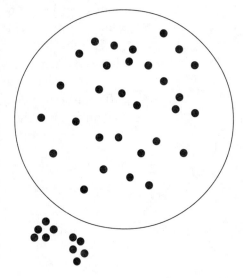

after doing the activity with the number 8, one group of second-graders was asked to estimate what would happen if the number 4 were chosen. Ron said that it "would be half, because 4 is half of 8." Jackie disagreed. She said it would be much more than half because four pom-poms are easier to grab, and "We're a lot better at doing this 'cause we've practiced!"

The Number Dance

Physical experiences can help children understand big numbers and place value. Greenes (1999) suggests that children can "feel" large numbers by using large circling arm movements for hundreds, forearm movements for tens, and finger flicking movements for ones. For example, children can model the number 431 by making four large circling arm movements, three forearm movements, and one finger movement. Similarly, children can model the number 134 by making one large circling arm movement, three forearm movements, and four finger movements. In this way children understand that 431 and 134 are very different numbers—because they "feel" different.

Because children are very interested in large numbers, an understanding of place value should be taught at an early age. Children love to do the number dance, and often create larger motions (such as jumping) for the thousands place.

Build the Numbers!

Wooden or plastic place-value blocks are common mathematics manipulatives. Small unit cubes represent ones; long 10-unit rods represent tens; 10-by-10 flat blocks represent hundreds; and large, 10-by-10-by-10 cubes represent thousands. Given the rods and unit cubes, children try to build 100 as many different ways as possible. Similarly, given the flat blocks, rods, and unit cubes, children build 1,000 a number of different ways.

Children often discover patterns in their solutions. For example, to make 100, one 100 block could be used, or one 10 block and 90 unit blocks, two 10 blocks and 80 unit blocks, three 10 blocks and 70 unit blocks, four 10 blocks and 60 unit blocks, and so on.

The children record their solutions by pasting cutouts of shapes representing the blocks to pieces of paper. A small square represents a unit cube, a long thin rectangle represents a 10-unit rod, a large rectangle represents the 100-unit flat block, and a very large square represents a 1,000-unit cube. By second grade the children are also usually able to draw the different ways they construct the numbers.

All the Ways to Make . . . 222

After children learn Build the Numbers! they are ready for this activity, which is more complex. Children find all the ways to make 222 using place-value blocks or all the ways to make $2.22 using coins. The number 222 (or 333, 444, etc.) is a good number to use because the same numeral is in each place value—children must have a real understanding of the difference between two units, two tens, and two hundreds.

After the children construct the number with blocks, the next step is to write equations or phrases illustrating all the possible ways to make or describe 222. This list can be added to throughout the year, emphasizing unique and creative solutions. Some possible solutions include "half of 444," "111 + 111," "a palindrome," and "more days than we are in school." One class came up with more than 100 different ways to describe 222!

In My Bag!

The teacher or second-grade child places some place-value blocks in a bag and tells the class how many. Children work as partners to figure out which place-value blocks are in the bag. To do so, they ask questions about the blocks' total value that can be answered *yes* or *no*. This game can also be played with coins.

For example, Mr. Emilio told his class that he had five coins in his bag. He asked the class to guess what the coins were. Mary Ann asked, "Is your bag more than a dollar?" Mr. Emilio responded, "No!" Willy whispered to his partner, "Well, they can't be all quarters!" Cameron asked, "Is it less than 50 cents?" Mr. Emilio said yes. Questions continued and children discovered with little trouble that Mr. Emilio had five nickels in his bag.

While the children in this example seemed to solve the puzzle easily, children often find the game very difficult when first learned. Over time, the teacher should observe that children refine their reasoning strategies by asking questions and listening closely to the answers.

Scavenger Hunt

At home, children hunt for numbers larger than 100. They record them by copying them and drawing a picture of where they found them, cutting them out (if possible) and pasting them on note paper, or photographing them. When the children bring the numbers to class, they can be classified by size (for example, numbers greater than 100 but less than 200, or numbers greater than 1,000) or by their use. The discovery of special types of numbers, such as zip codes and phone numbers, leads to discussions of number meaning and the fact that some numbers are used only as locators.

Roll and Make a Dollar

In this game for two players, two dice are used, one die featuring a picture of a coin on each side (one quarter, two dimes, two nickels, and one penny) and the other die featuring the numerals 1 through 6. Each player rolls both dice on his or her turn. The player then gets the number of coins shown. For example, if 3 is rolled on the number die, and a quarter is rolled on the coin die, the player gets three quarters. A player can stop at any time, but if she rolls the dice, she must take the indicated number of coins. After one or both players have rolled the dice ten times or both players decide to stop, the coins are totaled to learn which player has an amount closer to a dollar without going over.

This activity provides useful experience in estimation and reasoning, which occur as children decide whether to stop rolling or to continue. It is an excellent learning center game for first and second graders. If the sum is changed to 50 cents and the quarter is eliminated, kindergartners enjoy it as well.

A Million?

Children love to say large numbers, and children and adults frequently say "a million" to indicate a very large amount. When asked to guess or estimate *how many*, children often respond by saying the largest number they know, and *million* is often used with little understanding or meaning. Many library books use the word *million* in their titles or as part of their text.

The book *A Million Fish—More or Less,* written by Patricia C. McKissack and illustrated by Dena Schutzer, includes a picture of "a million" fish, which provides an interesting investigation of a *million*. After inspecting the picture, children count only 65 fish. Using a calculator to key in + 65 =, children are asked to see if they can add until they reach a million.

Children slowly begin to key in + 65 =. The teacher observes the group, saying, "Just tell me when you reach one million. Are you there yet?" After a few minutes, children begin adding very rapidly and soon realize that it will take a long time to reach a million. Most children stop at this point, put their calculators away, and go on to some other activity. However, there is often at least one child who takes the calculator with him throughout the day. After about three to four hours, he shouts, "I got a million!"

Ice Cream Shop

A creative dramatics center provides a wonderful opportunity for projects involving the use of number. An ice cream shop is set up by converting the housekeeping or store center. Bins filled with Unifix cubes represent scoops of ice cream; coins and cash registers (real or pretend) are used for monetary transactions; and paper hats and aprons are uniforms for the employees.

Ice cream prices, lists of flavors, store bills, and advertisements are written and illustrated. Customers are given numbers indicating the order in which they will be served. Making ice cream from recipes involving measurement is a great final event for the Ice Cream Shop project. This project takes some time, but the results are often quite beneficial to young children's understanding of mathematics and its use in everyday life.

Principles in action

The classroom examples in Chapter 4, "Number and Operations," reflect some of the curriculum, instruction, and assessment principles that form the basis for teaching mathematics effectively to young children. To clarify how specific principles look in practice, this chart highlights five instances in which selected principles were evident.

Curriculum Principle 3 Effective curriculum includes a mathematically rich environment with a variety of materials to help children explore key concepts.	Books, puppets, and the children's fingers were used for counting during the octopus activity (pp. 48–51). Using their own fingers was purposeful, demonstrating to the children that fingers—part of the child's everyday life—could be useful in a complex reasoning process.
Curriculum Principle 4 Curriculum decisions should take into account children's knowledge, abilities, and interests.	Because of their previous work with minibeasts, the children were interested in examining animals—especially in counting octopus legs.
Instruction Principle 2 Interacting with children and promoting interactions between children are key roles of the early childhood teacher.	The teacher's measured responses during the octopus activity were part of her strategy—she paused to think carefully about all the children's ideas before reacting. The teacher was also trying to keep the children from reading her reactions, as well as giving them more thinking time.
Instruction Principle 3 The teacher must orchestrate various contexts and ways in which children engage in mathematical experiences, such as whole group, small group, project teams, and other strategies.	Deciding how and when to intervene is important. In the housekeeping center, the teacher intervened by acting as a player, drawing in an onlooking child, and asking a simple number question that might be posed in a real-life situation (p. 52). In the block center, the teacher aide did not step in to resolve the children's dispute about who had more blocks (p. 54). Instead, she proposed a comparing strategy the children could use without relying on the counting sequence. This strategy helped to consolidate their understanding of number, counting, and perhaps measurement.
Assessment Principle 2 Observing and listening are essential skills for the early childhood teacher.	Children's different levels of understanding can be noted during the octopus activity. Jimmy's response to the "how many are hiding" question reflected his preoccupation with only what he sees. In contrast, Rachelle's response suggested that she understands the consistency of the number 10 because it always is "a 4 and a 6" (p. 51).

Chapter 5

Patterns, Functions, and Algebra in the Early Childhood Curriculum

"Look, it's a pattern!" is an exclamation often heard from young children just beginning to be explicitly aware of patterns. Children do not first encounter patterns in school. The young child enters the formal world of schooling having observed patterns in nature, at home, at play, and in stories. Children watch the sun setting every day; listen to stories, songs, and verses that follow patterns; notice how a puppy plays and sleeps on a schedule; jump rope to patterned chants; and skip over sidewalk bricks laid in patterns.

Mathematics is the science and language of patterns. Thinking about patterns helps children make sense of mathematics. They learn that mathematics is not a set of unrelated facts and procedures; instead, recognizing and working with patterns helps young children predict what will happen, talk about relationships, and see the connections between mathematics concepts and their world. Because the study of patterns is basic to all mathematical thinking, it has a close natural connection to the other math content areas. Patterns in number, geometry, measurement, and data analysis—all belong in the math curriculum for young children.

The teacher's role is to provide a bridge between children's informal observations of patterns and the more formal mathematical descriptions of patterns and changes. She encourages children to use their own language, representations, and symbols—forms of representing that they find meaningful. Subsequent teaching helps to move children to more formal school mathematics and conventional symbolic notations.

Perhaps more than any other content domain, the area of patterns, functions, and algebra can be emphasized throughout the young child's day. Opportunities to identify patterns occur frequently during spontaneous play episodes, routine activities, outdoor trips, literacy lessons, circle time, snack and lunch, shared reading, play with friends, and travel in a car. Understanding patterns, functions, and algebra is a continual process of connecting what is noted in the real world with planned pattern discovery activities in the classroom.

The following series of kindergarten classroom activities and routines illustrates an ongoing investigation of number and pattern. The events described here took place over several months in varied settings, including a learning center, a small-group lesson, transition time, and even at home. The children are 5 or 6 years old, and many have limited proficiency in English.

Number Hangers

First Event (early January)

Ms. Tinsley has set up a variety of number stations in her kindergarten classroom. Each station has a particular type of manipulative—Unifix cubes, color tiles, plastic chain links, strands of plastic beads, toothpicks and glue, golf tees and Styrofoam, foam cubes, pattern blocks, "squashed" marbles. The children, in groups of two or three, choose a station and create models of a given number.

At the links station three children use red and blue plastic links to make chains for the number 5. The teacher challenges them each to make as many different combinations as possible grouping red and blue links together in chains of five.

Amanda: I got a 5 chain! (*holds up a chain of five links, one red at the end and then four blue*)

Jorge: I got one! (*holds up a chain of four links*)

Amanda: Here's another one, two reds and three blues. And another one, one blue and four reds.

Mark: Mine is different. (*holds up a chain with alternating blue and red links*) See? It's a pattern.

The children continue to work, creating a pile of chains in the center of the table. Some chains have six links and a few have four, but most of the chains conform to the rules.

After about 10 minutes, the teacher comes over to the links center.

Ms. Tinsley: You three have certainly made a lot of chains. What number are you working on?

Amanda: Five. See, here's one! (*holds up a chain and counts the links*) 1, 2, 3, 4, 5.

Ms. Tinsley: You have all made so many chains; it would take a long time to count the links in every one. I wonder if we could tell by just looking if all the chains have exactly five links. (*lays out a few chains so that those with five links can be seen to match in length*)

Amanda, Jorge, and Mark soon begin matching chains and adding or subtracting links as necessary. As they work, the teacher picks up Mark's chain with the alternating colors. She remarks on the pattern but also reminds Mark that in the activity that day they are going to keep the colors together. The aim of the activity is for children to see and work with patterns that show basic number facts, in this case working with the number 5 (e.g., 2 + 3 = 5, 1 + 4 = 5, 3 + 2 = 5). Children will create and examine representations of these facts by staying within the teacher's constraint of "Keeping the colors together," as in a chain of two reds and then three blues—red, red, blue, blue, blue.

> **Ms. Tinsley:** Well, keep working. I wonder how you'll be able to tell if you have made chains showing all the different ways. I wonder how many ways there are.

Second Event (later in January)

Ms. Tinsley and seven children are sitting on the floor around a bucket of chains with five links that the children made the week before. Ms. Tinsley has a wire clothes hanger, some index cards, scissors, a hole punch, and paste.

> **Ms. Tinsley:** Here is the bucket of chains we made last week. Can anyone remind me what type of chains were supposed to go in the bucket?
>
> **Dana:** Five links.
>
> **Ms. Tinsley:** Yes, that's right. Five links on every chain. Show me 5 with your fingers. Great, now can you do it another way?

Ms. Tinsley watches as the children show various configurations of five: two fingers on one hand and three on the other, four on one hand and one on the other, and so on. She describes each child's response in words and numbers.

> **Ms. Tinsley:** Well, clearly you are ready to help me sort these chains. *(empties the bucket)* Everyone, take a few chains and check them. Remember, five links in every chain, the colors need to be together, and each chain should be different. Here's one with five links. I'll put it in the center of our circle so you can compare its length with the others.

Children begin to sort chains. Some children can tell simply by looking at a chain that it is not five links long; they put those chains aside. Others count individual links, often counting incorrectly as the links bunch together. Still others match their chains with the one in the center to check the number of links.

> **Amanda:** Ms. Tinsley, I know this one is right. It's got five, the reds are together, and it's different from the one you got.
>
> **Ms. Tinsley:** Oh, Amanda, show that one to Jorge and let him check it too. I'm going to arrange these chains in a very special way, and I want them all to have five links. Use your words to tell Jorge why you think that one fits.

Children share their "good" chains with each other, sometimes using words to talk about them. Soon Ms. Tinsley asks the children for their attention.

> **Ms. Tinsley:** You are doing a great job checking these chains, but I'm worried that we won't be able to tell if we have all the different ways a 5 chain could be made with our keep-the-colors-together rule. I brought

a hanger that I think will help us see the chains better. We can attach them here on the bottom wire.

Ms. Tinsley shows the children the hanger and then writes the number 5 on two index cards. She pastes the cards back to back, punches a hole at the top, and slips this sign over the neck of the hanger, making a "5 hanger." She then sorts through the pile of chains and begins attaching particular ones to the hanger so that a color pattern becomes evident. Index cards cut in strips, folded over, and pasted at both ends of the hanger keep the links from sliding. As each chain is placed on the hanger, Ms. Tinsley asks a child to describe it using numbers and color words.

When five or six chains are arranged on the hanger, Ms. Tinsley asks children to find places where chains are missing, using interruptions in the color pattern as a clue. Before adding a missing chain, the child describes it and tells where he believes it must go and why. ("This has two reds and then three blues. It goes after the one with one red and four blues.")

When the children declare the 5 hanger complete, it is hung from a large pushpin on the bulletin board by the door. In later lessons, children will make hangers for numbers 6, 7, 8, 9, and 10. The hanger model is easily moved to small-group settings for discussion or hung on a bulletin board for display.

Third Event (several times in February and March)

Children line up for lunch, standing next to the bulletin board with the number hangers. Four hangers now hold chains—a 5 hanger, a 6 hanger, a 7 hanger, and an 8 hanger. Ms. Tinsley has been notified that lunch is running late, so she decides to talk about the patterns seen on the hangers.

> **Ms. Tinsley:** Let's look at our hangers. I think we have found all the ways to make five, six, seven, and eight. Does anyone notice anything about our board that is special? Do you see any patterns?

Ms. Tinsley pauses a minute while children talk to each other about possible answers to the questions—a common occurrence in this classroom. Many children feel more comfortable discussing answers with one another before discussing them in front of the class.

> **Ms. Tinsley:** I would love to hear some of your discoveries. Who would like to be first?

> **Scott:** Chains on the 8 hanger are longer.

> **Amanda:** The red color goes down like this. *(models a diagonal)*

> **Jorge:** The chains are on hangers.

> **William:** It starts with a lot of red and then goes to a little red and then back again to a lot of red. Lots, little, lots.

> **Francis:** You add on blue each time, and then you start taking it away.

> **Sheila:** It's pretty because it looks like my belt.

Several weeks later a child initiates another discussion while lining up for lunch.

Jorge: Ms. Tinsley, Ms. Tinsley! *(excited)* There's a pattern on the board. Look at the colors. It's got the same on each hanger, just more!

Amanda: I already said that, Jorge! You copied!

Ms. Tinsley: I think both of your discoveries are important and slightly different. Jorge, can you show us what you mean?

Jorge points out the diagonal pattern he has just noticed in all four hangers. When asked for further clarification, Jorge goes to the housekeeping center and brings back a small quilt with a similar diagonal pattern.

Fourth Event (March and April)

In Ms. Tinsley's kindergarten many small-group meetings occur like the following one. Included in the group are children who are writing numerals, with understanding, for number quantities. Ms. Tinsley selects the 5 hanger and brings it to the small-group meeting. She also has red and blue markers and a stack of index cards cut in half lengthwise.

Ms. Tinsley: I know that the year is almost over, and I want you to remember months from now what we made on our 5 hanger. I think we need to write it down so you won't forget. José, why not pick one of your favorite chains and tell me about it?

José: *(taking a long time to select one)* This one.

When Ms. Tinsley asks José how many red links the chain has, he shows two fingers; for blue links he shows three. Ms. Tinsley records a red 2 at the top of a skinny card and a blue 3 in the middle of the same card.

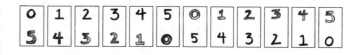

She places it on the desk. She continues to make the cards as the children describe the chains. When she is finished, the cards are in the same order as the chains with which they correspond.

While the two cards in the center indicate the same combination of links, the order of the numerals on the cards reflects their placement in the pattern.

Ms. Tinsley: *(replacing the 5 hanger on the bulletin board)* Does anyone see any patterns on the number cards?

Freddie: Yeah. On the bottom row, the numbers go high to low and high to low again: high, low, high, low.

Christie: See *(pointing to the top row)* it goes zero . . . one more . . . one more . . . one more . . . one more . . . one more, and then back to zero and start all over again.

John: Look, there are some matches: a 1 and a 4 here and a 1 and a 4 there. They are different 'cause they are different colors . . . That's cool. And there's a 4 and a 1 and another 4 and a 1. They all are on the 5 hanger. Cool.

Ms. Tinsley: Can anyone find any other patterns like the ones John found?

Discussion continues. At this point, no one has noticed the relationship between the two numbers on one card: when the top number gets larger, the bottom number gets smaller, and vice versa. That recognition comes later, after the cards have hung at the bottom of the chains on the bulletin board for a while.

When the discussion concludes, Ms. Tinsley punches a hole at the top of each card and asks children to hang the cards on the last link of the corresponding chains.

Fifth Event (April and May)

Six number hangers are displayed on the bulletin board, with matching number cards for each of the chains—hangers representing combinations for 5, 6, 7, 8, 9, and 10. Children work in various centers making things to take home for the summer so they won't forget kindergarten. At one center children make number hangers for home, using construction-paper strips for the chain links. Each child makes all the possible chains for a given number, along with the number cards to be pasted to the corresponding chains.

This activity helps to strengthen the school-home connection. Children will have the hangers at home to refer to, perhaps making further observations and discoveries. Parents and children may decide to make additional number hangers. Further, when parents see this representation of pattern and number relationships, they become more aware of the math connections children explore in class and are more likely to continue such conversations at home.

The children's work with the number chains over many months illustrates how ideas and knowledge develop over time. Thoughtful teacher planning creates this developmental sequence and makes possible in-depth learning.

Children at play—With patterns, functions, and algebra

Many patterns are evident in a calendar. Tommy, a first-grader in Mrs. Brown's class, discovered a new calendar pattern when he remembered a game activity from the day before.

In preparation for a game called Trump Seven, Mrs. Brown had asked Tommy and Jonathan to collect the manipulatives in sets of seven. As the boys collected the materials, Mrs. Brown counted by sevens: "Here's 7; seven more, 14; seven more, 21 . . ." This process was repeated many times until the boys began saying "7, 14, 21, 28" as they placed the manipulatives in plastic bags. Mrs. Brown wrote the numbers on the bags as they were collected.

A day later, January 28, during calendar time, Tommy was the calendar leader. Suddenly he interrupted the normal routine and exclaimed, "Hey, look! The 7 pattern! It goes 7 . . . 14 . . . 21 . . . 28." Pointing to the Tuesday column, he added, "It goes down!" At first many children did not understand Tommy's observation; but as he shared the 7 pattern eagerly with his classmates, recognition showed on their faces. Mrs. Brown said, "I wonder if any other months have that same pattern." She located an old picture calendar and, using a red crayon, circled the same 7 pattern on every month.

The children were very excited about their discovery, and other questions arose: Will there be 7 patterns next year? What about when their parents were children a long time ago, were there 7 patterns then? Why does the pattern stop? Does it ever go to 35? Why not? Why do the days of the month stop at 30 or 31?

While Mrs. Brown had not anticipated Tommy's pattern discovery, she built on it to extend all the children's learning by asking questions, getting out another calendar, and conveying an infectious spirit of wonder.

Another pattern discovery occurred quite spontaneously during circle time in Mr. Willis's 4-year-olds class. Seated on the floor, children were playing a counting game that emphasized the number 4. A child counted "1, 2, 3, 4" over and over again as he pointed to children one at a time clockwise around the circle. Each time he said the number 4, the child indicated stood up.

Gabrielle suddenly became excited: "I know who is going to stand! I know!" Mr. Willis asked, "How do you know?" "Look, it's a pattern: three sitting, one standing, three sitting, one standing. It happens every time!" The class continued the game and Gabrielle smiled as her predictions proved accurate. At the teacher's suggestion, she later drew a picture of the pattern in her journal. Thinking how to represent the pattern was a further challenge that extended Gabrielle's understanding.

Even young children can explore simple functions of this kind, using concrete materials or charts and other graphics that highlight patterns.

Promoting development of key skills and concepts

Research has shown that learning experiences focusing on the concept of patterns effectively facilitate children's ability to make generalizations about number combinations, counting strategies, and problem solving (Nummela & Rosengren 1986; Payne & Huinker 1993; Caine & Caine 1994; McClain & Cobb 1999). If children see patterns in their world and connect them to mathematics, they are better able to remember what they have learned and transfer the knowledge to new situations or problems. Preschoolers already recognize patterns in their environment. Although they cannot always verbalize or represent these with symbols, they are frequently able to predict what will happen next. A parent or teacher who changes a pattern gets a quick reaction from the child. Skipping a page in a story, forgetting the treat at the end of a meal, or not following the bedtime ritual to the letter brings a prompt protest.

What do the words *patterns, functions,* and *algebra* in the chapter title mean, and why teach these concepts to young children? A pattern is a regular arrangement of objects, numbers, or shapes. Many early childhood programs incorporate activities relating patterns, particularly simple repeating patterns such as *aab, aab, aab* or *ab, ab, ab.* In this content area (patterns, functions, and algebra), the primary objective with respect to patterns is for young children to be able to identify and analyze simple patterns, extend them, and make predictions about them (NCTM 2000).

Set A	Set B
1 lollipop	10 ¢
2 lollipops	20 ¢
3 lollipops	30 ¢
4 lollipops	?

Function, a key idea in higher-level mathematics, builds on the understanding of pattern that begins in early childhood. A *function* is a special relationship between the items in two sets. Here, for example, the number in Set B (number of cents) is 10 times the number in Set A (number of lollipops). In other words, the cost is a function of the number of lollipops.

Algebra is a branch of mathematics in which symbols are used to express general rules about numbers, number relationships, and operations. Is it being suggested that early childhood teachers actually include algebra in the curriculum? They certainly should not attempt to teach algebra at the level it is taught in high school. Rather, it is algebraic thinking that may be informally taught in the early grades.

Teachers help children recognize patterns, make generalizations, and then use symbols to represent solutions to problems. In the early years children construct their own symbols to represent their ideas. Then, with an introduction to more formal mathematics in school, children grow familiar with symbols used to express quantities and relationships. The "Early 'Equations'" box shows this progression from concrete to symbolic representation.

Early "Equations"

Working with a pan balance and Unifix cubes (singles and units made up of two, three, four, or more cubes), children get a wealth of concrete experience with the concept of an equation. For example, a child may place a two-cube unit on the left side of the scale and then one single cube on the right side. Finding the left side heavier, she balances the scale by adding another single cube to the right side. Now she has an equation.

If children don't start such play themselves, the teacher may ask, "How can I make the scale balance, Michael?" or "I have a four-cube unit on this side. Can we make it balance using these twos?"

After children have had extensive experiences balancing sets of concrete objects, the teacher can encourage them to explore various ways of representing their "equations" and at some point acquaint them with the conventional representation: 2 + 2 = 4.

Repeating patterns

In a *repeating pattern*, a certain sequence of colors, shapes, sounds, or other elements is repeated again and again, for example, red-red-blue or loud-soft-soft. Young children most readily grasp concepts and vocabulary relating to pattern when teachers introduce these concretely and in context. Instead of talking *about* a pattern, the teacher "reads" the pattern using simple vocabulary ("Circle, square, circle, square, circle, square") and engages the children in doing so.

The Young Child and Mathematics

Children often identify color patterns that repeat. Jenny, a 3-year-old, discovered that the caterpillar living in a tree by her house had an *ab, ab* pattern of gold, brown, gold, brown. Rui Chen was quite excited one day to discover that his "bestest shirt" had a pattern: red, light blue, dark blue; red, light blue, dark blue—which was an *abc* pattern. He was able to see that the pattern could also be stated as "red-blue-blue, red-blue-blue," an *abb* pattern.

Children found repeating color patterns in the number hanger activity (pp. 84–88). During the counting circle game, Gabrielle identified a repeating pattern of three sitting, one standing, three sitting, one standing—a repeating position pattern.

Although young children initially do not perceive the mathematical significance of visual patterns, such discoveries often bring them to greater awareness of number relationships and patterns. For example, Gabrielle may see that the pattern repeats itself in every group of four children and become more aware of the part-part-whole relationship of 3 and 1 as parts of 4.

Growing patterns

Growing patterns are patterns that change from one value to another in a predictable manner. The growth of a tree, adding one ring for each year, and the rapid (exponential) growth of the class gerbil population are both examples of growing patterns. While a bit more complex than repeating patterns, growing patterns are also useful and intriguing for young children to analyze. They often are not linear. A child can readily find them in natural settings.

Young children can generate growing patterns with beads, blocks, marbles, or other items. They start with a certain number of objects, representing the first *term* of the pattern. Then more objects are systematically added to the previous term, with the pattern that is established. For example, the adjacent marble configurations—based on a growing pattern—were created by 7-year-old Montie. He described the process he used to make his pattern, "I added four marbles each time, one on each end." His teacher helped him record descriptions of his terms using numbers and recording them on a chart. The chart look something like the one in the box at right.

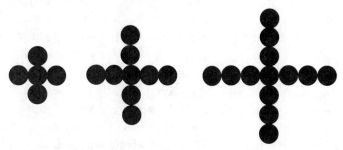

1	5 marbles
2	9 marbles
3	13 marbles
4	17 marbles
5	21 marbles

Using squashed marbles, Montie and one of his friends correctly figured out term 6 (25 marbles) and term 7 (29 marbles). When they finished, their teacher asked, "I wonder if anyone could figure out how many marbles would be in the next picture, or the next one, or even the one after that." The boys began making more pictures and quickly ran out of squashed marbles. When they asked for more, the teacher responded, "Sorry, we are all out. Is there any way you could figure it out without the marbles?" Using their fingers, the boys quickly calculated the eighth and ninth terms and announced the correct numbers.

In the creation of the number hangers, children also encountered growing patterns from one chain to the next. On the 5 hanger the number of blue links per chain starts at zero, increases to the middle of the hanger, and then decreases after the middle. Another growing pattern was the one Tommy discovered on the calendar (7, 14, 21, 28). If extended, this pattern can go on indefinitely in multiples of seven (35, 42, 49, 56, 63, 70 . . .).

Finding, copying, extending, and creating patterns

While children can find patterns easily, they may have difficulty copying or extending them. When they create their own patterns, they may not use a consistent rule throughout the pattern.

Louis described a pattern he created on the sidewalk with sidewalk chalk as "blue squiggly line, blue squiggly line, pink straight; blue squiggly line, blue squiggly line, pink straight; orange fire, red fire, yellow fire . . ." When asked about his pattern and specifically why he shifted to orange, red, and yellow fire, he declared that he was tired of making blue squiggly lines and the fire was more fun!

In this example it sounds like Louis chose not to continue the pattern. Often, however, when young children begin extending patterns, they add a new color, start completely new patterns, or leave out a part. Three-year-old Hardy was making a yellow, orange pattern with blocks, repeating, "Yellow, orange, yellow, orange, yellow, orange." When he began adding blue blocks to the end of his own linear pattern, the teacher asked him why. Surprised, Hardy answered, "Because blue's my favorite color!"

To help children create and copy patterns, teachers can provide them with materials that match the original materials in a pattern. For example, children can use cutouts that match the color and shape of pattern blocks to replicate or extend a pattern. When children have used all the cutouts, they can cut or draw more shapes to extend the pattern.

Remember Jorge and the number hangers? When the 5 hanger was first displayed, he was focused on the individual chains; he paid no attention at all to visual, color, or number patterns. Later, after more experiences, he was able to discover a rather intricate pattern and share his discovery with his class. In part he was able to do this because he had encountered the diagonal pattern in different places, sometimes with the teacher pointing it out, and was able to make the mathematical connection. Jorge had had classroom experiences with diagonal patterns, which lay the foundation for his discovery. These included activities and experiences in cooking (cutting square sandwiches into triangles) and in art (the Triangle Quilts pattern activity described near the end of this chapter).

Experiencing and representing patterns in various modalities

Patterns are everywhere in the curriculum. They may be seen in various modalities—auditory, tactile, and kinesthetic as well as visual. Inviting children to create a pattern physically (jump-jump-clap, jump-jump-clap) or musically (loud, soft-soft-soft; loud, soft-soft-soft) helps young children tune in to and understand patterns. Children can represent a pattern in movement, sound, or another medium with Unifix cubes or tiles. Children can draw or string beads to model the pattern, and they can describe it verbally. Auditory or movement patterns can also be represented with simple symbols. One dot might represent a hop on one foot, for instance, and two dots a jump with two feet. Children delight in interpreting ● **:** ● **:** as telling them to hop, jump, hop, jump. The use of all modalities—kinesthetic, auditory, and visual—facilitates the young child's understanding of pattern.

Dante, who had just turned 4, approached many learning tasks in a very physical way. Unless number or pattern was presented as a physical activity that involved his entire body, Dante did not understand it. When asked to show an *ab* pattern, he demonstrated an up-down, up-down, up-down pattern. His entire body shook, with his arms, legs, and head bobbing up and down. Doing this, he grasped the concept of pattern and was thrilled with his discovery! Although not every class has a Dante, there are many children who learn most readily through different modalities (Gardner 1983).

During the number hanger activity, many different modalities and representations were used. Finger representations for five, concrete chain links for five, numeral representations of number combinations for five, and many verbal discussions and descriptions for the quantity five were used. In another example, Gabrielle described a counting pattern using the terms "sitting, sitting, sitting, standing."

Skip counting can easily be done by using a physical pattern and an auditory pattern at the same time. Children in a second-grade class frequently counted using a prescribed routine. For instance, when counting by threes, the children said one number at a time as they first touched their head, then their shoulders, then their waist, and back again to their head. The numbers they said when touching their heads and shoulders were whispered, while the numbers said at their waists were shouted. The chant that resulted was "one, two, THREE, four, five, SIX, seven, eight, NINE, ten, eleven, TWELVE . . ." Children then recorded on a 100s chart the numbers they shouted. Working with partners, one child colored the shouted numbers while the other child did the gesturing and counting.

New counting routines can be created by extending the physical pattern: head, shoulders, waist, knees for skip counting by fours, and head, shoulders, waist, knees, feet for skip counting by fives. The figure at right is an example of a 100s chart completed when counting by threes and sixes.

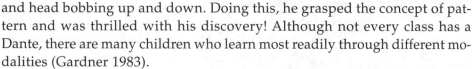

1	2	3	4	5	6	7	8	9	10
11	12	13	14	15	16	17	18	19	20
21	22	23	24	25	26	27	28	29	30
31	32	33	34	35	36	37	38	39	40
41	42	43	44	45	46	47	48	49	50
51	52	53	54	55	56	57	58	59	60
61	62	63	64	65	66	67	68	69	70
71	72	73	74	75	76	77	78	79	80
81	82	83	84	85	86	87	88	89	90
91	92	93	94	95	96	97	98	99	100

Counting by threes

Physical, musical, concrete (three-dimensional), pictorial, and verbal representations are all methods that can be used to help children recognize and represent patterns. The explicit connections made between the child's world and the real world are more effective when "the whole child" is involved. This multimodal approach to pattern also makes sense because individuals vary in their preferred learning modes, that is, in which of the various multiple intelligences (Gardner 1983) they demonstrate.

Use of symbols

Symbols are a major part of patterns, functions, and algebra. As described in *Principles and Standards for School Mathematics,* expectations for children in prekindergarten through second grade in the algebra standard suggest that "students should use concrete, pictorial, and verbal representations to develop an understanding of invented and conventional symbolic notations" (NCTM 2000, 90).

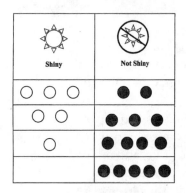

Children spontaneously sorted groups of five pennies into those that were shiny and those that were not. As children verbally described their pennies, the teacher decided to record their responses on a chart that looked something like the one on the left. Numerals were added to the chart along with the equal sign.

The circles represent the pennies. The first row shows there are three shiny pennies and two that are not shiny. The second row shows two shiny pennies and three that are not shiny. Representations for all the other combinations are recorded as well.

Later, the chart was transcribed in descriptive sentences: "3 pennies plus 2 pennies make five pennies" or "Five pennies can be three shiny pennies and two not-shiny pennies." Still later, symbolic equations were written $3 + 2 = 5$ or $5 = 3 + 2$.

The equal symbol (=) is probably one of the most commonly introduced symbols in early childhood classrooms. Yet to most young children, the symbol means "this is the answer." In fact, when given the three statements,

$$3 + 4 = 7$$

$$7 = 3 + 4$$

$$7 = 7$$

children usually say that the second and third equations are incorrect because they are not "written right."

The teacher's role is to give meaning to symbols by introducing them in context and sometimes providing a simple explanation or paraphrase. In the case of the equal sign, for example, the teacher introduces it as meaning *the same as.* He makes a point of illustrating it in a variety of equation forms ($7 = 3 + 4$ or $2 + 5 = 3 + 4$ or $7 = 7$). Concrete representations such as a scale in balance help too (see "Early 'Equations'" on p. 90).

Another example of gradually introducing mathematical symbols occurs in the sequence of hanger activities. When representing the blue and red links in the chains, the teacher first wrote the numerals by themselves on a card (p. 87) to allow the kindergartners to see patterns and relationships, the activity's initial focus. Later, when children could verbalize the patterns and relationships involved, the teacher laid each chain horizontally and wrote the number of each color link underneath, adding the plus (+) and *same as* (=) symbols to the numerals to express an equation. For example, on a chain with three blues and two reds, the sign would say 3 + 2 = 5.

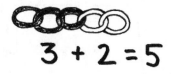

Making generalizations about number properties

Young children do no need to learn in a formal way about the properties of numbers, such as the fact that in addition the order of numbers does not affect the sum (the *commutative* property). But children may begin to recognize these properties in various ways. In the penny activity, for example, seeing on the chart 2 + 3 = 5 and also 3 + 2 = 5 helps them understand that the order in which the numbers are added does not affect the total.

The teacher can even more directly promote children's recognition of this property by using strategies that make the principle concrete. For example, he may ask them to hold the pennies in their hands (two in one hand and three in the other hand) and then crossing their hands so that the order is different, children can begin to see that the order does not change the total number of pennies. With this and other examples, children can begin to see that the sum is the same for 3 + 2 and 2 + 3.

While learning the concept of multiplication, second-graders were asked to solve a problem about chickens and eggs: There were 12 chickens and they each laid 7 eggs. How many eggs did the farmer collect that day? Most second-graders solved it by drawing a picture and then counting their representations of the eggs. However, counting by 10s and using seven fingers, Melani calculated that 10 chickens would lay 70 eggs (10, 20, 30, 40, 50, 60, and 70) and two more chickens would mean 7 + 7 more eggs, or 14. So, altogether there would be 84 eggs!

Melani generalized a number property from her experiences with algebraic thinking, which is one of the understandings that the teacher wants children to attain in this content area of the curriculum.

Describing change

Young children encounter change in many areas of their lives. They can describe change qualitatively ("He's taller than her") or quantitatively ("He's two inches taller than me"). The NCTM standards in the area of pattern, function, and algebra note, "The understanding that most things change over time, that many such changes can be described mathematically, and that many changes are predictable helps lay a foundation for applying mathematics to other fields and for understanding the world" (NCTM 2000, 94).

Describing changes that occur in science investigations and demonstrations is one of the easiest ways to introduce the idea of function to young children. Using comparison words (bigger, smaller; more, less; heavier, lighter; colder, warmer), children can describe what happens when something increases or occurs. For example, in an extended-day program, 4-year-olds were each holding tightly sealed plastic bags filled with varying amounts of baking soda and vinegar. When the container of vinegar was mixed with the baking soda, the bag filled with carbon dioxide—the bag "puffed up" and felt cold. The more soda and vinegar, the bigger and colder the bag. Children described what they found using their own words. This became a popular at-home activity.

Children can also describe changes quantitatively using numbers. Recording the height of bean plants, children can tell how tall their plants are after one week, two weeks, or three weeks. Weighing the class guinea pig, children can

Questions Specific to Patterns, Functions, and Algebra

Many of these questions connect to other mathematics content areas and can also be asked about stories, science, or experiences in other content areas.

To facilitate children's thinking about patterns, functions, and algebra, teachers may ask,

How are these alike? How are they different?

Do you see a pattern? Tell me about it.

What comes next? How could we make this pattern with these different materials? Could you tell a friend about this pattern and see if he can pick out which one you mean?

How can we remember this pattern? How can we make a picture that will help us? Could we use numbers? How?

Can you dance your pattern? What would you do first? Second?

What do you think will happen next? Why do you think so?

How did ___ change? Did something happen that made it change? Do you think it will change again?

Tell me about these two things: which one is bigger (heavier, smaller, lighter, more, less)?

What happens over and over again with these [beads]?

How can you read this pattern? Can you think of another way?

What would happen to the pattern if I changed ____?

evaluate the effectiveness of a particular diet or food supplement. Counting the number of cars passing the front of the school over a period of time, children can predict how the new road construction will affect traffic in the school zone. Describing and analyzing changes in various contexts helps children develop their algebraic thinking.

Providing a mathematics-rich environment

Many of the materials mentioned in Chapter 4 (focusing on number and operations) also help children learn about pattern, and recognizing and working with patterns help children understand more about numbers.

Even the youngest children begin to notice the patterns in routines that are repeated—put on coats, go outside, come in, take coats off—and anticipate the next action. Stories and poetry for young children are filled with patterns. Songs, of course, follow a pattern. Toys, furnishings, and children's own clothing often display bright, colorful patterns. Pattern scavenger hunts help children become more aware of patterns in their own classroom. Searching for patterns at home and bringing back information about these discoveries serve to connect home and school.

Many of the manipulatives used for number and geometry are useful also for considering pattern. In addition, pattern blocks (the colorful geometric shapes) are especially helpful. Children love to use them to cover large spaces. Because they fit together nicely and because of their regular shapes, the growing patterns created almost occur naturally. Other useful manipulatives include shape cutouts, Unifix cubes, base-10 blocks, plastic counters in a variety of animal shapes, and large beads.

The calendar is one staple in the environment that offers many opportunities to consider pattern. In addition to the 7 pattern that Tommy noticed in the Tuesday column of the class calendar (pp. 88–89), other natural calendar patterns include days of the week and months of the year. Even weather conditions and holidays can be described in terms of patterns. Creating a linear number line (like the one in Chapter 4, p. 63) to count the days of school yields many place-value patterns.

Children's errors often tell us what they understand about pattern. The child who predicts that 39 comes after 35 has little understanding of the pattern established with the order of the numbers 1 through 9. In contrast, the child who believes that 9010 ("ninety ten") comes after 99 seems to understand the pattern of counting and simply needs help with the conventional symbolic form.

Activities for exploring pattern and function and laying the foundations for algebra are described below. They are roughly in order of difficulty, but many can be simplified or extended to be more challenging.

Pattern People

Half of a group of children stands in a line, while the other half observes. The child leading the activity whispers instructions that follow a pattern to each person in line—for example, the first person in line is told to smile, the second to frown, the third to smile, and the fourth to frown. At the leader's signal, the children in the line carry out the whispered instructions while the audience guesses the pattern. Roles are then reversed, and the game is played again.

Several days after playing Pattern People, 4-year-old Erica drew a picture of four children frowning, smiling, frowning, smiling, and and declared that she had made a pattern.

Sidewalk Patterns

After studying patterns with two repeating parts—for example, red, blue, red, blue—children create their own patterns on the sidewalk with chalk. With a partner, each child draws one part of a repeating pattern. Patterns are copied onto black paper to share with the rest of the class when the children return inside.

Children often demonstrate understanding of position when describing patterns. As one kindergartner explained, "Our pattern starts with a purple squiggly line, then has a straight red line, then there is another purple squiggly line, and next there's a straight red line again."

Spin and Match

This activity requires game pieces of varying colors and features—attribute pieces work well—and spinners made by the teacher or children. The spinners are designed to reflect the features of the pieces and to correspond with the children's level of development. For example, if the children are learning to sort by *big* and *little*, a spinner divided in half with **BIG** on one side and LITTLE on the other can be used. If the children are learning to sort by color or shape, the spinner can be divided into wedges of color or sections with shape pictured. Sitting in a circle around the pieces and spinner, children enjoy taking turns spinning, reading the spinner, and selecting the indicated pieces.

For a greater challenge, the children can use more than one spinner. That is, the child spins one spinner for size, another spinner for color, and a third spinner for shape, then takes the piece described—a little red triangle. Play continues until the players have taken all the pieces. When all pieces are claimed, a spinner divided into *most* and *least* is spun. The winner of the game is the player with the most or least pieces, depending on the spin. To simplify the game or eliminate competition, this last step need not be used.

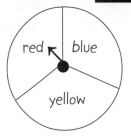

How Many Bird Wings?

Children enjoy learning about flying animals and insects, and this math activity is a good follow-up to an investigation of airborne creatures. The teacher wonders, "What if everyone in the class were a bird?" Children imagine they are birds and flap their "wings." The teacher points out that each bird has two wings and asks the children to guess the total number of wings there are in the class.

Kindergartners usually guess one more than the number of students in the class—each child realizes that he has two wings but does not take into account that everyone else does too. To resolve this misinterpretation, each child draws a picture of a bird with two wings, the pictures are posted, and the class counts the wings aloud. Later activities can investigate similar patterns by counting eyes, hands, or feet.

Moon Charts

Two small white paper plates are given to two different children every day for one month. The children are responsible for conducting a moon watch, cutting the plate to show the size of the moon that night and bringing it to class the next day. If the moon is not visible due to cloud cover, children can cover the plate with cotton balls or black paper, depending on the conditions.

The moons are posted daily on a calendar and the children discuss the pattern. The teacher introduces the descriptive words *full*, *half*, and *new* as they relate to each phase of the moon. Even with many cloudy nights, children can usually see a growing pattern. Children are generally conscientious about doing their "homework" and bringing in their moon assignments.

Dippy Patterns

Children fold white paper towels many times. They then dip the corners of the folded towels in water dyed with food coloring. After all the corners are dipped, they open the towels and set them out to dry. The dried towels are posted on a bulletin board.

Without indicating which towel is theirs, children take turns describing their patterns from top corner to top corner while the other children guess the towel being described. Afterward the teacher prompts the children to look at the towels from a different perspective, such as diagonally from top left corner to bottom right corner, vertically from top to bottom, or horizontally from side to side. A new perspective often fosters new and varied descriptions.

Photo Patterns

Photographs featuring patterns on buildings, sidewalks, and monuments around town are displayed in the block center. Children create their own versions of the structures in the photos by setting up block creations with similar patterns. They later draw the structures and post the drawings next to the appropriate photos. Photographs of the children's constructions can be taken to record the activity.

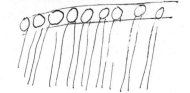

Children's creations are often remarkably similar to the buildings or structures in the photos. After doing this activity for a while, children find they can't go anywhere without seeing patterns inside and outside buildings!

Pattern Dance

Children take turns creating a dance using three different motions in sequence—for example, kick-spin-wiggle. The steps are repeated over and over again in an *abc* pattern. The child who creates the dance serves as the class's dance director, teaching the steps to the other children. When the music is turned on, everyone hops, wiggles, spins, kicks, jumps, flaps, or shakes in accordance with the pattern dance!

Building Block Blueprints

After viewing real building plans, children enjoy creating their own blueprints, using symbols and representations for their building block creations. These symbols may include a rectangle for a rectangular block or a square for a cube, as well as the child's own symbol for a doorway or stairs. (Young children cannot be expected to create keys for their plans, although some second-graders may wish to do so.)

Using white chalk, children draw buildings on blue butcher paper. They eagerly read and share each other's symbols and pictures and use them later to recreate their constructions.

Music Concert

Using musical instruments, children play an easily recognizable song featuring a pattern. "Bingo," for instance, is familiar to most children, and the chorus has a clear repeating pattern. *Clap, clap, clap-clap-clap!* represents the *B, I, N-G-O!* pattern and is easily grasped by children. Children enjoy hearing instruments playing in a pattern, and they enjoy performing songs with homemade instruments such as banjos created from plates and rubber bands, and shakers made from popcorn kernels and plastic tubs.

Pattern Music

In the music center, children decorate particular instruments with designated colors. For example, drums might be covered with blue stickers. Children compose music by creating patterns with different color stickers on paper printed with a musical staff. Each instrument plays in the order indicated by the pattern. This activity is great for small groups of children, who often like to pretend that they are musicians in a rock band.

The Lineup

In this activity, children see how a group (a *set* in mathematical terms) is formed from items that have a particular characteristic or do *not* have this feature. It is a good introduction to the *not* concept. When it is time for children to line up, they are shown a card with a symbol to indicate who goes first. The cards include symbols for shoe type, pet ownership, people wearing a specific color of clothing, and so on. Some cards have symbols with large black **X**s through them, meaning *not*. For example, the teacher might hold up a card with a red blob covered with a large black **X** and say, "Those children *not* wearing red should line up."

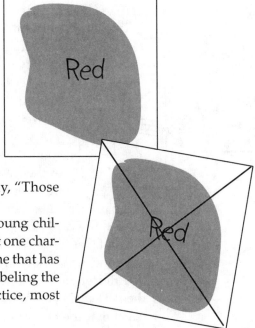

Initially, *not* characteristics are very difficult for young children to comprehend. To best teach this concept, select one characteristic and divide the children into two groups—one that has the characteristic and one that does not. Place signs labeling the characteristic in front of each group. After some practice, most young children master the *not* concept quite well.

Snake Patterns

After looking at pictures of snakes—or, better yet, an actual snake—and studying the snake's patterned skin, children make their own snakes from play-dough or paper. Snakeskin patterns can be created using cookie cutters, plastic tools, color construction paper, and other art materials. The completed snakes are displayed around the room.

Snakes made from paper cut first into a circle or oval and then into a spiral hang especially well from the ceiling, providing a new way to look at patterns. (Remind children to make a pattern on *both* sides of a paper snake.)

Straw Constructions

Children choose a number of small stirring straws of different lengths and stand them up in a piece of Styrofoam, arranging them in a line in order of height. They can adjust the height of the straws by snipping off the tops as necessary.

Children can take as many or as few straws as they wish; most choose about 10 straws. They tend to spend a long time making these constructions, reordering straws to make the pattern look just right.

Make an Equation

This activity helps children understand *equal* and *not equal* by comparing the quantities represented on two cards. The game also helps children recognize true and false equations.

Two decks of number cards are placed face down on the table. Each card represents a number, using a numeral or another type of representation such 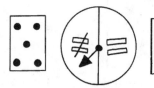 as tally marks, pips like those on dominoes, or a ten-frame. The spinner is divided into halves, one featuring the *equal* symbol (=) and the other, the *not equal* symbol (≠). The spinner is placed between the two decks of cards.

A player turns over the top card from each deck and then spins the spinner. Viewed together, the number on the top card of the first deck, the symbol indicated on the spinner, and the number on the top card of the second deck make an equation. If the player makes a *true* equation, he keeps the two cards. If the equation is *false*, the cards are placed face down next to the two decks, and the next player takes her turn. Play continues, using the discard piles when the decks are gone, until there are no more cards.

Children make interesting discoveries playing this game. They find that the *not equal* symbol usually works better than the *equal* symbol. They also learn that the equation 7 = 7 is true whether the numbers are expressed in numerals, tally marks, or pips.

Triangle Quilts

Children are given three paper squares of different colors. They fold the squares in half diagonally and cut each into two triangles. The children arrange the six triangles in patterns on a piece of paper and paste them down. They enjoy showing and describing the beautiful triangle "quilts" that result.

Covered Tiles

Using color tiles, groups of children create patterns with an additional property: the patterns become larger with each successive stage. Each pattern must have at least five terms laid out in tile. The teacher can check that patterns are consistent from one term to the next.

After the tile patterns are completed, one term is covered with a piece of paper. Other children view the pattern to try to figure out the missing section and then construct their guesses using tiles. The missing term is then revealed and the children who guessed correctly explain the strategies they used.

Due to its complexity, this activity is most appropriate for second- or third-grade children.

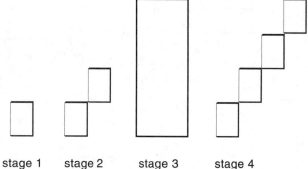

stage 1   stage 2   stage 3   stage 4

Marble Races

One end of a piece of PVC pipe (approximately one foot long) rests on the ground, while a child holds the other end. The child rolls a marble through the pipe, and everyone observes as the marble rolls out the other end and across the floor. The children record how far each marble rolls and how high the pipe was held, and then they raise or lower the pipe and try again. They take turns, seeing whose marble rolls the farthest. A discussion ensues about the best way to hold the pipe, and in the process, children learn about angles and functions.

In this beginning activity demonstrating function, children typically believe that the higher the pipe is held, the farther the marble will roll. This is not the case. In fact, when the pipe is held very high (almost vertically), the marble travels only a short distance because its impact with the floor slows it.

The children's recordings are highly dependent on their developmental level. Some may simply draw pictures of how high the pipe is held and then state that the marble went *far* or *not as far*. By second grade, children have developed measuring skills and some are able to give fairly accurate measurements for how high the end of the pipe is as well as how far the marble rolls. A child may make standard measurements with rulers if she is able, but she may also measure in relative terms. For example, a child might find that the end of the pipe was "as high as three books" and "the marble rolled five footsteps."

Principles in action

The vignettes and other teaching examples in Chapter 5, "Patterns, Functions, and Algebra," reflect the curriculum, instruction, and assessment principles that form the basis for this book. To clarify how specific principles look in practice, this chart highlights four instances in which selected principles were evident.

Curriculum Principle 2 Essential mathematical processes are solving problems, reasoning, communicating, making connections, and representing.	The connections between number and pattern have been modeled, discussed, and represented in a variety of ways during the activity involving index cards with number patterns (pp. 87, 95). Using the cards to represent numerals is important in helping children begin to understand the connection between number symbols and quantity.
Instruction Principle 1 To effectively plan experiences, teachers must make a variety of decisions based on their knowledge and focusing on the needs of individual children.	During the first number hanger event (pp. 84–85), the teacher arranged for the children to freely explore different ways to make chain lengths of five links, while establishing the rules so the children could readily see the number fact patterns. If the chains contained alternating colors, the number facts would not be recognized as easily.
Instruction Principle 3 The teacher must orchestrate various contexts and ways in which children engage in mathematical experiences, such as whole group, small group, project teams, and other strategies.	Since the patterns in number combinations featured in the second number hanger event (pp. 85–86) can be very complex and represented many ways, the teacher orchestrates this activity so the patterns can be viewed over a long period of time.
Assessment Principle 4 Teachers have a responsibility to assess their own teaching effectiveness as well as children's learning and development in mathematics.	The teacher was able to observe Jorge's growth in learning by comparing his first immature response to the hanger patterns ("The chains are on hangers") to his rather mature discovery about the similar color patterns on each of the hangers (p. 87).

Chapter 6

Geometry and
Spatial Sense in the
Early Childhood Curriculum

G*eometry* is the area of mathematics that involves shape, size, position, direction, and movement and describes and classifies the physical world we live in. Children's *spatial sense* is their awareness of themselves in relation to the people and objects around them.

Historically, geometry was one of the first areas of mathematics taught to young children. In the 1850s Friedrich Froebel, "the Father of Kindergarten," designed a curriculum with suggested instructional practices based on the use of geometric forms and their manipulation in space. In this curriculum Froebel designed "gifts" for kindergartners—special materials to enable them to explore and grasp basic forms and relationships. The first six gifts included balls of different colors, cubes, spheres, cylinders, and complex sets of geometric blocks that children manipulated and observed in a series of progressive tasks (Balfanz 1999).

In later years this geometric focus was largely lost. In fact, in an international comparison the United States's worst performance was in geometry (Beaton et al. 1996). Many reasons have been suggested for this dismal showing; however, everyone acknowledges that the study of geometry and spatial sense has not been a focus in the typical elementary or secondary school mathematics curriculum in the United States. This is especially true for early childhood classrooms. Shape definitions are typically the only prominent geometric ideas introduced, while manipulation of shapes and spatial exploration are generally neglected. Young children have worked with shapes in art activities and puzzles, and have constructed with Legos and unit blocks, which offer rich opportunities to explore geometry and spatial relationships. However, many teachers do not emphasize spatial concepts nor take advantage of natural connections to mathematics or other content areas.

As discussed here, the content standard on geometry and spatial sense involves much more than naming shapes. Key aspects of geometry and spatial sense, according to the NCTM standards for the early grades (2000), are

- analyzing characteristics and properties of two- and three-dimensional geometric shapes and considering geometric relationships,

- specifying locations and describing spatial relationships using coordinate geometry and other representational systems,

- applying transformations by recognizing and applying slides, flips, and turns as well as recognizing and creating shapes containing symmetry,

- using visualizations to create mental images of geometric shapes using spatial memory; to recognize and represent shapes from different perspectives; and to recognize geometric shapes and structures in the environment and specify their location. (p. 97)

Familiarity with shape, structure, location, and transformations and development of spatial reasoning enable children to understand not only their spatial world but also other mathematics topics. As children count the sides of two-dimensional shapes or the faces of a cube, they learn about number relationships. Patterns, functions, and even rudiments of algebra may be noted when children identify patterns in space or when they see the relationships between the number of faces, edges, and vertices of three-dimensional figures. When children compare shapes, directions, and positions in space, they develop concepts and acquire vocabulary that they also put to use in measurement. Grouping items, sometimes by shape or another geometric feature, is a skill also fundamental to data collection, and children may record and report shapes in an activity or in the environment.

Spatial sense and construction come into play in art, science, social studies, movement and music, and reading. For example, spatial thinking skills emphasized in geometry are critical to the making and reading of maps—essential skills in social studies. Children notice shapes in natural objects of all kinds. They discover many things about shape and geometry in their block play. Manipulating shapes in space introduces children to vocabulary words about position as well as other words necessary for reading and language arts. Even distinguishing between letters of the alphabet involves attention to shape and position. In art, spatial relationships and geometric forms are critical elements in both two-dimensional and three-dimensional creations.

Young children enjoy manipulating shapes in space, and their spatial capabilities often exceed their numerical skills (NCTM 2000). Three-year-old Jeffrey in Chapter 2 has a strong intuitive knowledge about shapes and how they relate to his world. While most of his knowledge is perceptual in nature, he is able to relate a two-dimensional circle to his uncle's basketball and to recognize that, unlike a basketball, the circle will not bounce.

As in the other content areas, the teacher's role is to bridge the young child's informal knowledge and formal school mathematics. This bridging often means using the child's own language and relating it to formal terms and definitions. It may also mean offering a position or shape word that describes what the child is doing or attending to. Jeffrey's teacher, for example, later referred to "the pizza shape," as Jeffrey called it, and compared it to a triangle. The teacher might decide to provide the word *sphere* for the basketball and engage Jeffrey in considering other differences between a ball and a two-dimensional circle.

Levels of Geometric Thinking

Describing children's development of geometry and spatial sense, researchers and educators often present Pierre Van Hiele and Dina van Hiele-Geldof's Levels of Geometric Thinking (van Hiele 1986). Most children up through the primary grades have not progressed beyond Level 1, and many preschoolers are operating at Level 0. Research suggests that to move through these levels, children must be exposed to many experiences and participate in numerous activities. Progress is often very slow.

Level 0: Children learn to recognize geometric figures such as squares and circles by their holistic physical appearance. For example, a given figure is a circle because it "looks like a clock." Children at this level do not think about the attributes or properties of shapes.

Level 1: Children begin to learn isolated characteristics or attributes of the forms, such as "a square has four equal sides."

Level 2: Children establish relationships between the attributes of a form. At this level, for example, children can determine that a square is a rectangle because it has all of a rectangle's properties.

Let's look first at a thinking activity that the teacher calls Look, Make, and Fix. Using an overhead projector, the first-grade teacher, Mr. Quintanilla, shows the children a model created from several tangram pieces. They study the configuration of shapes on the screen and then are given time to duplicate the figure with their own tangram pieces, look again, and fix their models to match the teacher's figure. Mr. Quintanilla encourages the children to help one another. As the configurations increase in difficulty, he gives the children as many tries as they need to correct their figures.

Playing Look, Make, and Fix in small groups, children who have difficulty with spatial skills can have more practice and learn new strategies. The game can also be played with attribute or pattern blocks. Children enjoy the activity so much that they like to play it on their own when they have the chance.

Look, Make, and Fix

Children are getting settled in the classroom as the school day begins. The message on the chalkboard directs them to select a set of tangrams. Seeing the projector, the children anticipate one of their favorite thinking activities and excitedly get their tangram bags together—seven tangram pieces that combine to make a large square. (See the diagram on p. 108.)

Mr. Quintanilla: Today we are going to get your thinking started by playing Look, Make, and Fix. First, let's check our tangram bags to see if we have all the shapes. Who remembers what we should have in our bags?

Tanya: Two big triangles and two little triangles.

Stanley: And one medium triangle. Five triangles!

Mr. Quintanilla: Right. That covers the triangles. What about the other shapes? There are seven shapes altogether, so how many more do we need to find?

Jane: There's a square and that funny shaped one, a squashed rectangle. I forget.

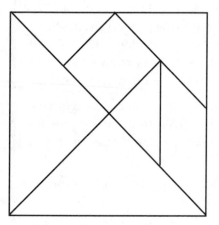

Seven tangram pieces combine to form a large square.

There is some discussion as the teacher pauses, listens, and observes children finding the parallelogram. Although the children have heard the words *parallelogram, rectangle,* and *quadrilateral,* they are not sure what they mean or how they relate to each other or to the particular "squashed rectangle" in the tangram set.

Mr. Quintanilla: Let's everyone look at Jane's squashed rectangle. Hold it up, and let's trace around it with our fingers. *(modeling with his parallelogram shape as he speaks)* Side . . . stop, tip. *(touches the vertex, the point where two sides meet)* Side . . . stop, tip. Side . . . stop, tip. Side . . . stop, tip. How many sides?

Children: Four.

Mr. Quintanilla: Then, although it can be called different things, like *squashed rectangle,* let's call it a *quadrilateral.* A quadrilateral is any shape that has four sides. In fact, let's use one of Jane's words and call it a *squashed quadrilateral.* Can you say it fast? Squashed quadrilateral, squashed quadrilateral, squashed quadrilateral. *(lots of laughter)*

Mr. Quintanilla decides not to further define a quadrilateral or identify the square as a special quadrilateral. Geometry and spatial sense are skills that develop over time, and those ideas will be introduced in future lessons. For the moment, the children have the words to help them identify the shape, and that is enough.

Mr. Quintanilla: All right. Check your shapes and see if you have every shape. *(places shapes on the overhead projector for children to see as he says the words)* Five triangles, two small, two large, and one medium; and one square and one squashed quadrilateral. A total of 2 . . . 4, 5, 6, 7 pieces. Is everyone ready?

One child locates a missing triangle on the floor and another gets a square from the box of extra pieces. Everyone is now ready.

Mr. Quintanilla: Place your pieces in a pile at the top of your table. Hands in your laps! Don't move them until I tell you to. Here we go.

Using the medium triangle and the square, Mr. Quintanilla makes a shape configuration on the projector.

Mr. Quintanilla: *Look!*

The Young Child and Mathematics

Children stare at the picture for a few seconds without touching their pieces. Mr. Quintanilla then covers the picture with a piece of paper.

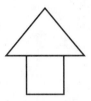

Mr. Quintanilla: *Make!*

Children select the pieces used and make the picture at their tables. Some look at others and copy or compare pictures. Most children make it correctly. A few use a different size triangle at the top of the picture. Mr. Quintanilla waits about 30 seconds while children continue checking, and then he removes the piece of paper covering the model.

Mr. Quintanilla: *Fix!*

Children check their creations against the shape projected. Most of the children who have used the wrong size triangle see their error and change pieces. Two children do not. Mr. Quintanilla reminds children to help each other, so one child helps another with the configuration, and Mr. Quintanilla quietly changes the incorrect piece of the other child.

Kimberly: *(raising her hand)* Mr. Quintanilla, Sara is looking at my picture and copying!

Mr. Quintanilla: That's fine! Remember, this is not a test; it is a game where we all help each other. Sara, I'm glad Kimberly has a good picture for you to look at. Thanks, Kimberly! Let's try another one. This one is harder!

Mr. Quintanilla repeats the process with three more examples. They get progressively harder, each adding more shapes in different configurations. The last task takes many "fix" steps for everyone to complete. It looks like this.

Mr. Quintanilla: Whew! That last one was a lot of work. Thanks for helping each other fix that picture. I noticed that Fernando was excellent at solving this one. Fernando, can you help us understand how you did it?

Fernando, whose home language is not English, tends to have difficulty verbalizing his thoughts. After a long pause, he shrugs and responds.

Fernando: I just thunk and thunk!

Mr. Quintanilla: I could see that you did! Did you think of a picture that the shapes made? Did it look like anything to you? A *gato,* maybe?

Fernando: *(laughing)* Not a cat—a turtle with no legs!

Mr. Quintanilla: Oh, what a good idea. What about you, Gina? You helped lots of people on that one. How did you do it?

Gina: I just worked on one part at a time. First I made the mountain *(pointing to the two large triangles)* and then I added the other stuff. The hardest part was that weird piece.

Mr. Quintanilla: The squashed quadrilateral?

Gina: Yeah. I looked at that a lot before I got it.

The discussion continues a few more minutes, then the tangram pieces are put away. Mr. Quintanilla will discuss more varied spatial tasks, strategies, and geometric terms at another time. Spatial sense takes a long time to develop, and this is just a beginning exploration.

Mr. Quintanilla's class does this basic activity in varied settings—large groups, small groups, and learning centers. Families can also play Look, Make, and Fix and other games relating to space and shape. During holiday time Mr. Quintanilla sends two die-cut tangram sets home as a gift so children can teach their families the game.

An interesting sidelight is that Mr. Quintanilla himself has never found spatial sense activities easy. Many teachers with this difficulty would say to themselves, "Some people have it and some don't," and either neglect spatial activities or convey a negative, defeated attitude toward them. Instead, Mr. Quintanilla highlights the importance of effort rather than luck or intelligence in demonstrating spatial sense. He talks about how hard children are working, and he offers the "fix" component of the activity as often as needed to allow children to succeed. Believing that spatial sense activities are important for all children to experience, Mr. Quintanilla has made sure to include plenty of them and become comfortable doing them.

The main purpose in assessing children's understanding is to tailor learning experiences to their needs. Mr. Quintanilla observes children in the whole-group setting and notes those who would benefit from small-group sessions. In small groups the children can observe the configurations more closely and even handle them. In this activity the teacher notes growth in Fernando's confidence and in Gina's use of strategies and continues to delight in Jane's descriptive vocabulary.

Children at play—With geometry and spatial sense

Young children naturally love to explore geometric and spatial aspects of the world around them. There are many opportunities for the teacher to scaffold children's understanding by asking questions, suggesting other activities, showing various transformations (such as two same-size right triangles forming a rectangle), and providing additional materials.

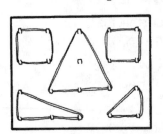

Denise, age 4, excitedly showed her teacher some shapes she had drawn in her journal. Mrs. Stipe gave her a geoboard with bands and asked if she could copy them on her board. Denise proudly demonstrated the result.

Ms. Patterson found three large plastic mirrors at a garage sale and placed them in the housekeeping center. She listened as a verbal 3-year-old gave everyone a guided tour: "Look in here. I can see two mes and two yous. These are called *magic windows*." For weeks children experimented with their mirror images and reflections.

Creations in the block center provide many opportunities to enhance children's understanding of geometry. Questions like, "How is your tower

The Young Child and Mathematics

different from Joe's?" or "What will happen if the bottom block is removed?" or "What if I try to make a building like yours without looking? Can you tell me what I need to do to make mine just like yours?" or "It will soon be time to clean up. How will you remember what you have built?" can facilitate thinking and experimentation. As a result of the teacher's questions and discussion with 7-year-old Frank, the balance and symmetry of his block creation were enhanced and noted more consciously by Frank and the other children looking on.

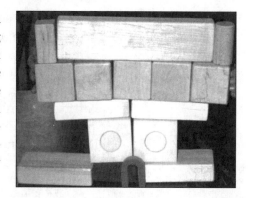

Geometry and Block Play

Using blocks presents children with many opportunities to make discoveries about two-dimensional and three-dimensional shapes. A multitude of configurations appear from children's spontaneous arrangements.

Four of the small triangles can make a square.

Four of the large triangles can make a rhombus.

Two squares and four small triangles make a hexagon.

Two triangles joined to a square or a rectangle make a parallelogram.

Or two small triangles and a square create a trapezoid (the long side of the trapezoid may be at the top or bottom; if the long side is at the top, the children may call it a boat).

Children also make many discoveries about shape when constructing objects they use in creative play.

Adapted from E. Hirsch, ed., *The Block Book*, 3d ed. (Washington, DC: NAEYC, 1996), 57–58.

Promoting development of key skills and concepts

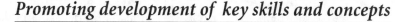

Although young children often demonstrate intuitive spatial abilities, many teachers virtually ignore geometry and spatial sense. The new *Principles and Standards for School Mathematics* (NCTM 2000) emphasizes geometry and spatial sense as an important content area for children in prekindergarten settings through twelfth grade. Let's look at the specific expectations for young children.

Shape

Children begin to form shape concepts in the years before school, and these concepts are fairly stable by the time children are 6 or 7. Clements (1999) suggests that an ideal period to learn about shapes is between 3 and 6 years of age. For the most part, young children do not develop their concepts of shape from looking at pictures or merely hearing verbal definitions ("a triangle has three sides and three angles"). Rather, they need to handle, manipulate, draw, and represent shapes in a variety of ways.

The study of shapes should focus on the attributes and properties of both two- and three-dimensional shapes. Initially, children must be given many opportunities to manipulate and sort shapes according to their own criteria. Particular sorting clues can easily be highlighted as children sort blocks and put them away on shelves that are marked with outlines for each type of block or by some other system. For example, tubs can be provided for children to sort pattern or attribute blocks according to number of sides (quadrilaterals vs. triangles). Matching or classifying objects by such properties helps children to focus on the critical attributes of each shape.

Research strongly supports the use of a wide variety of manipulatives to help children understand geometric shapes and develop spatial sense (Greabell 1978; Clements & McMillen 1996). Manipulating geometric solids helps children learn geometric concepts (Gerhardt 1973; Prigge 1978). Solid cutouts of shapes are more conducive to shape learning than are printed forms (Stevenson & McBee 1958).

Computer programs that allow children to manipulate shapes have specific advantages because, if designed correctly, they offer great flexibility (Clements & McMillen 1996). The best software allows children to instantly change the shape and the size of forms as well as save and later retrieve their work.

Beginning with shapes they can pick up and handle, children can familiarize themselves by tracing the outline of a shape with their fingers. When the child gets to the end of a side—reaches a corner or an angle—the teacher, and then the child, notes this verbally. For example, in tracing a rectangle one might say, "Side, stop, corner; side, stop, corner; side, stop, corner; side, stop, corner." By saying *corner* instead of *tip,* and by using a different or perhaps louder voice, the teacher can draw children's attention to a right angle as being different from other angles. A right triangle can be traced and described using *corner* at the right angle and *tip* for the other two angles. Children can go on to trace around cutouts or pictures of shapes.

At first, children recognize a shape by its appearance as a whole. Children may know that a triangle has three sides, and perhaps recognize the familiar equilateral triangle, yet be unable to identify triangles within a group of figures. Having a limited understanding of "triangleness," young children often do not recognize triangles that depart from the equilateral version they know and love! Four-year-old Daniel, for example, recognized the regular and irregular triangles in a group with all triangles, but he declared, "These are the really *good* triangles [pointing to the equilateral triangles resting on one of their sides] and these ones are *bad* ones [pointing to the fat, long, skinny, or irregular triangles standing on their points]!" Similarly, children see a triangle standing on its vertex as wrong and call a square sitting on its point a diamond.

Children most readily learn the critical attributes of a geometric shape when they see a variety of examples and nonexamples (Clements 1999). Examples of triangles shown in a variety of positions and sizes, as well as nonexamples (triangle-like shapes with curved sides, without sides, or with too many sides), should be shown, manipulated, and discussed. Most important, children benefit from practice in telling why a particular shape does or does not belong in a group.

At their level of development, young children do not easily categorize shapes in more than one way. Children tend to see squares and rectangles as two discrete shapes rather than seeing squares as a subset of rectangles; they expect a rectangle to have two long sides. A square is a special rectangle, of course, one that has equal sides. It is also a quadrilateral, a parallelogram, and a rhombus. Introducing all these words and concepts to young children is probably premature. However, teachers should keep the real meaning of such terms in mind and avoid giving children ideas that are actually wrong (for instance, by saying "No, that's not a rectangle—it's a square").

As Mr. Quintanilla uses the words *side* and *tip*, he models tracing the parallelograms with his finger to clarify their meanings. He discusses with the children Jane's *squashed rectangle* terminology and introduces a new word, *quadrilateral.*

Mr. Quintanilla combines tangram shapes, placing them in a variety of positions for the children to replicate. To be successful, a child must not only recognize various shapes but also note their positions in space. At this point the children are not asked to draw the shapes, but this is planned for later in the year.

Space

Thinking spatially—visualizing shapes in different positions and imagining movements—is important to young children's development as mathematical thinkers. Specifically, teachers need to help children develop "a variety of spatial understandings: direction (which way?), distance (how far?), location (where?), and representation (what objects?)" (NCTM 2000, 98). Of course, learning to think spatially is an evolutionary process. In the early childhood years, experiences with simple maps, position words, and opportunities to manipulate shapes into various positions are important to children's development of spatial sense.

These skills can be emphasized during routines or in specially planned activities. For example, children in a kindergarten class love finding their class puppet every week by reading a map the teacher gives them. The map includes direction words and arrows, geometric shape landmarks, distance between landmarks in number of footsteps, and a pictorial representation of the puppet to be found. Later in the year, the kindergartners make the maps to help their peers find the puppet.

The creative dramatics center is a good place to emphasize spatial vocabulary. As children act out stories like "The Three Billy Goats Gruff" or "The Three Bears," position words can be used as prompts for their movements. During guided reading activities, position words can be emphasized and used in context in other meaningful situations. Also, language expressing how something is moved (right, left, up, down) and what it looks like after it is moved (standing on one tip with the big part on the top) should accompany actions that involve moving objects in space. Using children's language combined with meaningful definitions, the teacher and the children can describe how movements are made and the resulting effect.

Spatial Vocabulary

Location/position words: on, off, on top of, over, under, in, out, into, out of, top, bottom, above, below, in front of, in back of, behind, beside, by, next to, between, same/different side, upside down

Movement words: up, down, forward, backward, around, through, to, from, toward, away from, sideways, across, back and forth, straight/curved path

Distance words: near, far, close to, far from, shortest/longest path

Transformation words: turn, flip, slide

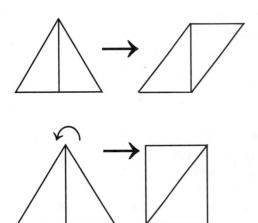

Transformations. Young children are often unable to visualize what the shape will look like when it is turned, flipped, slid, or transformed in some way. When a group of 4-year-olds practice folding a square diagonally and cutting it into two triangles, they often giggle in surprise when they can move the two triangles back and make a square. Similarly, when children flip up half of a triangle and make a parallelogram, they are delighted at the transformation and may practice it over and over again to see the changes. Moving puzzle pieces and making shapes fit exactly into frames require children to transform shapes by sliding, flipping, or turning them.

Lines of symmetry. A line of symmetry divides a figure into two parts that are mirror (reversed) images of each other. To further their understanding of symmetrical relationships, children can draw half of a picture—half of a person, half of a house, half of a flower. When they place the edge of a mirror (held at a right angle to the paper) against the unfinished edge of the image, the image will look complete. Children also enjoy holding a mirror to a family photograph, making Mom with two heads or brother Tom with four legs.

Another way for children to explore symmetrical relationships is to cut out two duplicate geometric shapes (squares are easy), then fold them each along the same line of symmetry (for squares, the line can be vertical, horizontal, or diagonal). When they hold one folded square against the other, axis to axis, children can see that the matching halves form a whole. Children also experiment with balance and symmetry while building with Legos, wooden blocks, and other materials. For young children, exploration should be the primary focus of experiences with symmetry.

Providing a mathematics-rich environment

More than any other content area, geometry requires certain specific types of manipulatives to help children learn. Attribute blocks (shapes in different colors with shape, size, and thickness attributes), pattern blocks (red trapezoids, orange squares, green triangles, yellow hexagons, and blue and white rhombi), and tangram pieces are important shape models that are helpful to children as they develop their understanding of shape and space.

Three-dimensional models are also important. A variety of wooden blocks with unusual shapes, along with the more typical shapes, help children develop their perceptions of shapes in space. Children can use clear containers (sphere, cube, cone, rectangular prisms, pyramids) filled with water to explore the water surface and provide opportunities for explorations of moving shapes.

Everyday objects also contribute to the development of children's understanding of geometry and spatial sense. The young child's world is filled with shapes in different sizes and positions. Basketballs, cereal boxes, and cans are examples of geometric models that children can compare to classroom models. Patterned material or artwork with shapes positioned in unusual ways can be displayed on classroom walls. Children can use string, pipe cleaners, and yarn to create the outlines of shapes or shape sculptures. The teacher can share books that involve children in looking at objects from different perspectives, or children can work on books of this kind on their own. Objects children bring from home to share may be excellent examples of shapes and add to a mathematically rich environment.

Young children also benefit from having many opportunities to climb in and out of big boxes, on or around equipment—going under, over, around, through, into, on top of, and out of different things to experience themselves in space. With an assortment of large hollow blocks, boards, saw horses, and the like (Cartwright 1996), children can build structures big enough to get inside, which allows them to experience their constructions from a very different spatial perspective.

Questions Relating to Geometry and Spatial Sense

Although experienced early childhood teachers ask many questions, they often overlook questions relating to spatial sense and shape. Here are some possibilities:

How is that shape like this one? How is it different?

Why isn't this shape an [oval]? What makes it a [circle]?

What if I turned this shape? What if I flipped it? What would it look like if I slid it from your paper to my paper?

Where have you seen this shape before?

Can you find something like this at home?

(When a child has made a picture out of shapes) How did you decide to use this triangle for the roof?

How did you decide what to copy/draw?

Can you tell me how to get to the [cafeteria] from here?

Can you tell me about the neighborhood you built with blocks? I'm going to draw a map of it without looking. So tell me what it looks like and what I should put where.

Do you think this shape would roll? Slide? Could we stack these?

How could you cut this paper to make another shape?

What shape could you make out of these shapes?

Could we make the cone roll straight, or would it roll crooked? What about the cylinder?

What would happen if I dropped this [cube, cylinder] and it broke in half? What would the parts look like? Could it break in half another way?

Have you found all the ways to put those shapes together? How do you know?

What would happen if I cut off an end of this? What would it look like?

Can you think of another name for this shape?

Can you make a square [a triangle, a rectangle] with pipe cleaners? How about a ball [a box, a cone]?

Some activities based on geometry and fostering spatial sense are described here. While these activities are roughly listed in order of difficulty, many can be expanded to be more challenging or can be streamlined to simplify them.

String Shapes

Three or four children hold a large string loop. They make a variety of shapes by adding or taking away a vertex or a side; changing the size of an angle, or increasing or decreasing the area of a shape.

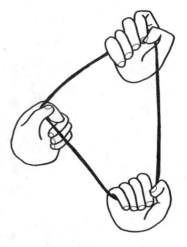

Children enjoy making shapes as the leader of the activity names them. They find that a triangle is easy to make because it can be skinny, fat, or "just right" and still be a triangle. A square is harder because all the sides must be exactly the same. Children are often surprised that a circle is one of the hardest shapes to make with string, as it is easy to draw. As one child explained, "Circles are easy to draw because you don't have anyone holding the line and making a point. They are much harder to hold."

Reenacting Stories

Children act out stories they have heard recently using position words such as *above*, *below*, *down*, *up*, *right*, *left*, *under*, *top*, *bottom*, *side*, *beside*, and *through*. Children either represent the characters in the stories themselves, or they model the stories by using storyboards.

The storyboards depict settings of recently studied themes or projects and can be used as backdrops for a variety of stories. Using objects to represent characters, children model stories by placing items appropriately on the storyboard. They use position words to describe the characters' actions.

"The Three Billy Goats Gruff" is a great story for children to perform; it is especially popular with prekindergartners. A small table can be used as a bridge. The narrator emphasizes many position words (such as *under*, *over*, *after*, *next*, *between*) and size words (such as *big*, *middle*, *little*) to describe the action as children act out the story. Afterward, the story can be rewritten with the characters in different locations (the troll on top of the bridge, the billy goats trotting under the bridge), which children often find amusing.

Kitchen Prints

Children use a variety of kitchen utensils to make paint prints in the art center. The prints must fill up an entire piece of paper, but the individual prints on the paper may not touch one another. Forks, spatulas, handles, plastic lids, the tops of pans, cheese graters, slotted spoons, and food brushes create unique prints in a variety of shapes and partial shapes.

Children generally take great care in spacing the individual prints so they do not overlap. When finished, they describe the paint prints using shape and position words and have fun guessing which tools made the prints in each other's pictures.

Domino Flash

With half of it covered, the pip side of a large domino is quickly shown to the children. Based on their fleeting view of the pattern of the pips, children 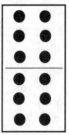 decide what number is displayed on that part of the domino. When children become comfortable with this activity, both halves of the domino face are shown and children must add the two amounts. (It is best to use a domino set with "double-six"—six pips on each half— as the highest value, as this activity may be too difficult for young children if higher values are used.)

Children quickly learn what the arrangement of pips for 1, 2, 3, 4, 5, and 6 look like. When asked how they recognize the numbers so quickly, their responses reveal their understanding of number as well as spatial sense. When Allen was asked how he knew five pips stood for 5, he said, "It's one in the middle and two up and two down. You don't even need to count—it's just there!" Jelani said that 2 was "so easy—there's one in one corner and one in the other corner. Easy!"

Making Frames

Children construct frames for three-dimensional shapes by bending pipe cleaners around objects found in the constructing center. (A section of the frame is lifted up to remove the object.) The frames are then displayed and children try to guess which shapes match which frames.

This activity fosters an understanding of shape and space. Children enhance their knowledge of edges, faces, and vertices when they resolve the problems of "making this part straight" or "getting all the pieces to meet at one point."

Treasure Map

Eric Carle's book *The Secret Birthday Message* is a delightful story about a boy searching for his birthday surprise—a new puppy. The book uses many direction and shape words. A map at the end of the book visually represents story events, using shapes and arrows to indicate directions.

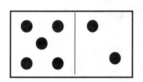

make a puppy

After listening to the story and studying the map, children make their own maps of the classroom, complete with shapes, arrows, and a hidden puppy. These wonderful maps can be created entirely using shapes. For example, the teacher's desk becomes a rectangle, the clock a circle, the doorway a rectangle, and the cabinet door a square. A puppy can be constructed by using two circles and cutting one in half to make ears.

When the classroom maps are finished, children "read" each other's to see if they can find the puppy. The maps are saved and often shared with other classes.

Quick Draw

Children are briefly shown one or two shapes, which they quickly draw. Afterward, children discuss and describe the shapes or draw pictures using them. These pictures can be kept in a special "shape journal."

This activity is especially well suited to prekindergarten classes, although older children also enjoy it. After drawing a shape, children often create more pictures to put in their shape journals by drawing patterns featuring that shape. Other shapes can be included in the pictures as well. Some children prefer to draw the circle because "it's easy." Other shapes like hexagons are harder for children to draw, but after tracing cutouts of these shapes, children recognize them more readily and their drawings improve.

Shape Pictures

In this excellent learning center activity, children compose pictures using specified numbers of circles, triangles, and rectangles. First, children cut multiples of these shapes in various sizes from construction paper. Using a spinner divided into thirds (labeled *circle*, *triangle*, and *rectangle*) and a die with pips from 1 through 6, children spin the spinner and roll the die, select the appropriate number of the shapes indicated, and repeat the process once more. They then make pictures using the shapes they selected. Children display their pictures and describe their constructions using shape and position words.

The pictures can be quite interesting. Squares become animals, houses, or robots. Circles are often used as parts of flowers, the sun, or spots on a dog. Triangles become people's heads, tops of buildings, or race cars.

Secret Socks

Children create their own "secret socks," which contain several mystery shapes. A child threads two or three shape beads onto a pipe cleaner, folding the ends so the beads will not fall off. He places the pipe cleaner and beads in a secret sock. The secret socks are then traded. Children feel the shapes inside the socks *without* looking, and in their own words, they describe what they think is inside.

Children's descriptions are typically connected to everyday objects. They describe the sphere as a round ball, the cube as a box, and the cylinder as round with flat like a can. Using another pipe cleaner and shape beads, the children then make a copy of the shapes they believe are inside. Finally, answers are checked by opening the secret socks. The teacher may need to explain that beads of the same shape match even if they are different colors.

Mystery Shapes

The teacher or a child hides a three-dimensional shape in a box. The teacher or child gives clues, and children try to guess the hidden shape. For example, a child's clues for a rectangular block might include, "It's shaped like a cereal box. What shape do I have?"

Tangram Creations

Using one or more sets of construction paper tangram pieces, children can create original designs or follow pictures from tangram shape books. Pictures are named, described, and displayed for everyone in the class to see. This is a great activity for 4-year-olds, as long as they have enough time to experiment with the shapes.

Picture Pie Books

Ed Emberley's series of *Picture Pie* books are filled with pictures made from circles, squares, and partial shapes. He gives step-by-step directions for making insects, puppies, flowers, letters of the alphabet, and a variety of real and pretend characters.

Children view the directions and make the pictures of their choice, tracing the shapes needed or following the templates provided in the book. The pictures are easy to adapt or simplify. When associated with a particular theme or story the children encounter in any part of the curriculum, these pictures help them make connections between mathematics and other areas—social studies, science, art, and so on.

Bubble Wands

Children bend pipe cleaners into bubble wands of different shapes, predict what shapes the bubbles blown with these wands will be, and then blow bubbles. How surprising that all the bubbles are spheres! The children try over and over again to make cube or pyramid bubbles. Alas, bubbles are always spheres!

This activity provides useful experience in constructing shapes and recognizing spheres, but at this level the children are not given any scientific explanations of this phenomenon.

Aka Backa Soda Cracker

The Aka Backa Soda Cracker game helps children learn to recognize shapes and pass an object from right to left. It may also help the teacher to assess children's understanding of shape words.

Children sit in a circle and pat their legs in time to "Aka Backa Soda Cracker." The song is sung "Aka backa soda cracker, Aka Backa BOO [at *BOO*, everyone claps his hands in the air], Aka backa soda cracker, pass to you!" After learning the words and rhythm of the song, each child gets a manipulative shape. The teacher models how to pass from right to left. (The teacher may also wish to explain that moving from right to left inside the circle is like the movement of the hands of a clock, and that this circular direction is called *clockwise*). When the words "Pass to you!" are sung, children pass their shape to the person on their left and receive a new shape from the person on their right. If done correctly, all pieces move one at a time in a clockwise direction. The game continues for as long as the class wishes.

Once the passing motion is error-free, the children are ready for a modification of the game. A leader for the activity is selected. Periodically, the leader says STOP at the end of a verse and then states the name of a shape. Anyone who has that shape holds it up in the air. Using descriptive terms like *side* and *corner*, the children holding that shape trace around it and describe it in unison, led by the leader. Those who do not have the shape hold their fingers up in the air and trace an imaginary shape.

Teachers should not teach this game too quickly, or the children may not master the passing motion. If passing from right to left is modeled step-by-step, then children learn it easily and never seem to tire of the game.

Creating a New Playground

Children in second grade design their ideal playground by constructing a model using blocks and other materials. The children draw building plans for their model, using a key of their own design with symbols that can be easily interpreted. Symbols might include a green rectangle to indicate a wooden plank or a red line to represent a metal bar. This activity is a good early exercise in symbolic reasoning.

Bubble Windows

In this popular activity, children from quadrilaterals from string and straws. After dipping these frames in a bubble solution of liquid soap and water, children investigate planes as well as the many different shapes that can be made from two or more bubble windows that intersect. Because of the surface tension of soapy water, bubble windows can be combined in interesting and unusual ways and can be manipulated easily. The children make fascinating discoveries about shape properties and planes.

What Am I Seeing?

Three-dimensional shapes—pyramids, cubes, spheres, cylinders—are placed on the overhead projector and covered with a thin piece of paper. The children try to guess what shape is on the projector by looking at the image on the screen. If a dark circle is on the screen, children may guess that a cylinder is on the overhead projector, since they know that cylinders have circles on both ends. Shapes such as a pyramid are more challenging; a pyramid can be set on its square base or on a triangular side on the projector, so a triangle or a square may appear on the screen.

This activity for learning about the relationship between two- and three-dimensional shapes is generally appropriate for children in second grade, or perhaps at the end of first grade. Children are able to see that three-dimensional shapes are made up of *faces* of different geometric shapes.

Straw Towers

Groups of children are challenged to make a tower one meter tall that can withstand a hurricane and an earthquake rated 7.5 on the Richter scale. The hurricane strikes when everyone blows as hard as possible on one side of the tower and then on the other side. The earthquake hits when the teacher shakes the tower's cardboard base as hard as possible seven-and-a-half times. The tower is made with a maximum of 25 straws, 10 paper clips, a foot of masking tape, and one cardboard base.

The teams design, build, and name their towers. The children are given many opportunities to try out their ideas before testing the towers against the elements. When one of the towers withstands the weather, the architects are very proud.

After analyzing the results, children typically hypothesize that triangular bases are the strongest. They begin to observe other buildings and structures to validate their findings.

Cube Constructions

Children are challenged to build different constructions from five cubes that attach to each other. There are 29 possible constructions. Each construction must be built so that it can be picked up, flipped, or moved in any way and not match any other construction. All cubes must be connected in each construction.

This is a good group problem-solving activity, as children can work in teams to make the different constructions. Children often find 29 different ways to connect the five cubes, but upon closer inspection the constructions they create may not all be different. Unique constructions are displayed so children can compare their efforts. This is an excellent task for persistent builders!

Principles in Action

The vignettes and other teaching examples in Chapter 6, "Geometry and Spatial Sense," reflect the curriculum, instruction, and assessment principles that form the basis for this book. To clarify how specific principles look in practice, this chart highlights four instances demonstrating selected principles.

Curriculum Principle 1 The mathematical content should be rich, varied, and relevant to children.	Shape and spatial sense are cultivated during the tangram activity, as are vocabulary words that might typically be introduced at more advanced grade levels (pp. 107–110).
Curriculum Principle 2 Essential mathematical processes are solving problems, reasoning, communicating, making connections, and representing.	Children's reasoning processes are emphasized when the teacher asks them to articulate their matching strategies for shape configurations during the tangram activity.
Curriculum Principle 4 Curriculum decisions should take into account children's knowledge, abilities, and interests.	A child-centered approach is demonstrated frequently during the tangram activity as the teacher uses children's vocabulary to describe shapes, values children's strategies for replicating shapes, and joins in the laughter when children play with the words squashed quadrilateral.
Instruction Principle 2 Interacting with children and promoting interactions between children are key roles of the early childhood teacher.	The teacher promotes children's interactions when he changes Kimberly's focus from copying to helping while emphasizing the importance of learning from others' shapes (p. 109).

Chapter 7

Measurement in the Early Childhood Curriculum

Even during the preschool years, children begin to encounter many situations in which they want to compare things or judge how big, how long, or how deep they are. And they also hear adults talk in terms of feet, quarts, miles, minutes and hours, and dozens of other units of measurement. My 4-year-old daughter once came home from preschool complaining everyone else at school was "4 and something" years old and she was only 4. In her mind, she was *shorter* than everyone! When I informed her that she was really "4 and $\frac{1}{8}$," she was quite proud of her new measurement and her smile reappeared.

Young children are constantly measuring how big, how tall, how much, how far, how old, and how heavy they are compared to their friends. In daily experiences such as choosing the biggest brownie or pouring juice into too small a glass and spilling all over the counter, children use and develop their intuitive notions of comparing volume, area, length, and other attributes they will eventually learn to measure. Adults often think of measurement in terms of formulas, rulers, and graduated cylinders. But young children encounter measurement in many contexts every day as they explore and try to make sense of their world.

In the discussion of the prekindergarten through second-grade standard for measurement in NCTM's *Principles and Standards for School Mathematics* (2000), the guidance for teachers states,

> Children should begin to develop an understanding of attributes by looking at, touching, or directly comparing objects. They can determine who has more by looking at the size of piles of objects or identify which of two objects is heavier by picking them up. They can compare shoes, placing them side by side, to check which is longer. Adults should help young children recognize attributes through their conversations. "That is a *deep* hole." "Let's put the toys in the *large* box." "That is a *long* piece of rope." In school, students continue to learn about attributes as they describe objects, compare them, and order them by different attributes. Seeing order relationships, such as that the soccer ball is bigger then the baseball but smaller than the beach ball, is important in developing measurement concepts. (p. 102)

Researchers still have much to learn about children's development of measurement concepts and skills. Piaget's work (for an overview, see Ginsburg & Opper 1969) showed that young children's intuitive concepts of quantity, volume, weight, and length are rather different from those of older children or adults. Although certain controversies persist regarding the development of children's understanding of measurement, including the ages at which they are able to comprehend various concepts, much is now known about the basics in children's understanding in this area. Moreover, the focus in this chapter is not on *when* children acquire measurement concepts. Rather we are considering the experiences that facilitate the young child's development and learning of these concepts.

As in other mathematics content areas, it is important that teachers not underestimate young children's capabilities and as a consequence limit their learning. Instead, recognizing that even young children have emerging concepts relating to measuring and comparing things, teachers should provide a variety of experiences and communication to help children explore and reflect on comparison and measurement.

Young children construct measurement ideas over an extended period of time and the process can be quite complex. The box "Steps in Comprehending Measurement" gives an overview of the development of concepts and skills in measurement.

Steps in Comprehending Measurement

An effective teaching sequence for measurement skills and concepts follows the five basic steps in children's learning about measurement (Inskeep 1976; Driscoll 1981; Hiebert 1984). Within any of the areas of measurement—length, area, volume, weight, and so on—children tend to follow these steps:

• recognize that objects have measurable properties and know what is meant by *How long? How heavy?* and other expressions referring to properties.

• make comparisons (*shorter, longer*, etc.)

• determine an appropriate unit and process for measurement

• use standard units of measurement

• create and use formulas to help count units

Research evidence (Inskeep 1976; Driscoll 1981; Hiebert 1984) suggests that teachers of young children should primarily promote mastery of the first two steps, as well as plan some activities to encourage exploration of unit, which is an aspect of the third step. Children typically progress through the last two steps in the upper elementary grades. However, exposure to standard measuring tools is certainly appropriate throughout the early childhood years.

The Young Child and Mathematics

In the Animal Watering Hole activity, children in Mrs. Wong's kindergarten class are engaged in a thematic unit on animals. In terms of mathematics learning, they are investigating numbers, telling animal number stories, and designing zoos using geometric shapes. They are enthusiastic about solving problems and have had some experiences making best guesses or estimates of amounts.

For this lesson, children work in a large area, separate from their regular classroom, that has room for movement. The activity integrates creative dramatics, physical movement, time measurement, estimation, science, and language arts.

Animal Watering Hole

Mrs. Wong has a bag of finger puppets: butterflies, bats, caterpillars, mice, and dragonflies—enough for every child. In addition to a bucket of Unifix cubes, she has five separate bags of cubes. (Unifix cubes are important props because they stack well.) Children sit on the floor around the reading chair.

Mrs. Wong: Today we are going to pretend to be animals and move like they do. Let's practice!

Mrs. Wong reads a poem by Evelyn Byer, "Jump and Jingle," from *Another Here and Now Storybook* by Lucy Sprague Mitchell. Children use their hands and voices to act out the movements described in the poem.

Mrs. Wong: Now I think you're ready to pretend *and* do something else, something that you are getting so good at—estimating. Does anyone remember what estimating means? *(waits while children look at each other or talk about ideas)* We estimated a few days ago when we were deciding about how many weeks we had until vacation. We estimated when we tried to decide if we had enough money to go on our field trip. We estimated when we told Mrs. Miller about how much carpet we needed for our library. We estimated in our store when customers wondered if they had enough money to buy their groceries. Do you remember what we did?

Children: We counted . . . We guessed . . . We said how many . . . We bought groceries . . .

Mrs. Wong: Yes, we made good guesses about how many or how much. Remember, a *good guess* is a guess that you think about. A good guess is an estimate. Today you will be estimating in a game. Each of you will pretend to be an animal going to the watering hole. This bucket *(holds up bucket of Unifix cubes)* will be the watering hole, and every cube is one drink of water. The watering hole is over here *(about 20 feet from the group)* and all of you animals will go to the watering hole to get a drink. Each time you get one, you'll bring it back here, and then you can go back for the next one.

Children: Can I be an elephant? . . . I wanna be a python! . . . A bee . . . Alligator . . . Vampire bat . . . Gorilla . . .

Mrs. Wong: I have a finger puppet for each of you in my bag to help you pretend to be an animal. We want to give everyone a fair chance to choose the animal they want to be. How do we usually do that?

The children review the rules for *fair chances,* and with eyes closed everyone chooses a puppet from the bag. No complaining is allowed. When everyone has a puppet, the children form groups—all the bats are together, all the dragonflies are together, and so on. The groups discuss and practice how their animal might move to the watering hole. When children seem ready, Mrs. Wong gets their attention.

Mrs. Wong: Remember I said you were going to estimate today? When it's a group's turn to go to the watering hole, all the other groups are going to estimate how many drinks of water the animals in that group will be able to take in 30 seconds. Let's look at the clock and I'll show you how long 30 seconds is *(indicates 30 seconds on the analog wall clock)* Each cube represents one drink. Now, before I give each group a bag of cubes to show your estimates, I'm going to pretend to be an animal and we'll see how many drinks I can get.

Mrs. Wong finds a turtle puppet, selects a child to act as timer, and slowly moves across the room toward the watering hole. In 30 seconds she doesn't even reach the watering hole.

Children: You were slow! . . . Not even one drink! I thought there would be more . . . My animal is faster than that!

Mrs. Wong: Well, let's see. Butterflies, come to this side of the room. How many butterflies are there? Four. I wonder how much water they will drink altogether. There was only one of me, and I didn't drink any. Of course, I was very slow. I want to make a good guess, an estimate. So, butterflies, could you show us how butterflies move, please?

Butterflies flit around the room and over to the watering hole. Mrs. Wong then distributes one bag of cubes to each group.

Mrs. Wong: It is your job to estimate how many drinks of water this whole group of butterflies is going to take in 30 seconds. Each cube is one drink. Talk about it, count out cubes, and make *one* tower showing how many drinks you think the butterflies will take.

Groups begin talking while Mrs. Wong rotates among them, helping with rules and listening to their ideas.

Bats: It's gonna be more than Mrs. Wong, she was slow. . . . O.K., let's make two . . . But there's more people . . . So? It's still just a little more . . . Let's make it a lot . . . Use all of our cubes, then we will win!

The bat group makes three different towers: one with two cubes, one with six cubes, and one with all the remaining cubes in their bag, about 20.

Mrs. Wong: Hello, bats, where is your tower? The butterflies can't begin until your estimate is ready.

Sewnet: James wouldn't do what I wanted, so he made the big one. Some of us thought little, and some thought bigger, so we have all three.

Mrs. Wong: Well, I only want *one* estimate from your group, so I guess we could just stack all of them together. Is that O.K.*? (some children nod, others look worried but want the game to begin)*

Soon every group has its estimate tower. Mrs. Wong comments about each group's estimation. The groups' estimates are very different: the bats' tower is the tallest, containing more than 20 cubes; some contain only 3 cubes; others, 10 to 15; and still others, 16 to 20.

The butterflies start when the timer says to begin. Moving like butterflies, each gets a drink of water (one cube per drink), brings it back to the other side of the room, then returns for more water. When time is called, each butterfly has gotten two drinks of water—a total of eight cubes. Mrs. Wong asks a butterfly to stack the cubes in a tower to show the class.

Mrs. Wong: Well, here it is. *(taking the tower around to other towers and comparing them)* Ooh, close! . . . Your estimate was too much . . . Too short . . . Almost . . . Whoa, way too big! O.K., now let's try the dragonflies. There are only three of them!

This time, before the dragonflies begin, Mrs. Wong asks every group to explain or defend the height of its estimation tower. Here is their reasoning.

Caterpillars: *(showing a tower of 15 cubes)* They are really fast, so it is big!

Bats: *(a tower of eight cubes)* They will get just like the butterflies.

Butterflies: *(a tower of six cubes)* See, everyone will get two drinks, so *(taking off two cubes, two more, and two more)* this is water for one . . . water for another one . . . and water for the last one!

Mice: *(showing a tower of seven cubes)* We did that too.

Mrs. Wong: Oh, how interesting! *(comparing the six- and seven-cube towers)* Why is yours one more?

Abdul: Well, see, dragonflies are just a little bit faster, so one of them will get just one more drink. Aaron didn't want to say seven, but I told him to!

The activity continues. Each time children check their advance estimates against what actually happens. The five caterpillars move so slowly that they don't get any water. The bats have to sleep upside down when the lights are on, so estimating their number of drinks is very hard. And the mice run fast but get frightened and stop to look around. Despite the fact that the movements change as well as the number of animals, children's estimates and reasoning improve. As the game progresses, comments such as these are heard.

Caterpillars: We think eight drinks for the bats because James and Karie thought nine and Shary and Arien thought seven, so we just kinda put our guesses together!

Bats: We just think this because it's almost as tall as the butterflies, and the caterpillars are slower, so it will be little.

Mice: We just decided it . . . It's like theirs! *(pointing to a group that was correct last time)*

Butterflies: We think everyone will get three, and that's three *(showing three fingers)*, three more *(showing six fingers)*, three more *(showing nine fingers)*, and then three more *(holding up one more finger and stopping to look at the 10 fingers)* So it's 10! Or maybe more. So we just made it this tall. *(13 cubes)*

The Animal Watering Hole activity called on children to relate an action to the time it takes to perform, that is, how many times a given action can be repeated in a fixed amount of time. Further, because different pretend animals moved over the distance at different speeds, children needed to take that into account in predicting how many drinks each set of animals, whether fast-moving or slow, could take in a 30-second period. Using a cube tower to record the children's advance prediction and another cube tower to show the actual number of drinks made both numbers concrete and allowed children to make a direct, visual comparison—"Did we guess too many, or not enough?"—and make adjustments in their subsequent predictions. At a practical level, children relate time, distance, and number as they participate in the watering hole game.

Children at play—With measurement

Mrs. Freehand's kindergarten class was returning from physical education period when she overheard Sari and Cori discussing the unfairness of the Best Sport award. Upon questioning them, Mrs. Freehand discovered that when children demonstrate good sportsmanship in physical education, they are allowed to reach into the treat jar and take one handful of treats. Sari and Cori had won that week; however, they were upset because their bags contained noticeably different amounts. Sari stated, "Look, I have a little bag, Cori has a lot more. It isn't fair!" Cori countered with, "You just didn't use your *whole* hand."

While Mrs. Freehand recognized that these comparison arguments are common between young children, she decided to use the opportunity to discuss capacity (how much a hand can hold) and the importance of fairness (different hands don't always hold the same amount). She also introduced

What my hand can hold:

nine cotton balls   *six teddy bear counters*   *six wooden blocks*   *five Unifix cubes*

hand investigations in the math center. Children counted the amount their hands could hold and recorded the results in their journals, as shown above. A few weeks later the class wrote a letter to the physical education teachers to suggest a fairer way to make the award.

Measurement opportunities occur often in children's creative dramatics. In one early childhood classroom, four 3-year-olds were preparing to enact the story "Goldilocks and the Three Bears." Blake was setting the table, Ashley was putting pillows on the chairs, and Valerie and Brandon were making the beds. To aid their play, Miss Emma introduced materials of different sizes into the center: big and small plates, cups, and saucers as well as big and small pillows. She used descriptive and comparative words for the items as she placed them in the area. Responding excitedly, the children promptly designated the big items Father Bear's, the items already in the center Mother Bear's, and the little items Baby Bear's. Then the children enacted their roles using the materials of different sizes and their "big" and "little" voices. Asking questions such as, "Is Mother Bear's bowl bigger than Baby Bear's bowl? But is it the biggest of all?" and "Why does Father Bear have a large pillow and Baby Bear a small one?" the teacher provoked further thinking about relative size.

Promoting development of key skills and concepts

In the early childhood math curriculum, measurement provides an ideal bridge between geometry and number, one that comes up frequently in everyday situations. To wrap a package, the right amount of paper (the surface area of the rectangular prism) must be estimated. To cover a table, the right size tablecloth (the area of a rectangle) must be found. To pour a glass of orange juice, the appropriate glass (one with a capacity that is not too small) must be selected. To send a package through the mail, one must gather the right amount of money, depending on how heavy the package is. When selecting a new pair of shoes, the shoe size (the width as well as the length) is important for a proper fit. All of these examples and countless others illustrate the use of numbers to measure the size of geometric figures.

Even young children have some intuitive notions of measurement, and the curriculum can build on these. Measurement activities in the early years should focus primarily on enabling children to identify and compare attributes of length, area, weight, volume, temperature, and time. As children learn measurement vocabulary and explore a variety of measurement tools and materials, they begin to develop a more formal understanding of measurement and the components of conservation, transitivity, and unit. The use of appropriate measurement tools to measure height, length, weight, size, volume, time, or temperature comes later as children practice their skills using nonstandard and standard measurements.

Comparison and ordering

To lay the foundation for measurement, teachers involve young children in a lot of comparing. In fact, comparison is the core activity and concept that starts children on the path to fully developed understanding and use of measurement. Children should have opportunities, for example, to compare two things with respect to length (longer, shorter), area (covers more, covers less), capacity (holds more, holds less), and weight (heavier, lighter). They can also compare with respect to time and temperature (warmer, colder). After comparing two items, children then can compare three or more items and put them in order from shortest to longest, from covers least to covers most, from holds the most to holds the least, from lightest to heaviest, from shortest time to longest time, and from warmest to coldest.

To compare objects, children begin by using nonstandard units ("My table is more than four hands long") and then standard units ("The table is almost three feet long"). *Comparing fairly* is an important concept for young children. They may mistakenly say that two objects are the same in length or the same in weight because they look only at one end of the object to be measured or they weigh two of an object rather than one. Until children learn to *conserve* (as Piaget terms it), their comparisons may be distorted by one perceptual factor or another.

Length and area

Linear measurement typically receives the most emphasis in the early grades. For young children, length concepts involve how long, how high, how far, how wide, or how far around something is. Rulers, measuring tapes, or metric sticks provide numerical measurements for length.

Area concepts are much more difficult for children because those concepts require that children look at more than one dimension. How much two-dimensional space is covered, that is, the area, depends on both the height (or length) and the width. However, even prekindergartners are able to understand that while they can measure length with linear tools, they cannot directly measure area this way (NCTM 2000). With appropriate learning experiences, they grasp that to measure area they need to use a unit of area such as a square tile.

Capacity and volume

While capacity and volume do not receive as much emphasis in many early childhood classrooms, they have many everyday applications. *Capacity* often refers to liquid measurement and describes the maximum amount that can be held by a container. *Volume* is the space occupied by three-dimensional objects (height, width, and length), which in the case of a container is also its capacity.

Young children often explore capacity and volume in the block center, at the sand or water table, and even in pouring juice for snacks. As they carefully stack blocks on the shelves, they are exploring the capacity of the shelves. As they pour sand from one container to another, they must notice and compare the capacities of the two containers. When they pour a friend's juice, they try to stop just before the glass is filled. Although young children do not yet use numerical measurements for determining capacity or volume, teachers can introduce common terms such as *liter, pint,* and *gallon* in context to describe something children see daily, such as a gallon of milk. In cooking and science experiences, children begin to learn the names of common measures of volume such as *teaspoon, cup,* and *ounce.*

First-grade children were asked to compare a tall bud vase with a wide, short dish to see which could hold more water. Like the children of whom Piaget and Inhelder ([1941] 1974) asked similar questions, most of these first-graders focused on the height of the bud vase. They said the tall container could hold more because "It looks like it" or "I just think so" or "It's tall!" But Ronnie, a 6-year-old who always asks questions, said, "I don't get it. Do you want the one that's tall [showing height with his hands] or the one that's like this [showing width with his hands]?" The teacher repeated, "I want to know which one will hold more water." Ronnie looked frustrated, and the other children seemed irritated with his continual questioning. Ronnie, however, was beginning to see that there are different ways of measuring a container; most of the other children had not even considered the possibility. Providing many more opportunities for children to measure capacity and volume at the water and sand tables and sometimes asking them questions as she did here, the teacher fostered their continued thinking about these aspects.

Weight

Weight is determined by the mass of the object and the effect of gravity on that object. For example, the weight of a 10-pound object would be different on planets other than Earth because of their differing forces of gravity. An object's mass, in contrast, is not affected by gravity; it is simply the amount of matter in the object. For young children, the comparison of objects to see which one is heavier or lighter should be the primary focus. Balances provide good measuring tools for comparisons ("We know this rock is heavier than that rock because the balance goes down on this side"). Scales allow children to put a numerical value to a weight ("Amir weighs 65 pounds because the scale shows that number").

Time

Because time concepts and measurement are very difficult for young children, teachers do not emphasize time measurement in the early years. The Animal Watering Hole activity (pp. 127–130) is an example of a planned learning experience that engages children in exploring aspects of time, such as the relationship of time, distance, and speed. Activities like this, planned and led by teachers, are helpful in introducing concepts and extending children's thinking; children then explore these ideas further in their play.

For the most part, however, young children learn about time in everyday routines and conversation with adults and other children. Teachers use time vocabulary, as Charlesworth and Lind (1998) describe:

• general words: time, age

• specific words: morning, afternoon, evening, night, day, noon

• relational words: soon, tomorrow, yesterday, early, late, a long time ago, once upon a time, new, old, now, when, sometimes, then, before, present, while, never, once, next, always, fast, slow, speed, first, second, third, and so on

• specific duration words: clock and watch (minutes, seconds, hours); calendar (date, days of the week names, names of the month, names of the seasons, year)

• special days: birthday, Passover, Juneteenth, Cinco de Mayo, Easter, Christmas, Thanksgiving, vacation, holiday, school day, weekend (p. 216)

Concrete representations of time passing, such as sand running through an egg timer, help children get a sense of how long a given period of time is. For example, the teacher might tell the children that they have five minutes to clean up and that the sand will all be at the bottom when five minutes are up.

Working with the calendar gives children the opportunity to understand *yesterday, today, tomorrow, next week,* and so on as they discuss recent and upcoming events. At first, young children use only general terms of comparison, describing one event as taking *longer* than another, for instance, or perhaps as taking longer than a minute, an hour, or a day.

Adults frequently use time words inaccurately or in a casual, nonmathematical manner. For example, many adults tell children they will "be back in a minute" to help them with a particular activity. When that minute unfortunately stretches to 20 minutes or an even longer time, the child may form an idea of a minute that is quite inaccurate.

Temperature

Temperature too should be taught in the context of the young child's world. *Hot, warm, cold,* and *freezing* are temperature words that may describe the temperature of food, weather, or even a child's warm or cool forehead.

Thermometers can be thought of as vertical number lines. Kindergartners in the upper peninsula of Michigan have no difficulty talking about the temperature being below zero and developing a beginning understanding of negative numbers. Conversely, kindergartners in Houston, Texas, understand from firsthand experience that 100 degrees Fahrenheit is very hot even before they really grasp the value of 100. Again, measurement vocabulary used in context is critical to the child's understanding of temperature and any comparisons that can be made.

Conservation

When a child *conserves* length, to use Piaget's term, she knows that even if an object changes shape—for example, a pipe cleaner is bent—its length is the same.

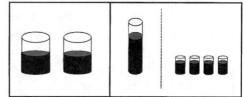

Based on his interviews of children, Piaget and his colleagues (Piaget & Inhelder [1941] 1974; Piaget, Inhelder, & Szeminski 1960) concluded that most children become conservers of length and area between the ages of 7 and 9 and conservers of volume a few years later. More recently researchers (for example, Gelman & Gallistel 1978) have reported that with careful questioning, they find children able to conserve at an earlier age. Further, it appears that children develop concepts of conservation by participating in and reflecting on measurement activities.

Transitive reasoning

Transitive reasoning refers to comparing one object to two others and then making a judgment about the relationship of the three objects. For example, a child demonstrating transitivity can make inferences of this kind: If Timothy is taller than James, and James is taller than Stephen, then Timothy too is taller than Stephen.

Researchers (Wilson & Rowland 1993) report that there is disagreement about the age at which children typically develop transitive reasoning. However, it is reasonable to conclude that young children's progress in transitive reasoning can be facilitated by experiences in the learning environment. Teachers can model such thinking by musing aloud, for example, "Let's see, your sister is older than your brother, and he's older than you. So I guess your sister's older than you, right?" Teachers can also provide situations that call for children to try working out such relationships themselves.

Unit

Critical to accurate measurement is consistency in the size of the unit used to make the measurement. In measuring and comparing, young children tend to consider only the number of units, overlooking the lack of consistency in the size of the unit used to measure. If young children measure distances using licorice sticks as the unit of measurement, for example, and one licorice stick has been partially eaten (as we saw in Chapter 2), the children may not make the connection between the differences in the measurements and the differences in the size of the licorice sticks. "Understanding of Unit" (below) briefly reviews research supporting this point.

Understanding of Unit

To estimate reasonably and measure accurately, children must understand that the unit of measurement makes all the difference. A particular distance could be accurately described as 144 inches, 12 feet, or 4 yards. The differences in number derive from the use of different units of measurement.

The National Assessment of Educational Progress (NAEP) reported that 8-year-olds have difficulty with this concept (Kouba et al. 1988). When children were shown a picture of three boxes of equal size and told that one would be filled with softballs, one with marbles, and one with tennis balls, two-thirds of the third-graders correctly said that the one filled with softballs would contain the fewest objects. However, on a similar task involving length, only 8% of the third-graders answered correctly. Researchers note that children do not gain this concept with the activities and instruction commonly provided by schools (Carpenter 1975; Carpenter & Lewis 1976; Hart 1984). More focus on both the number and size of units in measurement is needed.

Yet children are very concerned with *fair measurements*. In contest situations they may begin to see the importance of measuring with units. With first- and second-graders' natural love of competing with the teacher, appropriate contests engage their strong interest and provide opportunities for them to measure and thus encounter challenges and difficulties with measurement.

The teachers in Chapter 2 discussed an activity in which children release toy cars down a ramp to see which goes farthest, and then measure and record the distances. If set up correctly, the children's cars travel noticeably farther than the teacher's car. However, if the teacher uses a 4-link chain to measure his car's distance and the children use a chain with 10 links to measure theirs, the teacher will obtain a number (e.g., 30 chains long) larger than that of the children (e.g., 15 chains long). Wonderful discussions occur from this initially startling discrepancy. Cries of "That's not fair!" are heard, followed by "You have to measure using the same thing!" or "Do it again, and let's use something else." The teacher can then help children clarify their reasoning and follow up with other experiences relating to units of measurement.

The Young Child and Mathematics

In one kindergarten class, the teacher focused children's attention on the need for consistent units of measurement with an exploration activity. Mrs. Knapp attached a "totem pole" of medium-size bear cutouts to the side of a door frame. Children measured themselves by standing next to the door frame and asking a partner "how many bears tall" they were. The results were recorded on a poster sheet.

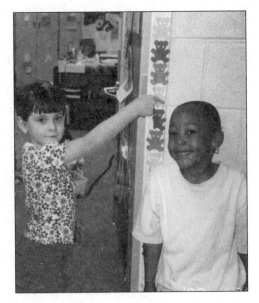

Several weeks later Mrs. Knapp put up a totem pole made from smaller bears on the other side of the door frame. Again, children measured their height in bears and recorded the results. Because of the smaller size of the bears, these numbers were almost twice those from the previous measurements.

When Mrs.Knapp interviewed the children, she asked about the two different measures. Five children referred to the size of the bears, noting that "they are different bears . . . See, the big ones get this much and the little ones get this much!" The other children had very different responses: "I just growed!" or "I ate lots of food this week!" or "I have been exercising with my dad!" or "I don't know, but I'm gonna tell my brother I am getting taller than him!"

A few weeks later Mrs. Knapp hung yet another totem pole of very large bears on another door frame and asked the children to measure their heights using the bears of their choice. Children measured themselves repeatedly against all three totem poles, exploring the differences. When asked to report their height in bears, almost all of them used the measurements from the small bears for their reports. However, more children talked about the differences in the size of the bears.

Mrs. Knapp demonstrated a very important role of the teacher. She set up experiences that confronted the children with a discrepancy—dramatically different measurements of the same child. The discrepancy provoked them to think further and eventually to work out that unit size makes a big difference in measuring.

Measurement processes

Besides core concepts in measurement, there are certain processes children must learn in order to actually measure. These include choosing or devising an appropriate tool and then using it in a way that yields an accurate measurement—not as straightforward as it may seem to adults.

Choosing an appropriate tool. Using a ruler to measure length, a scale to measure weight, or a clock to measure time is second nature to adults—it just makes sense. For a young child, however, measurement tools are not necessarily part of their everyday experiences. They may never have seen a scale or used a ruler, and they may not know what the numbers on a clock stand for. It is not uncommon to overhear children boasting about how old they are when they are on the scales ("I'm older than you are. I'm 78!") or how long their bus is according to the route number ("Our bus is really long. It's 112!"). Again, teachers' appropriate modeling of tools in real settings is key. More important, the tools must be available for children's experimentation and use.

The measuring process. Measuring processes and procedures can be rather complicated. For young children, the measuring process is primarily taught with length measurements. Two types of measuring can be used. The easier method for children to do involves using multiple duplicates of the unit of measurement (as with the teddy bear totem poles). In the other method the same instrument is used over and over again—an *iteration* process. In this method children must learn not to overlap the units nor leave gaps between the units. This type of end-to-end measurement can be done with nonstandard units (paper clips, licorice sticks, children's footprints, pencils) or with standard units (inch "worms," a 12-inch ruler, a meter stick).

In children's understanding of measurement, just as in other concept areas, the teacher plays a key role. Measurement may be overlooked or ignored because it is viewed as too hard or not fundamental. When perceived in the context of real-life situations, however, measurement is a bridge between other content areas and has important everyday applications. Among the teacher's roles with respect to measurement are to supply tools and resources, provide opportunities to measure, and encourage children to explain the results of their measuring activities.

Questions Specific to Measurement

Many questions can facilitate a child's thinking about measurement concepts. Teachers need to be sensitive to the pace of children's thinking and exploration, taking care not to interrupt with rephrasings or follow-up queries while the child is still pondering the original question. Questions are listed here as they relate to the different areas of measurement.

Length

Which one is longer? Shorter?

Can you find something that is longer/shorter than this? How can you show me?

How much ribbon will you need to go around this? How can you figure it out by just looking?

Can you put these three straws in order from the shortest to the longest? Show me how you know your answer is right. Where would you put this fourth straw? How did you know?

The table is three licorice sticks long. A toothpick is a lot shorter than a licorice stick. Would I need more toothpicks than licorice sticks to measure the table? Would I need fewer toothpicks to measure the table? Why do you think so?

The Young Child and Mathematics

You are measuring how long the desk is. What are you counting? Show me how you are measuring.

Area

Which shape can you cover with the most/least number of blocks?

Will it take more blocks to cover the table or to cover the book? Explain how you know your answer is correct.

To cover this book, would it take more cubes or more blocks?

I need your help in measuring how much space the rug is covering. *(later)* What are you counting? Show me how you are measuring.

Weight

Which is heavier? Lighter? How do you know?

How can you show which person weighs more/less?

Put these three blocks on the balance, one at a time. How can you tell which rock is the heaviest? The lightest?

You are measuring how heavy [the book] is. What are you counting? Show me how you are measuring.

Capacity

Which of these two containers holds more/less? Why do you think so?

How can you find out which container holds more water?

If you have three containers and you can only fill one of them, how could you find out which one holds the most water?

You are measuring how much the container holds. What are you counting? Show me how you are measuring.

Time

Will it take longer to walk to the door or to write your name?

Will it take longer than a minute to walk to the park? Why do you think so?

What do we do when we come to school? What do we do after that? Before lunch?

What do you think takes longer/shorter?

You are measuring how much time it takes to [wash your hands]. What are you counting? Show me how you are measuring.

Temperature

Is this [room] warmer or colder than [the hallway]?

Was the weather warmer last month? Yesterday? On Thanksgiving? During the Fourth of July?

You are measuring how hot or cold [the window pane] is? Show me how you are measuring.

Estimation

In many situations exact measurement is not necessary or even possible. Estimation is valuable in these situations and also when used as a check on whether the result one gets in measuring is reasonable. Because estimating measurement focuses children's attention on what is being measured and how, it contributes to development of spatial sense, number concepts, and a variety of other skills relating to measurement (NCTM 2000).

With young children the use of estimation vocabulary in the context of a measuring activity enhances understanding. Early childhood teachers can use words like *about, close to, almost, just a little smaller, too much,* or *way too high,* making their meanings clear in context. For instance, the teacher might ask the children how high the juice will fill up the pitcher when she pours every bit of it out of the carton, and then make her own prediction: "I think it will come almost to this line. Do you think that guess is way too high, way too low, or close?"

Estimation often involves numerical values. Children may estimate how many paper clips long an object is or how many marbles could be used to balance an object. Good estimations do not occur without exploration, many trial-and-error experiences, and numerous experiences in everyday situations.

Estimation was a prime objective of the Animal Watering Hole activity (pp. 127–130). Defining *estimation* as a "good guess" and providing opportunities for children to think about their answers helps children begin to construct estimation concepts.

Providing a mathematics-rich environment

Measurement instruments are usually specialized for gauging length, area, weight, temperature, capacity, or time. While measurement with standardized units is not the focus of young children's learning, standardized instruments should be part of every classroom. Children should be given opportunities to explore with balances, weights, scales, clocks, rulers, meter sticks, grid paper, measuring tapes, thermometers, gallon containers, cups, teaspoons, tablespoons, and graduated cylinders. In addition, a variety of nonstandard materials should be available. Children can use yarn, ribbon, blocks, cubes, timers, ice cubes, and a wide variety of containers to compare and measure to make sense of their world.

Some activities for measurement are described below in approximate order of difficulty. Many can be simplified or expanded to be more challenging.

Walking the Circle

This excellent transition or circle activity illustrates the meaning of comparison words, an important aspect of measurement. Children walk in a circle. The leader of the activity calls out a certain style of walking, such as "Walk faster!" and everyone does as directed until the next direction is given. Other possible directions include walking slower, higher (on tiptoes), lower, more heavily, more lightly, like an elephant, like a mouse, like a butterfly, swaying back and forth, noisily, and quietly. For greater challenge, the children can hold dowels and combine different directions, such as "hold the stick higher and walk faster!"

Family Links

Children bring photographs of their family to class. The children make paper or plastic chains, representing each family member with a different color plastic or paper link: a red link for an adult (male or female), a blue link for a boy, a green link for a girl, and a yellow link for a pet. The children display the chains next to their family's pictures. Children then compare the lengths of their chains or the chains can be combined into one large chain, representing the classroom family.

This activity, which connects number with length, can begin when children first come to school in the fall and continue throughout the school year. If the children's families grow, more links are added to represent a new pet, a baby, or another relative who joins the household. If a child moves away during the school year, she can take the chain with her or leave the chain with the class to symbolize that she is still part of the classroom community.

Measuring Me

In this long-term activity, children measure themselves at the beginning of the school year and the end. The children measure how tall they are using yarn or ribbon, and they trace their hands and feet to record their size. At the beginning of the year, each child's measurements are placed in a time capsule marked with the child's name. At the end of the year, the children measure themselves again. The time capsules are opened and comparisons are made between the two sets of measurements.

This activity can also be used to connect school and home. A child's family can provide copies of his hand- or footprint as a baby and help the child measure a piece of string to show how long he was at birth. The prints and the string are added to the time capsule, providing another set of measurements for comparison.

Water Graph

Two clear plastic cups are labeled Yes and No. The teacher asks the class yes/no questions, and the children individually answer by using a turkey baster filled with colored water to place a drop in the appropriate cup. The water levels in the two cups are then compared to determine the answer of the class as a whole.

This activity is relatively easy for children in kindergarten. For a greater challenge, an eyedropper can be used, but only to answer *no*. The turkey baster is still used for *yes* answers. The children then must decide if this is a fair system. Although they may be unable to verbalize their reasoning, children quickly decide that using both the eyedropper and the turkey baster is unfair. This indicates a developing understanding the importance of a consistent unit of measurement.

Balance Scale Graph

The teacher marks one side of a balance scale Yes and the other side No. In this variation of the Water Graph activity, children answer the yes/no question posed by the teacher by placing a unit block on either side of the balance. The side most weighted down indicates the answer given most frequently. After the imbalance is analyzed, the blocks are taken off of the balance and stacked as two towers. Amazingly, the children find that the heavier pile of blocks always makes the taller tower!

Measuring Earthworms

Each child observes and cares for an earthworm. As part of the children's observations, the earthworms are measured, and their measurements are recorded.

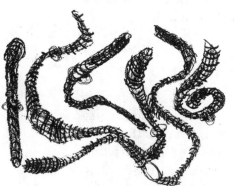

Children may measure and record in whatever way they wish. Some children measure their worms with string, while others draw lifesize pictures. First- and second-grade children are often able to use rulers to make fairly accurate standard measurements.

One first-grader measured and recorded his earthworm by drawing the picture at left. When the teacher asked why he drew so many versions of his earthworm, he replied "Because it kept moving! So I just drew it the way it looked." When asked which picture showed the best measurement, he said, "The straight one, because it's easier to see how long it is."

Shoe Store

Transforming the housekeeping center into a shoe store provides 3- and 4-year-olds with many opportunities to measure. Children take off their shoes, and a shoe clerk measures and matches feet with shoes of the correct size. Purses and wallets may also be sold at the shoe store, and children can decide which purse or wallet holds the most. Boxes of various sizes can be used as shoeboxes. The shoe store employees must be sure that both shoes in a pair can fit into one shoebox. In addition to measuring, children also sort, count money, write receipts for purchases, and develop language skills in this activity center.

Coin Match

In this game for a small group of children, bags containing pennies, dimes, nickels, and quarters are prepared and distributed to the players. Each bag has the same number and type of coins. The children hold their bags of coins behind their backs. The leader of the activity picks one coin from her bag and displays it to the group. The other players try to find a matching coin in their bags but are not allowed to look—they must find the matching coin by touch only.

Children quickly notice that the quarter is the easiest coin to find. It is biggest and, as the children say, "more different" than the other coins. The penny is often the hardest coin for the children to find.

Oobleck

Children mix two parts cornstarch with one part water to make a substance called *oobleck.* Oobleck is a strange mixture that shifts between a liquid and a solid state—it can be temporarily molded into a solid shape, but within seconds reverts to a liquid form. The mixture is an excellent cleaner for children's hands and can also be used to clean water or sand tables.

When cornstarch and water are mixed together, children have an opportunity to measure both a powder and a liquid as accurately as possible. Then they can practice measuring various amounts of oobleck and explore its properties at the same time.

Cup Drips

In this comparison and timing activity, children poke holes of varying sizes in Styrofoam cups. They hold their fingers over the holes while the teacher fills the cups with water. When the teacher gives a signal, the children uncover the holes and observe how rapidly or slowly the water empties out of the cups. They compare which cups emptied at what speeds and make predictions about which cups will empty fastest or most slowly the next time. Children in second grade and beyond enjoy more specific challenges, such as designing a water cup that will empty in exactly one minute.

Elephant Problem

The problem is this. A circus comes to town, but not everyone can go to see it. Some children are sick in the hospital. The circus decides to go visit the sick children and cheer them up. The clowns and acrobats race through the hospital, honking horns and doing flips, but the elephant is too big to come in. The children on the first and second floors open their windows and wave to the elephant, but the children on the third floor are too high to see him. How can the elephant get to the third floor to visit the children there?

Children discuss possible solutions to this problem and draw pictures showing their methods for solving it. These pictures portray the children's understanding of weight and balance concepts.

Snapping

Second-grade children estimate the number of times they can snap their fingers in one minute and record their estimates. Children then snap for 15 seconds. The results are added together four times and compared to the initial estimates. Children are often surprised that their estimates are lower than their actual results.

Children love this type of activity and are eager to discover how many other things they can do in one minute.

Balloon Rocket

Using string, a plastic straw, a balloon, a chair, and a doorknob, this experiment is set up as shown in the diagram at right.

The teacher blows up a large balloon for the children, holds the end so that the balloon does not deflate, and tapes it to a straw according to the children's directions. The teacher lets go of the balloon and it blasts off along the string. Marking the balloon's highest point on the string, the children measure the distance the balloon traveled using a full-size licorice stick.

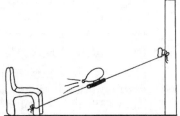

Next, the teacher inflates and blasts a much smaller balloon. This time, however, the distance the balloon travels is measured with a very small piece of licorice. The children loudly protest when the small balloon's measurement indicates that it traveled farther than the large balloon. In puzzling over the apparent discrepancy in measurement, children become more conscious of the importance of using a consistent unit to measure.

These activities, along with the classroom vignettes and other examples, emphasize the close connection between measurement and the content areas for geometry and number. Children have an impressive intuitive understanding of measurement culled from informal experiences with measurement concepts. The teacher's role in teaching measurement is to build upon these experiences and help children as they apply their understandings of measurement.

Principles in action

The vignettes and other teaching examples in Chapter 7, "Measurement," reflect the curriculum, instruction, and assessment principles that form the basis for this book. To clarify how specific principles look in practice, this chart highlights four instances in which selected principles are evident.

Curriculum Principle 3 Effective curriculum includes a mathematically rich environment with a variety of materials to help children explore key concepts.	Although the puppets used in the Animal Watering Hole activity (pp. 127–130) are not typical mathematics materials, their use made the activity more realistic to the children. In addition, the Unifix cubes provided a perfect link between length, number, and measurement. While this activity can be effective without the puppets, the Unifix cubes are necessary to facilitate learning of measurement.
Instruction Principle 2 Interacting with children and promoting interactions between children are key roles of the early childhood teacher.	The teacher began the Animal Watering Hole activity by modeling the process of estimation. She then asked children to estimate, talk about their decisions with friends, and listen to others' reasoning. She continually posed questions that prompted children's ideas yet did not give away answers or make corrections as they were exploring.
Assessment Principle 2 Observing and listening are essential skills for the early childhood teacher.	Because the teacher listened to the children's argument over the Best Sport award (pp. 130–131), she was able to use it as a learning opportunity for everyone.
Assessment Principle 4 Teachers have a responsibility to assess their own effectiveness in teaching as well as children's learning and development in mathematics.	During the Animal Watering Hole activity, the teacher was able to observe different levels of development in her children. The caterpillars who figured averages to arrive at their answer and the mice who said their tower was a good answer because it looked like their neighbors' tower are at very different levels of understanding.

Chapter 8

Data Analysis
and Probability in the
Early Childhood Curriculum

I n almost every early childhood classroom, you find examples of children displaying, collecting, and analyzing data. Graphs displayed on the wall, information on a This Is Me bulletin board, pictures of families, favorite pet books, and number tallies showing how many children want milk, ride the bus, or are in the block center are evidence of this content area. Directly related to the child's world and environment, this standard focuses primarily on different ways to help children collect, represent, and visualize information.

Statistics is the study of data. It involves collecting, sorting, representing, analyzing, and interpreting information. For the young child, the primary focus of this content area is informal experience with data collection and organization, and the display of those data. Ideas about probability at this level are also informal. Probability vocabulary, such as the words *impossible,* *maybe,* and *certainly,* can be introduced to describe data collection in experiences like throwing number cubes or selecting treats from a closed bag.

The data analysis content standard is illustrated with an activity that occurred in a prekindergarten (4-year-olds) classroom on St. Patrick's Day. The children had just cooked and eaten green eggs and ham after reading the popular book by Dr. Seuss. Each child had placed a picture of green eggs or yellow eggs on a poster to show which color eggs he or she preferred. A discussion about their opinions ensued. "We don't like green food," "Green food is yucky," and "I always throw away stuff that is green!" were the most common comments. Children were fascinated by the results of the green food coloring. The teacher asked if they would like the eggs better if they were red, purple, or blue. Children thought about that for a while and decided that red food was "really, really good."

To take advantage of the children's interest in colored food, the teacher initiated an experiment to test their hypothesis about preferring red food. With some organizational help from the teacher and a teacher aide, the prekindergartners conducted a taste test of a new kind of pudding. They used vanilla instant pudding mix and just the right food colorings to create red pudding, green pudding, and purple pudding. The puddings were placed in dishes outside the classroom along with matching squares of red, green, and purple paper. The young scientists distributed three clean spoons (one spoon per pudding, so there was no double dipping!) to kindergarten testers and directed them to the dishes of pudding. After testers had sampled the puddings, they each selected one paper square to indicate their favorite. The 4-year-old scientists collected the squares and brought them back to the classroom for a lively discussion. Red pudding *did* turn out to be the favorite, and many school-family connections resulted as children began to request red mashed potatoes rather than white ones!

The following vignette illustrates a routine graphing activity. Individual graphing activities take place daily in this kindergarten. This lesson occurs in March. It is led by Paulie, who was assigned the job of class grapher for the week.

"Graphing" with Blobs, Bars, and Circles

The classroom has a large circle area at the end of the room. There is also a free-form red "blob" of laminated construction paper on the floor in one corner and a similar blue blob in another corner. A red rectangle of laminated construction paper is on the floor near the door, with a blue rectangle next to it. The Question of the Week is on the board, and children study it as they settle in.

Do you have a cat?

YES
(written in blue)

NO
(written in red)

Paulie: The question is, "Do you have a cat?" Everybody, show your cubes. *(Most children, knowing the routine, have already selected either a red or a blue cube to show their response. The few who forgot to, go now to the cube box and select one.)* O.K., now let's form the red blobs and blue blobs.

Children go to the red or the blue corner, depending on the color of their cube, and stand on the red or the blue blob, forming two groups.

Paulie: Point to the blob that looks like it has the most people.

Most children point to the red blob, which looks as if it has several more children than the blue. Paulie addresses the children standing on the red blob, asking them to move closer together. He asks the group standing on the blue blob to spread out.

Paulie: Now, point again to the biggest blob.

Again, most children point to the red blob, and Paulie looks at the teacher and says, "You can't fool us!" He refers to a time early in the year when the teacher used a similar activity relating to conservation of number. On that occasion many children were misled when the groups were rearranged to look different.

Paulie: O.K., now make bars.

The children excitedly line up either on the blue rectangle or red rectangle by the door.

Paulie: I am going to walk between the red line and blue line. Shake hands with a different color partner across from you after I go by.

Paulie walks between the two lines of children and children shake hands with their counterparts across the rectangles. Four children, all in the red bar, do not have someone with whom to shake hands.

Paulie: *(after a short pause)* How many people didn't shake hands?

Children: Four! *(Paulie counts them to be sure.)*

Mr. Jordan: So, how many more people are in the red bar than in the blue bar?

Children: Four!

Mr. Jordan: How many more people don't have cats?

Children: Four!

Mr. Jordan: Which group has more people?

Children: The red group—people who don't have cats.

Mr. Jordan: Good! Paulie, back to you.

Paulie: O.K., everybody make a circle divided into red and blue.

Red-cube children hold hands and blue-cube children hold hands. The two lines join and form a circle. The children then sit in a circle, putting their cubes on the floor in front of them. They are going to pretend their circle is a pizza.

Paulie: *(bringing a plastic crate with red and blue chains to the center of the circle)* Blue kids, raise your hands.

Paulie takes a blue chain, attaches one end to the center crate, and gives the other end to a blue child sitting next to a red child, where the blue and red sections of the circle join. He then attaches another blue chain to the center crate and gives it to the blue child sitting at the other end of the blue section of the circle.

Paulie: Look how big the blue piece of pizza is. Now, red kids, raise your hands. *(repeats the process using the red chains)* Look how big the red piece of pizza is.

Mr. Jordan: Excellent job, Paulie! Before you go, boys and girls, let's look at the red piece of pizza together. Reds, raise your hands again. Can someone tell me about the red piece with words? I want to remember how big it is so I can make my pizza plate look like it.

Children: It's bigger . . . It's more . . . It's half of the pizza but just a little bigger . . . It's smaller than the whole pizza . . . It's how much I want if the pizza has pepperoni . . . It's almost like the one we had when we counted brothers, see? *(pointing to pictures on the board illustrating previous circle graphs)*

Mr. Jordan: Fantastic! Now, everybody, put this picture in your mind. Got it? Go to your cubbies and get your pizza plates and let's make them look like our circle.

The children made "pizza plates" at the beginning of the school year with red and blue paper plates. They cut slits (slightly longer than the radius) from the outside edge through the middle of both plates. Stacking the red plate on the blue, slits together, they turned their red plates clockwise, making the blue edge overlap the red and forming a blue wedge of pizza in a red pizza pie.

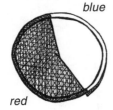

Children get their plates and adjust the colors to look generally like the red and blue sections of the circle the class made. Talking together and giving feedback to those whose plates need adjustment, the children work to get all the plates right.

Finally, getting a sheet of paper with a large circle outline from the graph box, Paulie colors it red and blue to approximate the proportions of the red circle to the blue pizza slice indicated by his red and blue pizza plate. He tacks it to the bulletin board under the Graph of the Day sign.

From beginning to end, the graphing activity takes about 20 minutes. The teacher reminds the children that they will be exploring the cat question the rest of the week, representing the results with different graphs and activities (one of which is the YES/NO bag activity in Chapter 2, pp. 25–27).

Materials in the early childhood classroom provide children with many opportunities for practicing the basic concepts and processes that underlie data analysis, especially sorting and organizing. Unit blocks are a good example. They frequently need to be organized and put away; curved blocks, for example, may be stored on one shelf and straight blocks on another. Pictorial labels help children with the organization.

When adding new blocks to the classroom supply, the teacher can ask, Where should these new blocks be placed? Which blocks are they most like? Why would you put them there? Are there more blocks on the curved-block shelf than on the straight-block shelf?

Sometimes the shelves need to be reorganized, and the children can help make decisions about rearranging materials. Telling the children that space needs to be cleared for new materials (water buckets and tubes), the teacher asks them questions such as, What blocks should we put away for a while? How can we find out which blocks everyone uses the most? You like the curved blocks the most, but does that mean everyone in the class does? How could we find out?

Responding to questions like these, children are eager to help decide where and how new materials should be stored. When children have input in aspects of classroom organization, they feel greater responsibility for and ownership of the classroom, and they are learning about classifying and data collection in the process.

Teachers can use classroom routines too to give children experiences with various skills and concepts that come into play in data analysis. During snack time children can collect data to find out who prefers apple juice and who likes orange juice, if more celery or carrot sticks are needed, or how many children use raisins or sunflower seeds on their peanut butter crackers. During circle time data collection takes place as the children post their names under an activity sign on the bulletin board to show the learning center in which they chose to work. During cleanup children classify and put things in groups as they sort materials and put them away. Labeled shelves in each center help children organize materials and naturally allow children to see if there are more big blocks than little blocks, more forks than spoons, and so on.

Question box

Children love to ask questions, but there is not always enough time to address them. A box for children's questions is a helpful addition to any classroom. Some of the questions may not lend themselves to data collection, but many will. Children learn a great deal in thinking about and discussing how to collect data on a variety of questions that are important to them.

The teacher can write out children's questions and put them in the box and add her own questions as well. Some children may draw pictures of their questions, others may write only their names or a brief statement and put them in the box for later interpretation—"I am getting a new baby" can translate into "Do you have a baby in your house?" Such questions are good for data gathering and can be used for weekly graphing activities. Children learn a great deal in thinking about and discussing how to collect data on questions that are important to them.

One day a week, a period of time can be designated for talking about the questions in the question box. (The teacher may want to look through the question box beforehand and select particular questions.) The class can choose the question for the following week's graphing activity and then talk about other questions as time permits.

Data from the classroom

In Mrs. Chen's first-grade classroom, children do a lot of counting, and each day a different child is named Counter of the Day. This classroom job provides another opportunity for data analysis. The counter distributes a set of stacking cubes for the item counted that day. If children's pockets are to be counted, for example, the counter places a cube in all the pockets of children in the class—pockets in shirts, pants, skirts, dresses, or any other item of clothing. When the count is made—each child reporting her or his own pocket count—the counter collects the cubes and stacks them. The tower of cubes can then be placed on the chalk tray with an accompanying picture or label. On Friday the children use these visual representations of their surveys to look at the results of a week's worth of counting and make comparisons and predictions.

Mrs. Chen's first-graders, for example, counted pockets on Monday (58 cubes), noses on Tuesday (23 cubes), ears on Wednesday (44—someone was absent), and earrings on Thursday (11 cubes—five girls wore pairs and one boy wore one). On Friday Mrs. Chen asked the children how tall the tower of stacking cubes would be when shoes were counted that day. Which other tower would it be most like? Why did they think so? Would the number of cubes be even or odd? Why did they predict that? Would the number still be even/odd if five children had chicken pox and stayed home?

Data from home

When children have collected, organized, and analyzed data from their peers, they often are interested in how their brothers, sisters, parents, or neighbors will react to their questions, so data analysis activities are a natural link between classroom and home. After completing favorite-color graphs in a prekindergarten classroom, children were to survey four more people at home about their favorite colors. The children asked the people surveyed to each write his or her name by an empty square. Then the 4-year-olds would color in the square with that person's favorite color.

The teacher was surprised when one child returned his paper with a drawing of a dog next to a square colored red. When she asked whose favorite color the red square represented, the child answered, "It's Champ's. He's my puppy and he doesn't talk to everyone. I asked him, and he told me it was red. Red's my favorite color too!" Champ's favorite color was then added to the class's graph along with the results of others' home research.

Teacher questions

Teachers can facilitate an understanding of data analysis by interacting with children as they engage in activities in various centers in the classroom. Asking children to tell about their favorite stories, toys, or food is a good beginning. Then children can discuss methods of recording and displaying favorites within the group for some purpose, such as showing to other classes or to parents. The graphs or representations can also be referred to later, for example, in planning foods for parties or selecting stories to read or act out.

Teachers will also find many opportunities to understand and extend children's thinking in situations in which they are sorting and grouping objects. Asking children to describe their choices is important: Why is the circle in that group and not over here with these triangles? How is the square like the other shapes in its group? How is this square different from the oval over there?

After they can sort or organize the objects in one way, for example, by size or color, children can be asked to sort the objects on a different basis or make more (or fewer) groups. For example, the teacher may ask such questions as, Is there another way we could put these into groups? What if this whole group of shapes were taken away, how would the rest of the shapes be sorted? What if this square and triangle are in a different group? What could the name be? What if I sorted them this way, what group would this object be in? Why do you think so? Such interactions help children learn to communicate their reasoning about sorting and organization and also provide meaning for data analysis.

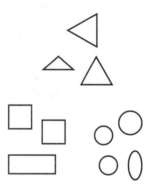

Promoting development of key skills and concepts

Skills and concepts relating to collecting and analyzing data and considering probability have wide applicability across the curriculum. Among these skills and concepts are posing questions and gathering data to answer them; sorting and classifying; organizing data; representing data; describing and comparing data; and beginning to grasp concepts and language of probability.

Sorting and classifying, for example, are important in every subject area—science, social studies, literacy, the arts. Language itself is based on classification. To learn a new word, we need to know which actions, descriptors, or objects the word applies to and which it does not. The learner typically begins by getting a general idea and then refines the knowledge of what does and does not fit the category of things.

When a young child first learns the word *dog*, for example, he may think it refers only to his own collie and others of that breed. Gradually he broadens his conceptual category to include a wide range of assorted canines, perhaps overextending *dog* to include wolves and foxes—and having no idea that a chihuahua is a member of the

class! Learning many new words every week, the young child is continually refining his knowledge of the class to which each of the words refers.

Reading and describing graphs or other representations through a child's perceptions and explaining the advantages and disadvantages of specific representations are skills that encourage language development. Probability vocabulary is important in contexts beyond mathematics, and the reasoning questions that naturally occur as data are interpreted help young children increase their use of precise and descriptive words.

Posing questions and gathering data

Young children have an endless supply of questions, and these questions often involve their own attributes or preferences: Do you like your sister? Do you like green ice cream? Do you like scary costumes? What kind of backpack do you have? Often, however, children's questions are difficult to answer: Why is the sky blue? Why don't airplanes fall down? Why do brown cows give white milk? How high are the clouds? Where did I come from?

The teacher's role is to provide opportunities for children to ask questions, help them formulate their questions (see the question box strategy, pp. 151–152), and then use these questions as catalysts for investigating and learning. Among the possible directions a teacher may go with such queries is to engage children in data analysis experiences so that they can help children answer their own questions.

Children can begin to understand data gathering by conducting simple surveys of attributes of children in their class or other classes (Do you have freckles? Are you wearing white sox?) and using tally marks, check marks, or numerals in YES or NO columns to indicate answers. They can make counts of object attributes or even survey the preferences of family members and neighbors. Young children may better understand the concept of data gathering when it is demonstrated physically or concretely—for example, having children actually standing in one group or another (the blue blob or the red blob) to indicate their answer or cast a vote by placing a marker or cube in a YES box or a NO box.

Young children often pose questions that are not easily definable, and at first they certainly do not know how to get the data that would answer a question. But these are learnable skills. Teachers can introduce children to a variety of data collection methods and model and discuss questions appropriately. They can and should provide many data collection experiences involving children's own questions. These are all important roles of the early childhood teacher in this content area.

In the blob, bar, and circle set of activities, the teacher used children's natural questions to decide on the Question of the Week: Do you have a cat? Every Friday children were asked to suggest and discuss possible questions for the following week. The teacher helped them pose their questions appropriately and, in addition, facilitated their discussion about the method that they predicted would work best.

Sorting and classifying

Sorting and classification are important processes in many content standards besides data collection and analysis. Particularly in algebra and the concepts that underlie it, classification is fundamental (see Chapter 5).

The usual developmental sequence for sorting can be seen in young children's spontaneous behaviors (Markman & Subert 1976; Copley 1998). First, a child separates objects from a pile or collection because they share a common attribute—for instance, they are all blue or fuzzy or round. Sometimes children can verbalize the reason for this selection; often they cannot. They do not apply one rule consistently throughout and may go on to separate objects on various other bases.

At the second level children are able to sort the entire collection of objects consistently by one attribute. They are capable of classifying things that have a certain attribute and those that do not. For example, children at this level can sort a collection into things that are red and things that are not red. This two-part type of classification—*has* versus *has not*—is fundamental in collecting certain kinds of data (children who have cats and children who do not have cats) and in graphing and other representations of data. Young children may need help to understand the meaning of *not,* so teachers can offer many experiences that allow them to separate objects into just two sets: those items that have a particular attribute and those items that do not.

At the third level children are able to sort a collection of objects in more than one way (color *and* size or shape *and* texture). A child approaching this level often shows confusion when another child uses a sorting rule that is different from his. The teacher can also look puzzled when viewing the collection and ask the sorter to talk about how she sorted her objects. At this level children need to hear other children's reasoning and sorting rules frequently.

The highest level of classification reached by young children is to be able to state the rule that accounts for a grouping, even when someone else has done the classifying. To do this, the child must perceive one or more common attributes of all the objects in the group and also determine that the attribute is not shared by objects outside the group. The child also is able to verbalize a rule to indicate whether a new object would be included or excluded.

To help children develop basic sorting and classifying skills, materials with easily identifiable characteristics are preferable. For example, there are many types of counters commercially available. The dinosaur, frog, or bug counters are excellent sorting materials if they have more than one attribute (different colors and sizes, for example) and the attributes are easily identified (type, number of legs, tail or no tail). Children move forward in classification when they encounter challenges and questions such as teachers asking, "Can you sort these another way?" or "What if they were all red, how would you sort them?"

Sorting and classifying activities promote reasoning skills. A specific lesson illustrating this type of activity is in the reasoning section in Chapter 3.

Organizing data

There are many methods for organizing data, and a number of these may be explored by young children. In an effort to help children be successful, some teachers determine the way that data will be organized by providing preprinted graph paper complete with labeled grids and titles. However, children miss a vital step in the handling and examining of data if they go directly to a more limited task like coloring a graph made by someone else.

For example, counting different color candies and then coloring corresponding squares on a preprinted graph is an activity lots of teachers use. In one early childhood classroom where children were completing this activity, they were asked to explain what they were doing. The typical response: "You color these squares and then you get to eat the candy." A limited understanding at best!

What is more effective is for children to collect data and then bring them back to the group (or to a small group of children within the class) to sort and organize in ways they work out themselves. When a child states, "This is a mess! I don't know what the answer is!" the teacher can seize the moment to offer ideas about how data can be organized and displayed so that at a glance we can find the answers we're looking for. While the resulting representation might not be as polished or organized as one using a commercially produced format, it is the child's own work and evidence of the child's budding understanding of organizing and displaying information.

Representing data using concrete objects, pictures, and graphs

Visual displays of data are actually direct extensions of sorting and classifying. With young children, the teacher's purpose is to help them see graphing and other such representations as ways of showing information so that people can "read" it just by looking and use it to make comparisons.

Using concrete objects is an essential first step in representing data. By standing with a group of Yes people or No people, each child shows his or her response, and collectively the groups of children form a simple physical representation of the data. Placing pattern blocks or other items in rows in ice cube trays (see, for instance the Ice Cube Tray Graphing activity, p. 163) or on ten frames, one per compartment, according to their attributes—orange squares, green triangles, and so forth—forms a representation of categories in a way that easily translates into horizontal or vertical bar graphs.

Teachers can have children make tags to indicate their opinions on an issue, with each child placing her tag by the answer she chooses. Another method is to create picture cubes by putting each child's photo on an empty carton (e.g., milk containers). Children cast their votes by stacking their cube next to the answer of their choice.

Another example is placing cubes or counters, all equal in weight, on one side (YES) or the other side (NO) of a balancing scale to represent children's votes. This procedure creates a different type of visual model: the side of the scale that is heavier has more votes. In all these examples, concrete objects represent data, and children then use their words to describe the data they see and make comparisons.

Representations of data can also be made with pictures depicting individuals' choices or answers. For example, the teacher may give children cards on which to draw their favorite pet. With these cards the teacher can show the children various ways to organize and examine the information. The pet cards can be placed in a horizontal or vertical bar representation, a blob representation, or a circle representation.

Different questions can be answered using the children's pet cards. A survey titled "Is a Dog Your Favorite Pet?" could result in a bar graph with picture cards of dogs making up one bar and picture cards of pets that are *not* dogs forming the second representation. For a survey of "What Is Your Favorite Pet?" the picture cards could be lined up as on a bar graph and compared in categories such as dogs, cats, fish, gerbils or hamsters, rabbits. Similarly, a graph showing responses to the survey "What Kind of Animal Makes a Good Pet?" could list categories such as mammal, fish, reptile, bird, and so on.

As young children work with organizing and representing data, they often reveal misconceptions. When this happens, teachers can take the opportunity to help children develop a better understanding of representing data. For example, a group of children were using Lego pieces to make bar graphs to show the number of children in the class who had younger siblings and the number who did not. The boy making the younger-sibling bar counted out 7 Legos and the boy making the other bar counted out 11, but they were a smaller size. When the bar of 7 loomed over the bar of 11 and thus seemed to contradict what the children knew to be true, they protested, "But there *aren't* as many kids who have little brothers and sisters!" The teacher then was able to pose questions to help them recognize the problem, and the children gained an understanding of the principle—that one must use units of equal size to allow for accurate comparison. The understanding they developed was far more solid than it would have been if the teacher had simply told them to always use equal-size units.

As they create representations using objects, pictures, or graphs, children also learn about labeling and describing parts of their representations. They learn that they need to write words and labels on graphs so that others can understand what the graphs say. When children create the labels for their own graphs, the graph and the graphing process become more meaningful to them as well as to others.

To help children learn how to label graphs, the teacher should emphasize the importance of remembering what the graph says and also the importance of communicating to others about their graph. He can pose questions like, How can we remember what those **X**s mean? How will we remember what those bars are? What should we call these marks here? What are those

How Many Pockets in Our Clothing?

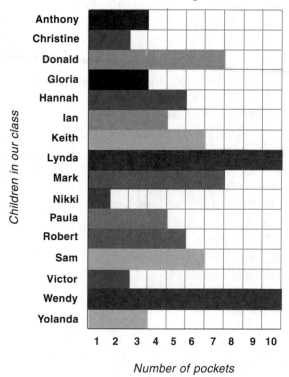

Number of pockets

(Children in our class: Anthony, Christine, Donald, Gloria, Hannah, Ian, Keith, Lynda, Mark, Nikki, Paula, Robert, Sam, Victor, Wendy, Yolanda)

How Many Pockets in Our Clothing?

Children										
			×							
		×	×	×	×	×	×			
	×	×	×	×	×	×	×			×
1	**2**	**3**	**4**	**5**	**6**	**7**	**8**	**9**	**10**

Pockets per child

A bar graph and a line-plot graph of the children in a second-grade class who have from one to ten pockets

squares? What should we call this graph? What was our question? Who did we talk to when we made this graph?

A variety of graph types is important, even for the same data. The two figures (NCTM 2000, 112) shown here illustrate two very different representations describing the number of pockets in a classroom. Although the data are presented differently, both graphs contain numbers, titles, and labels. Even young children can see the information conveyed in pictures, bars, lines, or circles and recognize differences and similarities between these representations.

Young children like to share the graphs they make with others, for example, with parents or other classes in the school or center. At a large primary school, each class made one graph a week without a title and put it in the hallway. Other classes in the school had fun reading the graphs and guessing the title just from looking at the organized and labeled data. In the process the children learned more about interpreting graphs and saw the importance of titles and labels on graphs.

Describing and comparing data

Clearly comparisons are an important part of data analysis. Teachers can ask questions that require children to make comparisons based on information shown in a graph. They can ask about part of the graph, for example, "Do kindergartners have more bicycles than first-graders?" referring to a graph showing the number of bikes belonging to children in each primary grade. Teachers can also pose questions involving the data set as a whole, like, "What is the most popular TV show?" or "What sport do most kids like best?" or "What is the least popular way to get to school?"

Number lines also help children analyze and describe data. For example, in the estimation activity in Chapter 2, children used a number line to find the mode and median of their answers to the question of how many finger snaps each child could do in one minute. Although the concepts of mode and median are often reserved for older children, the children in Ms. Henekee's second-grade class easily understood these terms because they were presented in a meaningful manner.

The children in Ms. Henekee's class lined up left to right, from smallest estimate to largest. Each child stated her number in turn, and everyone paid attent!ion to the number repeated most often. The most common answer mentioned was designated the mode. The number line was used to find the median when children returned to their seats two at a time, one from each end of the line. The answer of the last child left standing in the middle was the median. (If two children remain standing, a number halfway between their answers is the median.)

Acquiring the concepts and language of probability

With respect to probability, the early childhood curriculum focus is on the most basic concepts, such as certainty, impossibility, and probability, and the vocabulary used to express these ideas. Teachers can discuss situations where an event is *certain, impossible, more likely,* or *less likely* to occur using those words in the context of experiences in everyday life as well as mathematical events. Teachers may comment on the weather ("Looking at those dark clouds, I think it is likely to rain today"), class routines ("It is 12 o'clock; where do you think we will probably go next?"), or events ("We have 22 in our class. Do you think Ethan's mom is likely to bring 100 cupcakes for us?").

For young children, difficulty in understanding probability words may result from the way adults often use them with children. The prediction "You can *probably* go" may end up meaning *yes* if Mom and Dad are in a good mood but something totally different if they are not. Grandma's declaration of "Impossible!" seldom means *never* when directed at her two grandchildren.

Providing a mathematics-rich environment

In working with children on classification, data collection and analysis, and probability, teachers find a variety of materials useful: animal counters, attribute blocks, buttons, plastic trees, cloth swatches, attribute people, sorting rings, large plastic tarps for real graphs, predrawn graph paper, and prelabeled posters for graphs. While some items are quite helpful (especially the attribute blocks and people with three types of attributes), many materials are not necessary. Instead, objects from dollar stores, old wallpaper books, buttons, tops to milk containers, rocks, pebbles, old keys, garbage ties, straws, and so on provide opportunities for sorting and classifying. In addition, sorting trays can be purchased from restaurant suppliers, discount stores, or dollar stores.

Predrawn paper or plastic gridded tarps are not necessary when children create their own organization of data. If children standing in a red bar graph representation shake hands with corresponding children standing in a blue bar graph representation (as in the "Graphing" with Blobs, Bars, and Circles activity earlier in the chapter), they don't need a printed grid to tell them where to line up. Sticky notes are useful for data collection because each note can be used to record one piece of data. The individual notes can then be moved and reorganized to form the best possible visual representation.

A small selection of activities pertaining to this content standard are listed below. They are roughly in order of difficulty, but the degree of challenge is highly dependent on the child's construction of the activity and the specific way the activity was introduced and/or extended.

Color Sort

Red, yellow, green, and blue boxes are placed in an activity center. Children cut out pictures of different colors from magazines and place them in the matching box. Objects can also be used instead of pictures. This is an excellent activity for 3- and 4-year-olds.

Haves and Have Nots

This transitional or circle activity is a variation of the Lineup activity in Chapter 5. The leader of the game (either the teacher or a child) selects a characteristic, such as red. She whispers her selection to one other person, who helps her remember what she has chosen and ensures that the chosen characteristic will not change arbitrarily (this is often a problem with young children). The leader then tells each child if he or she has or does not have the characteristic. If red is the attribute, then all children wearing red sit inside the circle (or line up, if the game is being used as a transitional activity), and those children not wearing red remain outside of the circle (or do not line up). Children try to guess what characteristic has been selected by comparing the children sitting inside the circle with those sitting outside.

Children soon realize that it is as important to observe those outside the circle as it is to observe those inside. Clothing color is often the first type of characteristic children select; however, they soon progress to other characteristics, such as smiling or sitting cross-legged. The teacher should guide children away from selecting physical characteristics.

Marching Band

Children march in a band, playing homemade instruments such as rubber band guitars, percussion shakers, and kazoos. The musicians are grouped together by type of instrument, such as sound blowers (like kazoos and homemade trumpets), string instruments, and percussion instruments. The conductor directs the band, having those in each group march in a particular way, such as swaying back and forth or taking giant steps while playing.

The musicians sound their instruments when the conductor signals. For example, the conductor blows a whistle to signal the musicians: one whistle for the string players, two whistles for the sound blowers, and three whistles for the percussion players. Band members exchange instruments periodically.

This activity is very popular with 4- and 5-year-olds.

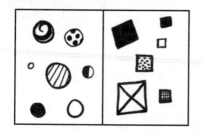

Sorting Collages

Each child divides a piece of paper in half and picks a category for each side. For instance, the left side of the page might be for round items and the right side for square items. From a variety of materials, the children select items that fit their categories and paste these items onto the paper.

Veggie Robots

Children bring a variety of vegetables to class, such as broccoli, carrots, celery, cauliflower, and sweet peppers. The children help clean the vegetables and, while the teacher cuts the vegetables into various size pieces, the class discusses which types of vegetables come from the flower, stem, seeds, leaves, or root of a plant.

Children then create veggie robots using toothpicks and pieces of vegetables. They describe their creations and classify the vegetable parts they used. The teacher asks questions like, "Whose robot has a round head?" or "Does anyone have a robot with a body made from a triangle-shaped root?" If a child's robot has that characteristic, she stands up. After describing and classifying her creations, the child eagerly eats the robot.

People Sort Book

At the beginning of the school year, each child creates a book about him- or herself. Each page of the book contains a description of a different attribute. For example, a child might draw a picture of himself with his two brothers.

During circle time or a transitional period, the teacher selects one book without revealing whose it is. The entire class stands up and, as the teacher reads or describes each page, children who do not have that attribute sit down. Children enjoy seeing which of their classmates are similar to them. By the end of the book, only the author remains standing.

These popular books can be made in various ways; report covers with three fasteners work well because new pages can be easily added. Pages need to be updated as the children's lives change. Near the close of the year, the teacher can also make her own book about a child's attributes. For instance, the teacher's book may describe a child who "works very hard," "is such a good scientist," or "is one of my favorite students." The teacher's book describes everyone! Children of all levels can participate in this activity, but some may need more assistance than others.

Ice Cube Tray Graphing

Children use an ice cube tray to sort two different types of small objects; one object is placed in each compartment, with one type of object placed in each side of the tray. If a child has four ladybug magnets and two marbles, his ice cube tray would look like the one at left.

A line drawn down the center of the ice cube tray helps children interpret the tray as a bar graph representation. If the tray is turned sideways, it can be interpreted as a horizontal graph. When placed vertically, it represents a vertical graph.

Buried Treasure

Plastic bugs, fake jewels, shapes, and other items are buried in a large storage containers filled with sand. Children pretend to be scientists and archaeologists, searching for rare antiquities and precious gems. The children use plastic spoons as shovels to dig out the hidden treasures, and then they clean the items with brushes. Afterwards, the children record their discoveries by classifying them in different categories and drawing pictures showing how the items were sorted.

Minibeasts

This activity is a variation of the Where Are the Minibeasts? activity in Chapter 4. Armed with magnifying glasses, children go outside to discover minibeasts—creatures smaller than a child's pinky finger. After observing the creatures in their natural environment, the children return to the classroom and draw pictures of those they have seen. The children's minibeasts are named and classified into different categories, such as eight-legged spiders, six-legged ants, four-winged moths, and worms with no legs. Then children create their own minibeasts from play-dough, classify them, and describe them in their own words.

Counting Walk

With partners, children count objects in the school, such as windows, desks, wastebaskets, chairs, flags, and chalkboards. Each pair of children counts a particular item. The children record their findings on sticky notes, making up to five tally marks per note. For example, a pair of children documenting the number of doors in the school may find that there are 20 doors. These children return to the classroom with four sticky notes labeled Door, each note having five tally marks.

When the children are finished counting, all of the sticky notes are stuck to the classroom's chalkboard, and the children discuss how to organize their results. The children assign items to categories such as Furniture or Things That Can Be Opened. The results are used to make graphs.

People in Your Hand

This probability activity emphasizes matching and introduces the concept *impossible*. The attributes of a set of figurines are written on index cards. For example, attributes for the figurines below would include the colors Blue, Red, Yellow, and Green; words describing age and gender such as Girl, Boy,

 Woman, and Man; and adjectives describing size such as Big, Medium, and Little. Besides these attributes, several others that do not belong—such as Dog and Purple—should be added as well.

Each child selects a figurine and covers it with her hands. The teacher selects an attribute card that the children's figurines might have and shows it to the children. Children holding figurines with the selected characteristic say yes (or whisper yes if in a large group) and stick up one of their thumbs. Children holding figurines without the attribute say, "Oh, well," and shrug. After a period of time, the teacher selects an attribute that no figurine could possibly have, such as purple polka dots. When every child says, "Oh, well," the children soon realize that no figurines match the teacher's attribute. At this point, the teacher introduces the concept of impossible. The next time the teacher picks an attribute that no child's figurine could have, the children reply, "Impossible!"

Children love the word *impossible* and use it often. Their knowledge of impossible is often transferred to other activities, such as the Haves and Have Nots activity described earlier. If "children who are dogs" are asked to line up, many children will reply, "Impossible!"

Number Activities

Number activities are a natural place for introducing probability concepts in second grade or beyond. Tossing two cubes with faces numbered from 0 through 5, children predict the most (or least) probable sums to come up. Teachers encourage the investigation by challenging children to "keep rolling until you get a sum of 11" (*impossible* with two dice numbered 0 to 5) or to "keep rolling until you get a sum of 0, 1, 2, 3, 4, 5, 6, 7, 8, 9, or 10" (a *cer-*

tain event since all of the sums tossed would fall within this range). Children describe their tossed sums and share their frustrations with rolling a sum that is impossible or absolutely certain.

In addition to fostering skills pertaining to this content area, this activity offers many opportunities to facilitate language use. The process standards described in Chapter 3 are also evident as children communicate the results of their data analysis, discuss reasons for these results, and represent their findings so that others can understand them.

Principles in action

The vignettes and other teaching examples in Chapter 8, "Data Analysis and Probability," reflect the curriculum, instruction, and assessment principles that form the basis for this book. To clarify how specific principles look in practice, this chart highlights six instances in which selected principles were evident.

Curriculum Principle 1 The mathematical content should be rich, varied, and relevant to children.	During the blob, bar, and circle "graphing" activity (pp. 148–150), the children used circle graphs, which are not typically a part of the mathematics curriculum for young children. However, because of the meaningful presentation of the data, the children were easily able to handle this type of representation and discuss the results.
Curriculum Principle 3 Effective curriculum includes a mathematically rich environment with a variety of materials to help children explore key concepts.	The plates, chains, and color unit cubes all contributed to the success of the blob, bar, and circle "graphing." While the chains and cubes are generally viewed as mathematics manipulatives, the plates are not. Easily purchased, one set of disposable plastic plates generally lasts all year and can go home with children for further investigations.
Instruction Principle 1 To effectively plan experiences, teachers must make a variety of decisions based on their knowledge and focusing on the needs of individual children.	The progression from blob to bar to circle representation and the subsequent review of all three stages demonstrated that the teacher knows how children develop understanding. His questions also helped the children link the visual representations to prior knowledge and experience.

Instruction Principle 3 The teacher must orchestrate various contexts and ways in which children engage in mathematical experiences, such as whole group, small group, project teams, and other strategies.	The teacher's consistent routine and good management skills in the blob, bar, and circle activity foster self-regulation in the children and promote a child-centered approach to learning. This is especially true for the class grapher; the child is able to direct the classroom activity through predictable and understandable questions and answers.
Assessment Principle 1 The primary purposes of mathematical assessment are to benefit children and identify their strengths and specific needs.	Although it is not apparent from the blobs, bars, and circles vignette, Paulie's enthusiasm and ability as grapher reflects his overall growth and development throughout the year, fostered by his teacher. Paulie was a child who did not experience much success at the beginning of the year; he rarely spoke in front of his peers and did not want to be a leader. Because of the many opportunities for children to share their learning in this class, Paulie developed some new strengths. This was his first time as grapher. The teacher prompted him throughout the week about his day and how well he would do. He was as pleased as Paulie was about his success as grapher.
Assessment Principle 3 To best assess mathematical understanding, teachers should use multiple sources of evidence collected on a systematic basis.	The graph documentation produced daily by the "graphers" in the blobs, bars, and circles vignette was a way for the teacher to document and collect children's representations. Later, these pages were made into a book that showed data collections over a month's time. Graphers always signed their work so it could be identified.

Chapter 9

Questions . . . and Some Answers

I enjoy sharing my teaching experiences with other early childhood teachers. Every time I do, questions abound. While the questions have remained similar over the past 20 years, my answers have often changed or at least expanded. I continue to learn and to explore new ways of teaching various aspects of math. Because I study young children and listen to what they say and think, my teaching has become more child focused and less directive, more holistic and less segmented.

In addressing frequently asked questions in this chapter, I offer my personal responses as an individual who has spent many hours watching children as they experience math in various contexts, teaching and interacting with them, and observing other teachers in action. I also point out others' work that has been particularly valuable to me in relation to a given issue. My own learning is very much a work in progress; my responses here are simply my best thinking at the moment. I offer them as personal perspectives that readers can reflect on and perhaps synthesize with their own thinking and experiences.

Q: How should early childhood teachers organize math instruction? For example, should I teach the whole group or work only with small groups and at learning centers?

A: Sometimes I work with all the children as a group; for some experiences, that makes sense. But in small groups I see children really thinking and learning math particularly well, I can follow up more, *and* I see those experiences carrying over to children's play, their daily routines, and all areas of the curriculum. So I make sure to do lots of small-group work, especially in first and second grade, and I hear other teachers say they find it helpful too.

When making decisions about forming groups, I first focus on what the children will be doing and learning. Sometimes what we are going to be doing requires children to have learned certain concepts and yet not be well beyond for the activity at hand. In these cases, I group children with roughly similar knowledge and skills.

In other instances, having mixed groups of children can be a plus. For instance, if children are creating quadrilaterals from pattern blocks, they might work with a mix of other children to create the shapes. The teacher would provide vocabulary or offer questions and remarks that cause children to notice, check, or describe aspects of what they are doing. In this activity, children with varying knowledge and experience are able to identify shapes together, pick up ideas from one another, and transform their creations into new ones.

Teachers often wonder how they can work with small groups and at the same time have ample opportunity to observe, orchestrate other children's activities around the classroom, and interact with them as they work and play. Many classrooms do not have a teacher aide or other adult, or have such help only on a limited basis. This is challenging, but teachers with too many children and not enough help don't have to resort to only whole-group instruction or free play. This situation calls for creativity.

Dana is a case in point. She uses third-grade "math buddies" to help the children in her prekindergarten class. Each 4-year-old is paired with a third-grader, and they meet twice a month to do special activities and then later work together in center activities. "There are so many things we can do that are much harder with 20 children by myself," Dana says. "The older kids help me tremendously, and my children love the interaction. And I really benefit from the third-graders' help in writing down what my children say about their math ideas."

Q: There is so much to do in an early childhood classroom. How do you fit in mathematics?

A: Mathematics belongs in any part of the day and connects with all other curriculum areas. The more you observe children doing mathematics and become aware of mathematics content and processes, the more connections you see and the more mathematics "fits into" your day.

Q: What part should technology play in early childhood math programs?

A: NCTM's *Principles and Standards for School Mathematics* (2000) states that technology is essential in teaching and learning mathematics, influencing the mathematics that is taught and enhancing children's learning. Early childhood educators have had doubts about whether, how, and how much to use technology with young children, particularly in the prekindergarten years. Yet positive results are reported by researchers and practitioners who make judicious use of developmentally appropriate software (for example, Davidson & Wright 1994; Clements 1999; Haugland 1999, 2000). Weighing the evidence from research and practice, NAEYC adopted a position statement (1996a) in support of computers and other technology in the early childhood classrooms, when these are appropriately and effectively used. The tools of technology can enhance mathematical thinking and, also important, contribute to children's proficiency as users. Clements (1999) provides a useful synthesis of recent research on technology use in early childhood classrooms, with implications for practice.

Q: To improve math curriculum and instruction here at our school/center, what is the best program we can adopt?

A: There is no *one* program that best fits the needs of young children as they learn mathematics. However, there are many good programs and resources that provide ideas and activities and also help teachers understand children's mathematical thinking. Children's books, such as those listed in Appendix B, are excellent resources connecting children to mathematics.

In NAEYC's *Reaching Potentials*, volumes 1 and 2, Bredekamp and Rosegrant (1992, 70–73; 1995, 18–19) present a model for "Tranformational Curriculum" (see diagram below), which I find helpful in making decisions about math resources. I have included questions that reflect each part of the model and can be used in considering a teacher resource or math program.

The child at the center of the sociocultural context

Does the program

- take children's experiences and interests into account?
- allow children to make choices and contribute ideas about mathematics?
- suggest resources, games, experiences, and literature from various cultures?
- provide supporting research that was conducted in diverse settings?

Content and the discipline of mathematics (disciplines)

- Does the program do justice to all the key content areas, as defined by NCTM (2000) and elaborated in this book?
- Do learning experiences and teaching strategies challenge children to think, solve problems, communicate their thinking, and represent their solutions? Are these processes integrated with mathematics content?

Age appropriateness (child development knowledge)

- Are suggested teaching strategies and activities consistent with the knowledge base about children's development?
- Are examples of children's work included in the program? Are activities described as they relate to young children's development and learning?
- What assessment strategies are presented in the program? Would they be helpful in considering children's development and mathematical thinking?

Individual appropriateness (continuum of development and learning)

- How does the program meet the individual needs of learners? Are there adaptations for children who have special needs and strengths, and suggestions for children with different learning styles?

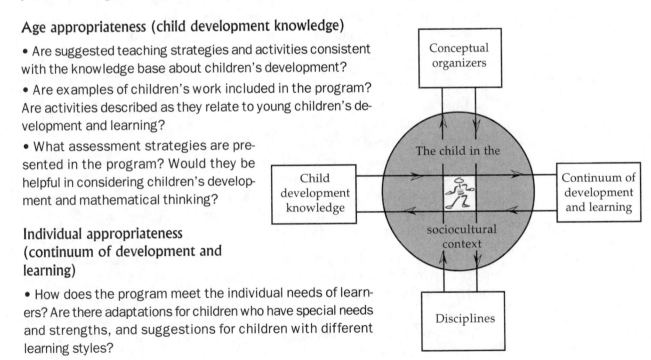

• Are there suggestions for integrating mathematics into circle time, centers, small groups, everyday routines, and other learning contexts?

Meaningful connections (conceptual organizers)

• How is mathematical knowledge introduced? Are math concepts and skills related to the real world of the young child?

• Do the curriculum and teaching strategies make mathematics content meaningful for young children? Do children explore concepts, use manipulatives, and connect their knowledge to more abstract forms?

• Are children given enough time to investigate and construct their ideas? Do materials give teachers useful and clearly described strategies for promoting children's learning?

• Is there research evidence that indicates young children's meaningful learning in this program?

Q: What sequence in the mathematics curriculum should be used over the year's time? Should some content areas receive more emphasis than others?

A: These are especially difficult questions. For years researchers, curriculum experts, teachers, parents, and others have considered and debated issues of scope and sequence in mathematics education. In *Principles and Standards for School Mathematics* (NCTM 2000), NCTM identifies the big ideas, the key areas, in mathematics and describes what children within various age ranges should know and be able to do (see Appendix A of this book for a list of NCTM math standards as they apply to young children). For children in prekindergarten through second grade, NCTM guidance strongly emphasizes number and geometry. About half as much emphasis is given to the areas of measurement and data analysis. Algebra receives the least attention, although pattern awareness and understanding, which are fundamental in algebraic thinking, are a strong thread throughout the early childhood standards.

Of course, we should remember that the five content areas and five processes in mathematical thinking are not isolated domains. In solving problems, people usually draw on concepts from several areas of mathematics and use at least two or three of the processes. Because I consider integration essential to an effective math program, I have given many examples of making connections throughout the book.

Beyond this question of *what* mathematics, there is also the question of *when*. Is there a natural sequence for introducing math content to young children? Decisions about order and timing need to take into account the needs, experiences, and interests of the particular children, but I can offer a few general guidelines and ideas.

• Some mathematics is naturally sequential. In these cases, children typically acquire one concept or skill before they acquire the next, which builds on the first. In the preceding chapters, I have pointed out such sequences.

• In any discussion of sequence of instruction, we need to remember that math areas should not be taught as separate, discrete units, that is, data analysis, then number, and so on. Rather, children should visit and revisit the content areas throughout the year.

• Learning and teaching follow a sequence—a cycle, actually (Bredekamp & Rosegrant 1992)—which is important to children's development of mathematical understanding. First, they become aware of a concept, and then they explore it. Then comes inquiry, and, finally, utilization of the concept. This sequence (see model in Chapter 2, p. 19) is elaborated in the "Cycle of Learning and Teaching" box on the next page.

• The primary decisionmaker in determining the sequence of mathematics curriculum is the teacher, and teachers know that the sequence of teaching and learning cannot be definitively mapped out at the start of the year and closely adhered to. Although the most effective teachers have an overall plan of what builds on what, they must continually assess children's knowledge, interests, and learning needs to plan what is next—in math or any area.

Q: How is math for preschoolers different from math for second- or third-graders?

There is no easy answer to this question. Throughout this book, I have emphasized the impressive mathematical understanding of young children rather than what they lack because of the egocentrism or illogical reasoning often attributed to them. In fact, I would prefer to tell you about the similarities in the mathematics for young children of various ages. Common to all classrooms, from prekindergarten through second grade for example, are teachers' careful observing of children as they solve problems, teacher-child and child-child language that scaffolds and connects ideas, extensive exploration of mathematical concepts through play, and real-life contextual learning.

As discussed in this book, the young child enters school, and even preschool, with considerable informal knowledge of mathematics. The teacher's job is to build a bridge from this informal knowledge to the more formal knowledge of school (Ginsburg & Baron 1993). The bridge is not the same for all children of a given age, say, for all 4-year-olds or for all 7-year-olds. However, just as there is a continuum for physical development and psychosocial development, there are developmental trajectories in cognition that need to be considered in math education.

First, math *content* naturally differs with children's age. Concepts and skills build on previously acquired concepts and skills. Generally, mathematics in a prekindergarten class involves experiences with basic number concepts, counting and sorting objects, and building with two-dimensional and three-dimensional geometric shapes. Preschoolers can also find and create patterns, make comparisons, create simple graphs or other representations of information, and play reasoning games. These areas of mathematics—number and operations, geometry and spatial sense, and so on—are also present in the primary-grade curriculum, but children work with them on a different level. They are learning about place value, combining and separating larger numbers, identifying the attributes of shapes and their transformations, and estimating and measuring distance, area, weight, and volume. At 7 or 8 years,

Cycle of Learning and Teaching

	What children do	**What teachers do**
Awareness	Experience Acquire an interest Recognize broad parameters Attend Perceive	Create the environment Provide opportunities by introducing new objects, events, people Invite interest by posing problem or question Respond to child's interest or shared experience Show interest, enthusiasm
Exploration	Observe Explore materials Collect information Discover Create Figure out components Construct own understanding Apply own rules Create personal meaning Represent own meaning	Facilitate Support and enhance exploration Provide opportunities for active exploration Extend play Describe child's activity Ask open-ended questions—"What else could you do?" Respect child's thinking and rule systems Allow for constructive error
Inquiry	Examine Investigate Propose explanations Focus Compare own thinking with that of others Generalize Relate to prior learning Adjust to conventional rule systems	Help children refine understanding Guide children, focus attention Ask more focused questions—"What else works like this?" "What happens if . . . ?" Provide information when requested—"How do you spell . . . ?" Help children make connections
Utilization	Use the learning in many ways; learning becomes functional Represent learning in various ways Apply learning to new situations Formulate new hypotheses and repeat cycle	Create vehicles for application in real world Help children apply learning to new situations Provide meaningful situations in which to use learning

Source: Reprinted, by permission, from S. Bredekamp & T. Rosegrant, "Reaching potentials through appropriate curriculum: Conceptual frameworks for applying the guidelines," in *Reaching Potentials: Appropriate Curriculum and Assessment for Young Children, Volume 1*, eds. S. Bredekamp & T. Rosegrant (Washington, DC: NAEYC, 1992), 33.

children are able to generalize about patterns on the 100s chart; collect, analyze, and display data; and approach reasoning problems more strategically.

The *materials* in the learning environment differ to an extent with grade level. For one thing, children of 3 or 4 do not have fine motor skills as well-developed as those of primary-grade children. So materials in preschool settings tend to be somewhat larger and more easily manipulated, such as links, pattern blocks, unit blocks, and geometric shapes. Also, many of these materials are open ended in their uses. Although such versatile materials still have a place in the primary grades, children then begin to encounter more materials designed for specific purposes, such as base-10 blocks (with rods made of exactly 10 cubes and flats made of exactly 10 rods).

Teachers are able to make different use of *language* because of children's own language development over the period from age 3 or 4 to 8. With young children, teachers use many contextual references to concrete items and a wide variety of labels for concepts and ideas. They also make use of children's own descriptive phrases, such as "a box with one end squashed" to describe a square pyramid.

By second or third grade, teachers are making more use of conventional math vocabulary. To a greater extent, verbal explanations can be helpful to children, although teachers should never rely on language alone to convey math concepts.

Children's increased linguistic skills also enable them to explain their own concepts and reasoning, not with perfect clarity but far more effectively than younger children are able to do. Thus, teachers can learn more about children's understandings and misunderstandings from their verbalizations and written language than is possible with younger children, and this changes assessment.

Over this age span of 4 to 7, children also become increasingly capable of abstract thinking and representation. In solving problems, for example, younger children are likely to use concrete objects to count, add, or subtract. By second grade, children make greater use of simple pictures, tally marks, or other representations to work through a problem and its solution.

In teachers' roles and interactions, there is both continuity and change. At any point within the early childhood span, teachers should give children opportunities to explore materials and generate their own activities and ideas. But in preschool settings, more time is devoted to exploration and play, with the teacher looking for opportunities to extend and connect the play to mathematics. Relatively less time is spent in planned activities. Although teachers will find value in math-oriented small groups throughout the early childhood years, they will typically make more extensive use of them in the primary grades.

Q: How do you assess young children's mathematical understanding?

A: As discussed previously, the primary purpose of assessment is to benefit children. The assessment principles presented in Chapter 2 support that purpose. They are based both on the position taken by NAEYC along with National Association of Early Childhood Specialists in State Departments of Education (1990) and on NCTM's assessment principle, "Assessment should support the learning of important mathematics and furnish useful information to both teachers and students" (2000, 372).

Of course, recognizing the importance of assessment is one thing; implementing effective assessment is quite another. Several sources have strongly influenced my perspective. Among these is Herbert Ginsburg's work, particularly *Entering the Child's Mind: The Clinical Interview in Psychology, Research, and Practice* (1997) and *The Teacher's Guide to Flexible Interviewing in the Classroom: Learning What Children Know about Math* (Ginsburg, Jacobs, & Lopez 1998), which emphasize the importance of interviewing children, listening to their responses, and planning instruction to build on their knowledge. In Chapters 3 through 8, I have included questions I find useful in talking with children in each area. Of course, it is essential not only to pose good questions but also to follow up, after listening carefully to the child's response.

Many excellent strategies for documenting children's work are described in *Windows on Learning: Documenting Young Children's Work* (Helm, Beneke, & Steinheimer 1998). These ideas, significantly shaped by the intensive use of documentation in Reggio Emilia, have further changed my teaching and helped me to focus on bridging children's informal knowledge and more formal school mathematics. My own efforts to document children's work appear in the dialogues and work samples throughout this volume.

Finally, *Assessing and Guiding Young Children's Development and Learning* (McAfee & Leong 1997) is very helpful in providing the organization and analytic strategies that teachers are looking for to improve the usefulness of their assessment. The book details many different strategies and procedures for assessing young children's cognition and learning as well as physical and social development. Procedures for collecting work over time, designing checklists, and interpreting anecdotal records provide practitioners with the specific, practical help needed to plan for the group as a whole and for each individual child.

To select and design assessment methods that accurately reflect what children know and can do, teachers and assessment specialists must consider the age, experience, and individual needs of all the children. For instance, English-enhancing and bilingual techniques should be used to support students who are learning English (NCTM 2000).

Q: Many parents feel children are learning more if they come home with worksheets. How do I show them the benefits of the kind of math program you describe and activate them to share math with kids at home?

A: Just as teachers need to be informed about key goals and learning experiences in mathematics, so do parents. In addition, family members have images of proper math instruction, based on recollections of their own school experiences. These are often dramatically different from the images of learning presented in this book. Even more problematic is the fact that many parents have low expectations for their children's mathematical achievement because they themselves "were never good at math."

To address these obstacles, teachers need to emphasize to parents the value of meaningful learning: it sticks with children, enables them to solve real problems, and lays the solid foundation of understanding they will need in order to tackle more advanced mathematics later on. These points can be communicated in parent meetings, workshops, parent-teacher conferences, newsletters, and sharing of children's portfolios.

Teachers, schools, and early childhood programs may want to use existing resources to help get families on board with math learning. Among these are parent materials from NCTM, programs such as Family Math (Coates & Thompson 1999), and resources available on the Internet (see "Web Resources," p. 184). Such approaches focus parents' attention on children's learning and understanding. When they see evidence of children's investigating, learning, and applying math concepts, both in and out of the classroom, they will value it.

Q: How can we put into action the philosophy that all children can learn mathematics successfully?

A: A combination of high expectations and strong support for all children is the position of both NAEYC (1996b; [1996] 1999) and NCTM (2000). To make equity a reality, certain things must happen. First, young children must have ample opportunity to learn mathematics. For the teacher, this imperative means constructing a solid curriculum based on what children at a given grade level should know and be able to do, providing the learning experiences to achieve these goals, and individualizing instruction to meet the needs of all children.

Second, high expectations for children must be conveyed by the adults in their lives, family members and teachers alike. Wanting children to understand that through their *efforts* they will be able to learn mathematics, we emphasize and reinforce effort rather than focus on math aptitude. Teachers can also model and emphasize persistence, flexibility, and effort in their own working through problems.

Educators who notice a gender gap in math performance and interest, often in high school and beyond, speculate about whether early experiences with math can help close this gap (see "Gender Equity in Math" box, p. 176). Many of the proactive suggestions made here are applicable to any group of children who tend to have lower math achievement or expectations, for example, children of a particular cultural group.

Finally, access to mathematical resources is key to equity. To teachers, that means being aware of manipulatives, technology, and other resources that help children develop mathematical understanding. Recognizing the value of such materials and resources, early childhood teachers can advocate for equitable resources within the school, district, and community.

Gender Equity in Math

Girls seem to start out on a par with boys in math ability, but somewhere during the later school years, many lose confidence in their ability and tend to stay away from upper-level math classes. For this reason far fewer women than men go into science and technology—math-related careers.

When young children develop a negative attitude toward math, it's extremely difficult to change this mind-set in subsequent years. What can teachers do to build each young child's interest in math and confidence in her ability?

1. Set a good example. Let children see how we use math in our daily lives: we look at the clock, measure things, use money, think about numbers of objects, notice patterns. We have fun with math! As people say, attitude is contagious; is yours one you want children to catch?

2. Structure math learning activities so that each child will be able to achieve success.

3. Give as many turns to girls as to boys—turns of equal length. Practice is critically important in creating comfort and confidence.

4. Compliment each child on her or his accomplishment. "You figured that out very well." "You're learning! You remembered! With a little more practice, you'll understand it." Give equal attention and encouragement to girls.

5. Encourage cooperation within mixed-sex small groups. Encourage children to help each other—especially girls to help boys rather than vice versa.

6. Place books containing pictures of women mathematicians, scientists, and engineers in the math center, as well as pictures of men—and pictures of women as well as men on the math center bulletin board. Talk a little about the women's careers and contributions.

7. Avoid using *he* more than *she* when talking about mathematicians and scientists. We need to counter in boys as well as in girls stereotypes of math as a masculine, not feminine, subject. Many girls say they avoid math in high school because of male peer pressure.

8. Alert parents to stereotypes about math being masculine and encourage them to make math seem as important and accessible for girls as it is for boys.

Source: Adapted, by permission, from P. Greenberg, "Ideas that work with young children. How and why to teach all aspects of preschool and kindergarten math naturally, democratically, and effectively (for teachers who don't believe in academic programs, who do believe in educational excellence, and who find math boring to the max)—Part 2." *Young Children* 49 (January 1994): 18.

Expectations for Prekindergarten through Second Grade, from NCTM's Principles and Standards for School Mathematics

Number and operations standard

Instructional programs from prekindergarten through grade 12 should enable all students to—	**Expectations for grade pre-K–2** *In prekindergarten through grade 2 all students should—*
Understand numbers, ways of representing numbers, relationships among numbers, and number systems	• count with understanding and recognize "how many" in sets of objects • use multiple models to develop initial understandings of place value and the base-ten number system • develop understanding of the relative position and magnitude of whole numbers and of ordinal and cardinal numbers and their connections • develop a sense of whole numbers and represent and use them in flexible ways, including relating, composing, and decomposing numbers • connect number words and numerals to the quantities they represent, using various physical models and representations • understand and represent commonly used fractions, such as ¼, $\frac{1}{3}$ and ½
Understand meanings of operations and how they relate to one another	• understand various meanings of addition and subtraction of whole numbers and the relationship between the two operations • understand the effects of adding and subtracting whole numbers • understand situations that entail multiplication and division, such as equal groupings of objects and sharing equally.
Compute fluently and make reasonable estimates	• develop and use strategies for whole-number computations, with a focus on addition and subtraction • develop fluency with basic number combinations for addition and subtraction • use a variety of methods and tools to compute, including objects, mental computation, estimation, paper and pencil, and calculators.

Note: The full text of these principles and standards for pre-K–2, with examples and guidance for instruction, is available online at www.nctm.org.

Source: Reprinted, by permission, from National Council of Teachers of Mathematics, "Standards for Grades Pre-K–2," *Principles and Standards for School Mathematics* (Reston, VA: NCTM, 2000), 78, 90, 96, 102.

[Patterns, functions, and] algebra standard

Instructional programs from prekindergarten through grade 12 should enable all students to—	**Expectations for grades pre-K–2** *In prekindergarten through grade 2 all students should—*
Understand patterns, relations, and functions	• sort, classify, and order objects by size, number, and other properties • recognize, describe, and extend patterns such as sequences of sounds and shapes or simple numeric patterns and translate from one representation to another • analyze how both repeating and growing patterns are generated
Represent and analyze mathematical situations and structures using algebraic symbols	• illustrate general principles and properties of operations, such as commutativity, using specific numbers • use concrete, pictorial, and verbal representations to develop an understanding of invented and conventional symbolic notations
Use mathematical models to represent and understand quantitative relationships	• model situations that involve the addition and subtraction of whole numbers, using objects, pictures, and symbols
Analyze change in various contexts	• describe qualitative change, such as a student's growing taller; describe quantitative change, such as a student's growing two inches in one year

Geometry standard

Instructional programs from prekindergarten through grade 12 should enable all students to—	**Expectations for grades pre-K–2** *In prekindergarten through grade 2 all students should—*
Analyze characteristics and properties of two- and three-dimensional geometric shapes and develop mathematical arguments about geometric relationships	• recognize, name, build, draw, compare, and sort two- and three-dimensional shapes • describe attributes and parts of two- and three-dimensional shapes • investigate and predict the results of putting together and taking apart two- and three-dimensional shapes
Specify locations and describe spatial relationships using coordinate geometry and other representational systems	• describe, name, and interpret relative positions in space and apply ideas about relative position • describe, name, and interpret direction and distance in navigating space and apply ideas about direction and distance • find and name locations with simple relationships such as "near to" and in coordinate systems such as maps
Apply transformations and use symmetry to analyze mathematical situations	• recognize and apply slides, flips, and turns • recognize and create shapes that have symmetry

Geometry standard continued on page 179

Use visualization, spatial reasoning, and geometric modeling to solve problems	• create mental images of geometric shapes using spatial memory and spatial visualization • recognize and represent shapes from different perspectives • relate ideas in geometry to ideas in number and measurement • recognize geometric shapes and structures in the environment and specify their location

Measurement standard

Instructional programs from prekindergarten through grade 12 should enable all students to—	**Expectations for grades pre-K–2** *In prekindergarten through grade 2 all students should—*
Understand measurable attributes of objects and the units, systems, and processes of measurement	• recognize the attributes of length, volume, weight, area, and time • compare and order objects according to these attributes • understand how to measure using nonstandard and standard units • select an appropriate unit and tool for the attribute being measured
Apply appropriate techniques, tools, and formulas to determine measurements	• measure with multiple copies of units of the same size, such as paper clips laid end to end • use repetition of a single unit to measure something larger than the unit, for instance, measuring the length of a room with a single meterstick • use tools to measure • develop common referents for measures to make comparisons and estimates

Data analysis and probability standard

Instructional programs from pre kindergarten through grade 12 should enable all students to—	**Expectations for grades pre-K–2** *In prekindergarten through grade 2 all students should—*
Formulate questions that can he addressed with data and collect, organize, and display relevant data to answer them	• pose questions and gather data about themselves and their surroundings • sort and classify objects according to their attributes and organize data about the objects • represent data using concrete objects, pictures, and graphs
Select and use appropriate statistical methods to analyze data	• describe parts of the data and the set of data as a whole to determine what the data show
Develop and evaluate inferences and predictions that are based on data	• discuss events related to students' experiences as likely or unlikely
Understand and apply basic concepts of probability	

Making Math Meaningful through Children's Books

A great many books, both fiction and nonfiction, are wonderful for exploring mathematics with children, providing meaningful connections to powerful mathematics. In addition to offering my own selected booklist below, I refer readers to these three teacher resources, helpful in finding good books relating to mathematics:

Burns, Marilyn. 1992. *Math and literature: K-3, Book 1.* Sausalito, CA: Math Solutions.

Sheffield, Stephanie. 1994. *Math and literature: K-3, Book 2.* Sausalito, CA: Math Solutions.

Thiesen, Diane, Margaret Matthias, & Jacqueline Smith. 1998. *The wonderful world of mathematics: A critically annotated list of children's books in mathematics.* Reston, VA: NCTM.

The annotated booklist offered here includes only a few favorites that I have found to connect especially well to various areas of math. Although each book is listed under a single area of mathematics, most connect to other math content as well. Also, the books could be used with virtually any young child, but I have found some to be especially well suited to children from 3 to 6 years old while others work well with primary-grade children. For each annotation, the age group with whom I most often use the book is indicated as * for prekindergarten and kindergarten children and ** for first-through third-grade children

Number and operation

*Anno, Mitsumasa. [1977] 1986. *Anno's counting book.* Reprint, New York: Harper Trophy.

This artistic and effective picture book features the numbers 1 to 12, represented by numerals and illustrations of manipulatives.

**Appelt, Kathi. 1996. *Bat jamboree.* New York: Morrow.

Some creative bats dance and sing at a production of the Bat Jamboree. The pyramid that they make at the end of the production is an excellent introduction to numbers that are multiples of three.

**Axelrod, Amy. 1994. *Pigs will be pigs.* New York: Simon & Schuster.

This humorous story features a hungry pig family who uses addition, subtraction, multiplication, and division to help family members find money and pay for their meals. Opportunities for problem solving, counting money, and reasoning are presented throughout.

*Bang, Molly. 1983. *Ten, nine, eight.* New York: Greenwillow.

Children count backwards as they get ready for bed. This Caldecott Honor book has beautiful illustrations and can help make bedtime a soothing experience.

*Boynton, Sandra. 1996. *Hippos go berserk!* New York: Simon & Schuster.

Beginning with "one hippo all alone," many hippos come to a party until there are so many that they go "berserk." The hippos then leave to return to their homes until one hippo remains alone again. Children love to act as hippos and create their own stories, which involve adding and subtracting.

*, **Crews, Donald. 1986. *Ten black dots.* New York: Mulberry.

What can you do with 10 black dots? This book is filled with pictures made with up to 10 dots. Children love to create their own pictures made with black dots.

**Cuyler, Margery. 2000. *100th day worries.* New York: Simon & Schuster.

Jessica worries about what collection of 100 things she can bring in to celebrate the 100th day of school. The story is filled with many possible solutions and encourages children to make their own collections.

*Dorros, Arthur. 2000. *Ten go tango.* New York: HarperCollins.

In this counting book, animals participate in 10 different dances, which require counting in sequence to do the different steps.

*Ehlert, Lois. 1990. *Fish eyes: A book you can count on.* New York: Scholastic.

Readers of this book see the ocean through a fish's eyes and count fish of different sizes and shapes. The pictures and descriptions of brightly colored fish provide many possibilities for problem-solving situations and interesting questions.

**Garland, Sherry. 1993. *The lotus seed.* San Diego: Harcourt Brace Jovanovich.

This is a tale of a Vietnamese family who travels to a new country with some lotus plant seeds. Learning about how the lotus plants grow provides children with a beginning understanding of multiplication as the seeds of one plant make many new plants.

**Hort, Lenny. 1991. *How many stars in the sky?* New York: Mulberry.

This beautifully illustrated book tells the story of a city boy who wants to know how many stars are in the sky. His father takes him on an adventure to the country to find out.

*Hutchins, Pat. 1982. *1 hunter*. **New York: Mulberry.**

This humorous counting book features a lone hunter who is chased by up to 10 animals. The book also provides a background for problem solving.

*Lyon, George Ella. 1994. *Five live bongos*. **New York: Scholastic.**

This delightful book connects music, language, and mathematics. Children play their own music with "five live bongos" they have made using found instruments.

Mathews, Louise. 1979. *Gator pie*. **Littleton, MA: Sundance.

Children learn about division in this story as an army of alligators fight over one gator pie, which is divided into 100 slices. The discussion between the two alligators dividing the pie is an excellent introduction to fractional concepts.

McKissack, Patricia. 1992. *A million fish...more or less*. **New York: Knopf.

This beautifully illustrated story about one boy's day fishing in the Bayou Clapateaux contains many exaggerations of number, weight, and length. The story is an excellent discussion starter on estimation.

*Micklethwait, Lucy. 1992. *I spy two eyes: Numbers in art*. **New York: Greenwillow.**

Paintings from great works of art are presented so that children can find particular numbers of items in the masterpieces. For example, Rubens's *The Gerbier Family* contains 9 children, and Hasan's *Squirrels in a Plane Tree* pictures 12 squirrels.

Owens, Mary Beth. 1993. *Counting cranes*. **Boston: Little, Brown.

This book contains beautiful watercolor illustrations of the whooping crane. As children count from 1 to 15 cranes, they discover that at one time there were only 15 whooping cranes left in the world and that now this population is increasing.

Pallotta, Jerry. 1992. *The icky bug counting book*. **Watertown, MA: Charlesbridge.

Beginning with 0 and ending with 26, this counting book pictures different bugs and scientific information about them. Many counting questions can be explored using this book as a starting point.

Rylant, Cynthia. 1993. *The relatives came*. **New York: Macmillan.

This Caldecott Honor book presents interesting mathematical problems. When relatives come to visit, suddenly there are many more people sleeping in the beds, sitting in the front room, eating up the strawberries and melons, and making noise. The problems in this story involve addition, subtraction, multiplication, and division.

*Schlein, Miriam. 1996. *More than one*. **New York: Greenwillow.**

This book is an introduction to sets. Some specific sets featured illustrate that one pair is two items, one baseball team is nine players, and one week is seven days. Both text and illustrations help children understand vocabulary that describes numbers of items.

*Walsh, Ellen Stoll. 1991. *Mouse count*. **San Diego: Harcourt Brace Jovanovich.**

A story of a snake's capture of ten mice and their escape. Children love to act out the story, counting and "uncounting" the mice.

Wells, Rosemary. 1991. *Max's dragon shirt*. **New York: Dial.

Max Rabbit wants to spend his money on a dragon shirt rather than on the pants he was supposed to buy, and he doesn't have enough money for both. This story features many opportunities for counting coins and solving problems.

*Wood, Jakki. 1994. *One tortoise, ten wallabies: A wildlife counting book*. **New York: Bradbury.**

This beautiful wildlife counting book pictures adult and baby animals. The incomplete sequence of numbers (1, 2, 3, 4, 5, 6, 7, 8, 9, 10, 11, 12, 15, 20, 25, 50, 101) provides opportunities for children to predict what number will come next and add new pages to make a complete counting book.

Patterns and algebra

Emberley, Ed. 1984. *Ed Emberley's Picture Pie 1: A circle drawing book*. **Boston: Little, Brown.

A variety of pictures and designs are illustrated using whole circles, half circles, quarter circles, and eighths of circles. Children can easily create their own designs using the circles and circle segments.

*Grossman, Virginia. 1991. *Ten little rabbits*. **San Francisco: Chronicle.**

Ten rabbits, pictured by illustrator Sylvia Long, wear authentic Native American blankets from five different tribes. The patterns woven into the blankets are beautifully colored and are labeled with the name of the corresponding tribe and information about its cultural traditions.

Paul, Ann Whitford. 1991. *Eight hands round: A patchwork alphabet*. **New York: HarperCollins.

Patchwork quilt patterns are illustrated, labeled, and described in this beautiful book. Twenty-six patchwork patterns—one for each letter of the alphabet—are pictured along with a written description of the pattern.

*Wallwork, Amanda. 1993. *No dodos: A counting book of endangered animals*. **New York: Scholastic.**

Although this is a counting book, it also pertains to patterns and algebra. In addition, each page uses shape and color to create patterned borders, a technique that children can easily copy.

Geometry and spatial sense

*Carle, Eric. 1986. *The secret birthday message.* **New York: Harper Trophy.**

This book requires children to read a map to find a birthday surprise. The map contains shapes, arrows, and other directions.

*Cohen, Caron Lee. 1996. *Where's the fly?* **New York: Greenwillow.**

A fly on a dog's nose is viewed from a variety of perspectives. This beautifully illustrated book helps children develop an understanding of spatial relationships.

*Crimi, Carolyn. 1995. *Outside, inside.* **New York: Simon & Schuster.**

A little girl plays inside and outside and finds many new friends in this story with many position words. Children will love to tell their own similar stories using position words to describe what they discover.

*Crosbie, Michael, & Steve Rosenthal. 1993. *Architecture: SHAPES.* **Washington, DC: Preservation Press.**

Shapes are featured with line drawings opposite photographs of architectural elements.

Ehlert, Lois. 1989. *Color zoo.* **New York: Harper Collins.

This colorful book introduces shapes children can both see and touch by introducing animals made out of differently colored shapes as well as shapes that are cut out of the pages.

Emberley, Ed. 1996. *Ed Emberley's Picture Pie 2: A drawing book and stencil.* **Boston: Little, Brown.

Pictures of animals, plants, and characters are illustrated using circles and squares and shape segments. Children can make similar pictures or create their own and use shape vocabulary to communicate their designs.

*Ernesto, Lilly, & Linda Hendry. 1993. *Look inside.* **Lexington, MA: D.C. Heath.**

The book simply and clearly illustrates the spatial concept *inside* as a young child travels to an airport, a post office, a school, a zoo, a hospital, a supermarket, a restaurant, and his house.

Grifalconi, Ann. 1986. *The village of round and square houses.* **Boston: Little, Brown.

This is a true story of the village of Tos in Central Africa, where the men live in square houses and the women live in round houses. The story provides opportunities for investigating square and round shapes.

*MacDonald, Suse. 1994. *Sea shapes.* **San Diego: Harcourt Brace.**

This book illustrates how pictures of the sea and its inhabitants contain many shapes.

*Rotner, Shelley, & Richard Olivo. 1997. *Close, closer, closest.* **New York: Simon & Schuster**

Photographs are enlarged to show what things look like from three different distances: close, closer, and closest. Patterns, three-dimensional shapes, and textures are evident in the magnified pictures.

Walter, Marion. 1971. *Look at Annette.* **New York: M. Evans.

Walter, Marion. 1971. *Make a bigger puddle. Make a smaller worm.* **New York: M. Evans.

These wonderful books introduce the ideas of reflection, flipping, and symmetry. Children can solve problems by placing mirrors on simple pictures.

Measurement

*Allen, Pamela. 1982. *Who sank the boat?* **New York: Coward-McCann.**

Animals attempt to balance their weight in a boat in this delightful story. Unfortunately, it sinks. This book is a wonderful introduction to weight and balance experiences, which children can use at the classroom water table.

Carter, David A. 1988. *How many bugs in a box?* **New York: Simon & Schuster.

This pop-up counting book contains a variety of boxes, each holding a specific number of bugs. It provides an introduction to the concept of capacity and leads children to similar investigations.

*Hirschi, Ron. 1994. *A time for playing: A how animals live book.* **New York: Cobblehill.**

Photographs of playing animals provide an excellent backdrop to discuss seasons, temperature changes, and times of day in realistic settings.

Leedy, Loreen. 1993. *Tracks in the sand.* **New York: Bantam Doubleday.

This story of the life cycle of the sea turtle features vocabulary used to measure time, such as full moon, night, day, season, and years.

*McBratney, Sam. 1994. *Guess how much I love you.* **Cambridge, MA: Candlewick.**

In this beautiful book, little and big nutbrown hares show their feelings for one another by jumping, running, and describing many different length measurements. Children love to make and record their own measurements to tell parents how much they love them.

*Miller, Margaret.1996. *Now I'm big.* **New York: Greenwillow.**

Filled with photographs of babies and 3- and 4-year-olds, this book talks about what children can do now that they are big. It is a good beginning to a discussion of how children have grown and of measurement concepts.

Say, Allen. 1982. *The bicycle man.* **Boston: Houghton Mifflin.

Japanese children holding a sports festival in their country schoolyard are charmed by two American soldiers' bicycle tricks. This engaging story suggests how many measurement skills are necessary in judging sports events.

**Silverstein, Shel. 1964. *Giraffe and a half.* New York: HarperCollins.

"If you had a giraffe and he stretched another half . . ." is how this humorous story begins. The book provides a wonderful introduction to measuring length and measuring half of a given length. Children love to make models of their bodies that are half of their real height.

**Singer, Marilyn. 1991. *Nine o'clock lullaby.* New York: Harper Trophy.

This book is a wonderful introduction to the idea of time zones across different continents. As a bedtime lullaby is read to children in Brooklyn, New York, other activities are described as simultaneously occurring in 16 other places.

*Tompert, Ann. 1993. *Just a little bit.* Boston: Houghton Mifflin.

Mouse and Elephant went to play on a seesaw. The delightful illustrations and text of this story encourage several possible measurement discoveries for the young child.

Data analysis and probability

*Franco, Betsy. 1997. *Sorting all sorts of socks.* Mountain View, CA: Creative Publications.

This humorous book introduces many ways to classify socks. Real-life situations for sorting and classifying are important to provide a good connection between mathematics and the child's world.

**Giganti Jr., Paul. 1988. *How many snails?* New York: Greenwillow.

Each page in this book is filled with pictures of snails, books, dogs, toys, or cupcakes. Children are asked to classify the objects by attributes listed on each page. This book provides a good model for stories children can write themselves.

*Hoban, Tana. 1978. *Is it red? Is it yellow? Is it blue? An adventure in color.* New York: Greenwillow.

This wordless book contains photographs of everyday objects. Colored dots on each page help children begin to classify colors.

*Morris, Ann. 1993. *Bread bread bread.* New York: Mulberry.
*Morris, Ann. 1989. *Hats hats hats.* New York: Lothrop, Lee & Shepard.
*Morris, Ann. 1995. *Shoes shoes shoes.* New York: Lothrop, Lee & Shepard.

These books contain photographs of bread, hats, and shoes from cultures all over the world. The pictures can be classified according to their similarities and differences or by other criteria.

**Nagda, Ann Whitehead, & Cindy Bickel. 2000. *Tiger math: Learning to graph from a baby tiger.* New York: Henry Holt.

Graphs are used to tell the story of the growth of a Siberian tiger born at a zoo in Denver, Colorado.

Web Resources

National Association for the Education of Young Children (NAEYC)
http://www.naeyc.org—Provides text of all position statements (e.g., curriculum and assessment; developmentally appropriate practice) and describes professional development opportunities.

National Council of Supervisors of Mathematics (NCSM)
http://ncsmonline.org/OtherResources/links.html —Gives links to organizations and educational groups, governmental entities, reports, and commercial links for accessing professional development workshops, videos, and classroom materials.

National Council of Teachers of Mathematics (NCTM)
http://nctm.org—Details professional development programs focused on helping teaching professionals put the *Principles and Standards for School Mathematics* into practice; books and other resources for teachers.
http://www.standards.nctm.org—Provides the principles and standards themselves, teacher guidance to enable children to achieve each standard, and electronic examples.

Conference on Standards for Preschool and Kindergarten Mathematics Education
http://www.gse.buffalo.edu/org/conference/— Provides complete text for some papers presented at the Spring 2000 conference, including several describing National Science Foundation-funded curriculum development projects in early mathematics.

U.S. Department of Education, Office of Educational Research and Improvement (OERI) National Institute on Early Childhood Development and Education
http://www.ed.gov/pubs/EarlyMath/—Offers engaging, practical ideas for parents and other caregivers. An online copy of *Early Childhood: Where Learning Begins—Mathematics* includes mathematical activities for parents and their 2- to 5-year-old children.

References

Balfanz, R. 1999. Why do we teach young children so little mathematics? Some historical considerations. In *Mathematics in the early years,* ed. J.V. Copley, 3–10. Reston, VA: NCTM; Washington, DC: NAEYC.

Baroody, A.J. 1987. *Children's mathematical thinking.* New York: Teachers College Press.

Baroody, A.J., & D.J. Standifer. 1993.Addition and subtraction in the primary grades. In *Research ideas for the classroom: Early childhood mathematics,* ed. R.J. Jensen, 72–103. New York: Macmillan.

Baroody, A.J., & J.L.M. Wilkins. 1999. The development of informal counting, number, and arithmetic skills and concepts. In *Mathematics in the early years,* ed. J.V. Copley, 48–65. Reston, VA: NCTM; Washington, DC: NAEYC.

Beaton, A.E., I.V.S. Mullis, M.D. Martin, E.J. Gonzales, D.L. Kelly, & T.A. Smith. 1996. *Mathematics achievement in the middle school years: IEA's Third International Mathematics and Science Study,* 41. Chestnut Hill, MA: Center for the Study of Testing, Evaluation, and Educational Policy, Boston College. Available: http://timss.bc.edu.

Bergen, D. 1997. Using observational techniques. In *Issues in early childhood educational assessment and evaluation,* ed. B. Spodek & O.N. Saracho, 108-28. New York: Teachers College Press.

Bjorklund, D.F. 1995.Piaget's theory. In *Children's thinking: Developmental function and individual differences,* 54–94. Pacific Grove, CA: Brooks/Cole.

Bredekamp, S., & C. Copple, eds. 1997. *Developmentally appropriate practice in early childhood programs.* Rev. ed. Washington, DC: NAEYC.

Bredekamp, S., & T. Rosegrant, eds. 1992. *Reaching potentials: Appropriate curriculum and assessment for young children, volume 1.* Washington, DC: NAEYC.

Bredekamp, S., & T. Rosegrant, eds. 1995. *Reaching potentials: Transforming early childhood curriculum and assessment, volume 2.* Washington, DC: NAEYC.

Caine, R., & G. Caine. 1994. Principles of brain-based learning. In *Making connections: Teaching and the human brain.* Menlo Park, CA: Addison Wesley.

Carpenter, T. 1975. Measurement concepts of first- and second-grade students. *Journal for Research in Mathematics Education* 6 (1): 3–13.

Carpenter, T.P., E. Fennema, M.L. Franke, L. Levi, & S.B. Empson. 1999. *Children's mathematics: Cognitively guided instruction.* Portsmouth, NH: Heinemann.

Carpenter, T., & R. Lewis. 1976. The development of the concept of a standard unit of measure in young children. *Journal for Research in Mathematics Education* 7: 53–58.

Cartwright, S. 1996. Learning with large blocks. In *The block book,* 3d ed., ed. E.S. Hirsch, 133–41. Washington, DC: NAEYC.

Charlesworth, R., & K.K. Lind. 1998. Math and science for young children. 3d ed. Stamford, CT: Delmar.

Clements, D.H. 1999. The effective use of computers with young children. In *Mathematics in the early years,* ed. J.V. Copley, 119–28. Reston, VA: NCTM; Washington, DC: NAEYC.

Clements, D.H. 1999. Geometry and spatial thinking in young children. In *Mathematics in the early years,* ed. J.V. Copley, 66–79. Reston, VA: NCTM; Washington, DC: NAEYC.

Clements, D., & S. McMillen. 1996. Rethinking "concrete" manipulatives. *Teaching Children Mathematics* 2 (5): 270–79.

Coates, G.D., & V. Thompson. 1999. Involving parents of 4- and 5-year-olds in their children's mathematics education: The FAMILY MATH experience. In *Mathematics in the early years,* ed. J.V. Copley, 205–14. Reston, VA: NCTM; Washington, DC: NAEYC.

Copley, J.V. 1998. Notes of classroom observations in sorting activities in kindergarten classrooms. Typescript.

Copley, J.V., ed. 1999. *Mathematics in the early years.* Reston, VA: NCTM; Washington, DC: NAEYC.

Copley, J.V. In press. *Pre-K–K TEXTEAMS Institute.* Austin: University of Texas at Austin.

Davidson, J., & J.L. Wright. 1994. The potential of the microcomputer in the early childhood classroom. In *Young children: Active learners in a technological age,* ed. J.L. Wright & D.D. Shade, 77–91. Washington, DC: NAEYC.

Driscoll, M.J. 1981. Measurement in elementary school mathematics. In *Research within reach: Elementary school mathematics.* Reston, VA: National Council of Teachers of Mathematics; Washington, DC: National Institute of Education.

Flavell, J.H. 1985. *Cognitive development.* 2d ed. Englewood Cliffs, NJ: Prentice-Hall.

Fuson, K. 1988. *Children's counting and concepts of number.* New York: Springer-Verlag.

Gardner, H. 1983. *Frames of mind.* New York: Basic.

Gelman, R., & C.R. Gallistel. 1978. *The child's understanding of number.* Cambridge, MA: Harvard University Press.

Gerhardt, L.A. 1973. *Moving and knowing: The young child orients himself in space.* Englewood Cliffs, NJ: Prentice-Hall.

Ginsburg, H.P. 1977. *Children's arithmetic.* New York: Van Nostrand.

Ginsburg, H.P. 1997. *Entering the child's mind: The clinical interview in psychology research and practice.* New York: Cambridge University Press.

Ginsburg, H.P., & J. Baron. 1993. Cognition: Young children's construction of mathematics. In *Research ideas for the classroom: Early childhood mathematics,* ed. R.J. Jensen, 3–21. New York: Macmillan.

Ginsburg, H.P., S.F. Jacobs, & L.S. Lopez. 1998. *The teacher's guide to flexible interviewing in the classroom: Learning what children know about math.* Boston: Allyn & Bacon.

Ginsburg, H., & S. Opper. 1969. *Piaget's theory of intellectual development: An introduction.* Englewood Cliffs, NJ: Prentice-Hall.

Greabell, L.C. 1978. The effect of stimuli input on the acquisition of introductory geometric concepts by elementary school children. *School Science and Mathematics* 78 (4): 320–26.

Greenberg, P. 1994. Ideas that work with young children. How and why to teach all aspects of preschool and kindergarten math naturally, democratically, and effectively (for teachers who don't believe in academic programs, who do believe in educational excellence, and who find math boring to the max)—Part 2. *Young Children* 49 (2): 12–18, 88.

Greenes, C. 1995. Mathematics learning and knowing: A cognitive process. *Journal of Education* 177 (1): 85–106.

Greenes, C. 1999. Ready to learn: Developing young children's mathematical powers. In *Mathematics in the early years,* ed. J.V. Copley, 39–47. Reston, VA: NCTM; Washington, DC: NAEYC.

Hart, K. 1984. Which come first—Length, area, or volume? *Arithmetic Teacher* 31: 16–18, 26–27.

Haugland, S.W. 1999. What role should technology play in young children's learning? Part 1. *Young Children* 54 (6): 26–31.

Haugland, S.W. 2000. What role should technology play in young children's learning? Part 2—Early childhood classrooms in the 21st century: Using computers to maximize learning. *Young Children* 55 (1): 12–18.

Helm, J.H., S. Beneke, & K. Steinheimer 1998. *Windows on learning: Documenting young children's work.* New York: Teachers College Press.

Hiebert, J. 1984. Why do some children have trouble learning measurement concepts? *Arithmetic Teacher* 331: 19–24.

Hills, T.W. 1992. Reaching potentials through appropriate assessment. In *Reaching potentials: Appropriate curriculum and assessment for young children, volume 1,* eds. S. Bredekamp & T. Rosegrant., 43–63. Washington, DC: NAEYC.

Hirsch, E.S., ed. *The block book.* 3d ed. Washington, DC: NAEYC.

Hopkins, L.B. [1972] 1995. Treasure. In *Good rhymes, good times.* New York: Curtis Brown.

Howden, H. 1989. Teaching number sense. *The Arithmetic Teacher* 36 (6): 6–11.

Inskeep, J. 1976. Teaching measurement to elementary school children. In *Measurement in school mathematics (1976) yearbook,* eds. D. Nelson & R. Reys, 6–86. Reston, VA: National Council of Teachers of Mathematics.

Kouba, V., C. Brown, T. Carpenter, M. Lindquist, E.A. Silver, & J.O. Swafford. 1988. Results of the fourth NAEP assessment of mathematics: Measurement, geometry, data interpretation, attitudes, and other topics. *Arithmetic Teacher* 35 (9): 10–16.

Markman, E.M., & J. Subert. 1976. Classes and collections: Internal organization and resulting holistic properties. *Cognitive Psychology* 8: 561–77.

McAfee, O., & D. Leong. 1997. *Assessing and guiding young children's development and learning.* Needham Heights, MA: Allyn & Bacon.

McClain, K., & P. Cobb. 1999. Supporting students' ways of reasoning about patterns and partitions. In *Mathematics in the early years,* ed. J.V. Copley, 112–18. Reston, VA: NCTM; Washington, DC: NAEYC.

McLeod, D.B., & V.M. Adams. 1989. *Affect and mathematical problem solving.* New York: Springer-Verlag.

Nelson, G.D. 1999. Within easy reach: Using a shelf-based curriculum to increase the range of mathematical concepts accessible to young children. In *Mathematics in the early years,* ed. J.V. Copley, 135–45. Reston, VA: NCTM; Washington:,DC: NAEYC.

National Association for the Education of Young Children (NAEYC). 1996a. Position Statement: Technology and young children—Ages three through eight. *Young Children* 51 (6): 11–16.

National Association for the Education of Young Children. 1996b. Position Statement: Responding to linguistic and cultural diversity—Recommendations for effective early childhood education. *Young Children* 51 (2): 4–12.

National Association for the Education of Young Children (NAEYC). [1996] 1999. Developmentally appropriate practice in early childhood programs serving children from birth through age 8 (summary of the position statement). In *NAEYC position statements,* 25. Washington, DC: Author. See also "Position Statements" online at www.naeyc.org/resources/catalog.

National Association for the Education of Young Children (NAEYC) & National Association of Early Childhood Specialists in State Departments of Education (NAECS/SDE). 1990. *Position statement: Summary of guidelines for appropriate curriculum content and assessment in programs serving children ages 3 through 8.* Washington, DC: NAEYC.

National Council of Teachers of Mathematics (NCTM). 1989. *Curriculum and evaluation standards for school mathematics.* Reston, VA: Author.

National Council of Teachers of Mathematics (NCTM). 1991. *Professional standards for teaching mathematics.* Reston, VA: Author.

National Council of Teachers of Mathematics (NCTM). 1995. *Assessment standards for school mathematics.* Reston, VA: Author.

National Council of Teachers of Mathematics (NCTM). 2000. *Principles and standards for school mathematics.* Reston, VA: Author.

National Research Council. 1989. *Everybody counts: A report on the future of mathematics education.* Washington, DC: National Academy Press.

Nelson, G.D. 1999. Within easy reach: Using a shelf-based curriculum to increase the range of mathematical concepts accessible to young children. In *Mathematics in the early years,* ed. J.V. Copley, 135–45. Reston, VA: NCTM; Washington, DC: NAEYC.

Nummela, R., & T. Rosengren. 1986. What's happening in students' brains may redefine teaching. *Educational Leadership* 43 (8): 49–53.

Payne, J.N., & D.M. Huinker. 1993. Early number and numeration. In *Research ideas for the classroom: Early childhood mathematics,* ed. R.J. Jensen, 43–71. New York: Macmillan.

Piaget, J. 1965. *The child's conception of number.* New York: Norton.

Piaget, J., & B. Inhelder. [1941] 1974. *The child's construction of quantities: Conservation and atomism.* Translated by A. J. Pomerans. London: Routledge & Kegan Paul.

Piaget, J., B. Inhelder, & A. Szeminski. 1960. *The child's conception of geometry.* New York: Basic.

Pólya, G. 1957. *How to solve it; a new aspect of mathematical method.* 2d ed. Garden City, NY: Doubleday.

Prigge, G.R. 1978. The differential effects of the use of manipulative aids on the learning of geometric concepts by elementary school children. *Journal for Research in Mathematics Education* 9: 361–67.

Renga, S., & L. Dalla. 1993. Affect: A critical component of mathematical learning in early childhood. In *Research ideas for the classroom: Early childhood mathematics,* ed. R.J. Jensen, 22–37. New York: Macmillan.

Richardson, K., & L. Salkeld. 1995. Transforming mathematics curriculum. In *Reaching potentials: Transforming early childhood curriculum and assessment, volume 2,* eds. S. Bredekamp & T. Rosegrant, 23–42. Washington, DC: NAEYC.

Shane, R. 1999. Making connections: A "number curriculum" for preschoolers. In *Math in the early years,* ed. J.V. Copley. Reston, VA: NCTM; Washington, DC: NAEYC.

Stevenson, H.W., & G. McBee. 1958. The learning of object and pattern discrimination by children. *Journal of Comparative and Psychological Psychology* 51: 752–54.

Van de Walle, J., & K.B. Watkins. 1993. Early development of number sense. In *Research ideas for the classroom: Early childhood mathematics,* ed. R. Jensen, 127–50. New York: Macmillan.

van Hiele, P.M. 1986. *Structure and insight: A theory of mathematics education.* Orlando, FL: Academic.

Wilson, P.S., & R.E. Rowland. 1993. Teaching measurement. In *Research ideas for the classroom: Early childhood mathematics,* ed. R. Jensen, 171–94. New York: Macmillan.